D0505935

ARGENTINA UNDER PERÓN, 1973–76

ARGENTINA UNDER PERÓN, 1973–76

The Nation's Experience with a Labour-based Government

Guido di Tella

St. Martin's Press   New York

ISBN 0-312-04871-8

Library of Congress Cataloging in Publication Data

---

di Tella, Guido, 1931–
    Argentina under Perón, 1973–76.

    Includes index.
    1. Argentina – Politics and government –
1955–. 2. Peronism. 3. Argentina –
Economic conditions – 1945–. I. Title.
F2849.2.D5   1982   982'.064   81-23281
ISBN 0-312-04871-8   AACR2

To those
who believed with hope
and remember with sorrow

Contents

List of Tables

Acknowledgements

It is difficult to acknowledge properly all the people and institutions who have helped to improve the stories here told.

It is inevitable that I should start by thanking my colleagues during my brief stay in the Government in a most troubled period from August 1975 to January 1976, when I was Deputy Minister of Economic Affairs. Although some have made learned contributions to economics, I am here thanking them for having helped improve the events of the time – or at least for having avoided worse – through a dedication and selflessness not always fully appreciated in Argentina.

In the academic realm I want to thank Raymond Carr, Warden of St Antony's College, Oxford, and Professor Christopher Platt, Director of the Latin American Centre, and his colleagues for having allowed me to join a privileged group of scholars with whom I have been able to discuss, in a relaxed atmosphere and far away from the events, the extraordinary developments of the 1973–6 period.

In Argentina I have been able to pick the brains of many scholars, mainly from several leading institutions: the Centro de Estudios Monetarios y Bancarios (CEMYB) and the Gerencia de Investigaciones y Estadísticas Económicas, both of the Banco Central de la República Argentina (BCRA); the Institute for Development Studies (IDES); the Centro de Estudios Macro-económicos de Argentina (CEMA) of the Fundación PAÍS; the Instituto de Estudios Económicos de la Realidad Argentina y Latinoamericana (IEERAL) of the Fundación Mediterránea; and what I could call – if I am forgiven the licence – my *alma pater*, the Centro de Investigaciones Económicas (CIE) of the Instituto Torcuato di Tella.

I have had the invaluable assistance, for the statistical parts of this work, of a group of outstanding junior colleagues, Oscar Baccino, Pablo Guidotti and Mario Vicens, without whose superior skills I should have been unable to tackle the analyses made in Chapters 6 and 7. Sara Caputo, Balbina Fernández, Ana Quaglia and María Cristina San Román have also to be thanked for their invaluable help in the collection of information and data which I would otherwise have been unable to obtain, having for most of the time been far away from the country.

I acknowledge the permission given by the editors of *Desarrollo Económico* and *World Development* to reproduce some parts of articles I published with them, and by Macmillan for the use of parts of my contribution to the book edited by Rosemary Thorp and Laurence Whitehead, *Inflation and Stabilisation in Latin America*.

I have to thank Leonardo Auernheimer, Héctor Diéguez, Alberto Petrecolla, Maurice Scott, Paul Streeten, Rosemary Thorp and Laurence Whitehead for their illuminating and useful comments on the more economic chapters of this book, and Juan Carlos de Pablo, author of an excellent book on the same subject, the first to come out in Spanish. I have also to thank, very specially, Malcolm Deas, who has commented, with his usual wit, on substantial parts of the more political chapters.

John Blackwood, for his part, has struggled to improve my English and I am most grateful to him for his skill and patience.

My last and warmest thanks go to my wife, partly for the usual reasons, but especially because, having never shared any of the hopes, she has had more than her share of the sorrows.

1 Introduction

[handwritten margin note: historian does not have gift of hindsight.]

(To write about recent events is a most risky affair.) Dust requires a long time to settle and the consequences of the events described continue to emerge over a long span of time. Nevertheless, a reflection on things not long past may hasten understanding of what really happened, and may even help quieten some of the passions that underlie the misunderstanding of so many of the important issues. Undoubtedly the subject-matter of this book touches one of the open wounds of Argentine society. (The whole issue of Peronism still divides people of all conditions.) It has probably been the source of more bitterness than the split which took place at the origin of constitutional government after the downfall of Rosas. The divide dates from 1946 to 1955, the time of the first Peronist governments. The second stay of Peronism, from 1973 to 1976, which is the subject of this book, changed the shape and form of the antagonism, but did not diminish it.)

The analysis of such a period is not made any easier by the fact that the author is not neutral, having for a brief period held public positions of some importance. As a consequence, the whole exercise may be dismissed as biased and worthless. Nevertheless, it is hoped that the views which are put forward will be judged on their own merits.

The title of this book may be misleading. Juan Perón was only one of the (four Peronist presidents) and was in power during ten of the thirty-four months that the second Peronist experience lasted. Moreover, the first president, Héctor Cámpora, and the last, Isabel Perón, followed substantially different policies,)which is (crucial to an understanding of some of the problems experienced.) The (whole period, however, was marked by the influence of Juan Perón, through either his presence or his absence.) Thus, while our title is not fully descriptive, we feel it is justified.

I do not pretend to have understood all the ins and outs of this story. I certainly do not want to fall into the common trap of explaining in too clear a fashion an intrinsically confusing reality. In the

1

social sciences there is such a thing as too good an explanation. Reality allows itself to be unveiled up to a point. Beyond that point one risks making unwarranted generalisations and ignoring – whether consciously or unconsciously – contradictory facts. Moreover, it has to be admitted that things do not happen in a clearly determined way. There are many instances where personalities, chance happenings, coincidences, have changed events significantly.

I have tried to probe into some of the causes underlying the actions of certain groups and certain people. I have tried to uncover the more immediate reasons for their actions, stopping short of an attempt to probe into the ultimate reasons, which – fortunately – are likely always to elude us. Economic motives and interests must come into the picture, but cannot exclude others, as human nature is more complex than that. Human nature is so complex that we must leave a significant proportion of actions without an explanation.

Although the main purpose of this work is to analyse some of the economic developments of the 1973–6 period, I have been forced to devote the next two chapters to an analysis of the political and social developments of the period. This in itself is a recognition of the intimate interplay between non-economic factors and the more purely economic developments of the period, or, for that matter, of any period. Much of what went on economically cannot be understood without reference to a broader point of view.

Some consideration is given, particularly in the political analysis, to little instances and small details. This may be a bit disappointing to those more inclined to *grande histoire*. I believe, however, that some of the apparent 'misunderstandings' of the period by various groups arose from the impact that these little happenings had. At times it may be difficult to understand why socially progressive groups did not support a labour-based government. If one stops to remember that the leader of this government once said in a most important public speech that to 'our enemies not even justice should be granted', one can understand one of the many reasons why these groups reacted in a 'non-structural' way. If at the same time one asks how it was that when several hundred people were killed in the 1955 uprising the fact went practically unrecorded, while Peronism with its half-dozen killed was subjected by the press to accusations of brutality, one may begin to understand the resentment at unfair and discriminatory treatment felt among partisans of the popular movement up to this day.

This attention to details has its risks, as one may end by giving undue attention to trivia and gossip. Nevertheless, this approach may come closer to the real world with its contradictions and incoherences than a more abstract one. It is a real pity that reality behaves in such an unruly way.

SOURCES AND REFERENCES

In order to transmit the flavour of the period, particularly when analysing political developments, I have made generous – if at times rather awkward – use of quotations from what was being thought and said at the time. There were so many changes in public mood during the period, so many changes of heart, that memories easily become blurred and judgements *ex post* a bit suspect.

The viability of Perón's return, the significance of the guerrilla movement, the choice between persuasion and repression, the accession of four presidents in one year, the death of the Leader, the 900 per cent inflationary outburst of mid-1975 and the final military coup created heated discussions and have left behind very faulty memories of what had been believed in and said at the time. Some kind of selective amnesia has taken place, frequently a mechanism of self-defence.

In order to cope with this problem, I have analysed the four leading newspapers – *La Prensa, La Nación, Clarín, La Opinión* – and *Mayoría*. The first represents the somewhat fanatic anti-Peronist view. In its own exaggerated way, it had one of the most consistent lines, and its permanent pessimism was proved right more often than not. *La Nación* also had a clear anti-Peronist point of view, but was much less intolerant and represented a much wider spectrum of opinion. As most people, civilian or military, did, it too changed its views during the period. In many instances *La Nación* gave the Government the benefit of the doubt, and only at the end did it give up all hope of redress. *Clarín* exhibited a wavering political attitude, rather along the lines of its political mentor, ex-President Frondizi, but on the other hand followed a clear – indeed the clearest – economic line, representing many of the protectionist views of the industrial establishment. *La Opinión* followed an ambivalent political view, if anything reflecting the slightly left-of-centre attitude characteristic of some intellectual sectors, and was particularly forthright in its campaign for human rights at a time when this was not easy. Finally, *Mayoría* appeared just before the 1973 elections; it was clearly pro-Government, representing the middle of the road, intellectual, Catholic brand of Peronism. Although it was not one of the major newspapers, it has been included as it reflects one of the few pro-Government views among an otherwise hostile press.

A full transcription of the most significant news and editorials appearing in these newspapers from January 1972 until March 1976 has been made elsewhere (di Tella *et al.*, 1981).

The choice of these newspapers, national in scope and published daily during the whole period, is representative of the opinion of the media, which were as a whole against the Government. This selection is representative of what the common reader was exposed to every day: this could not have been provided by a haphazard collection of short-lived newspapers, still less of short-lived weeklies. Nevertheless, this leaves out such significant opinions as those expressed in *Noticias, El Descamisado* and *La Causa Peronista* on the extreme left, or *El Caudillo* on the extreme right. These are quoted sparingly or not at all. Although they did not have a wide and lasting circulation and were bought only by the politically minded reader, they too make interesting reading.

For analysis of the economic developments I had initially to rely on my own resources. Several books and articles have appeared in the meantime which have thrown light on different aspects of the period. There is no doubt that even where I disagree I have benefited from them, and this is acknowledged as we go along. The economic data on the period, as is usual in Argentina, are not very good. Some problems are owing to old statistical samples. Although the cost of living is, fortunately, based on a 1970 sample, the more crucial wholesale price index is based on a 1953 sample. And, as if this were not bad enough, the extraordinary relative price variation has meant that no substitution effects have been taken into consideration either in production or in consumption, when in fact they have been very important – a problem which, as we all know, has no proper solution. Different base years with different relative price sets may give rise to quite different series, depending on the sensitivity to relative price variations and to different weightings.

The Research Division of the Central Bank has been publishing some new series which improve the methodology of the national accounts since 1960, and particularly since 1970 for the financial, agricultural, construction and foreign sectors (BCRA, 1979–80), a process which will continue. Oddly enough, some of the foreign trade series are among the weakest, to the point of having embarrassed the negotiations with the International Monetary Fund (IMF) in 1974.

The terms-of-trade series are particularly bad: the two available show significant and opposite movements in 1974, a puzzle of some significance. A choice of the more reliable series has been made in order to make up the Statistical Appendix. It must be kept in mind that some of the conclusions depend on weak series that may be changed at some time in the future.

THE OUTLINE OF THE BOOK

The next two chapters deal basically with political matters. Chapter 2 is devoted to the analysis of some of the more significant developments which have taken place since the advent of Peronism in the mid-1940s. It begins by recalling not only the economic but also the political and psychological base built up during the 1945–55 period for the extremely enthusiastic loyalty of the working classes towards Perón. This is recalled rather briefly, as it has become widely accepted by authors such as Germani (1962), Halperín (1964) and Romero (1946). The reader is reminded of some of the ways and means in which the process took place. It is claimed that some of the excesses and peculiarities of the Peronist regime hindered its acceptance among groups which would otherwise have accepted it more willingly. The view is taken that these problems were not trivial and are worth remembering if we are to understand in part (although only in part) the bitter feelings to which the period gave rise. The question is raised of whether the reaction of the established groups showed a lessening of the openness to change which had characterised their behaviour at the turn of the century.

In the same chapter, an analysis is made of some aspects of the evolution of Peronism – and of the country as well – that took place after its downfall. Particular emphasis is placed on the increased independence of the trade union movement, which had to endure the daily problem of the distant leader, whose more radical rhetoric soon became identified as 'the opposition' to the system. The consequences of the military coup of 1966, its leaders' initial expectations of a very long stay in government, its modernising, 'developmentalist' economic policies, the internal quarrels among the military followed by the surprising dissolution of the regime and the even more surprising 1973 comeback of Perón, are also analysed. A crucial factor here is the appearance of subversion. Violence in this particular instance was a contributory factor in accelerating the withdrawal of the military. One should be careful not to jump to an easy conclusion, as this withdrawal was not made to favour any of the aims of subversion; it favoured instead a regime that, no matter how much it was disliked by the military, was expected to deal with subversion in a politically more effective way.

The electoral summons, and the creation of a government legitimate in the eyes of most people, was an attempt to undercut the alleged basis of terrorism. It was to be a political solution to the subversion problem – an expectation that was brutally disproved soon after the elections. As had been foreseen, the fact that an electoral solution was tried took away much of the diffuse support enjoyed up to that moment by subversion, isolating it from the mainstream of political life. Later on, the continuation of subversion produced just the opposite result, accelerating the downfall of the popular coalition and the return of the military. Chapter 2 is mainly political and should serve to describe the setting and the initial conditions of Perón's come-back. It should be particularly useful to the non-Argentine reader.

Chapter 3 attempts to analyse the political evolution of the Government coalition during its hectic existence of nearly four years, from May 1973 to March 1976. Some authors take the view that the chaotic developments of these years and the sorry finale are the consequence of the intrinsic contradictions of a populist coalition incapable of handling a much more complex country than the one it had handled twenty years before. In this view, the situation was fundamentally aggravated by the physical decline and eventual death from old age of Perón himself, coupled with the absolute incapacity and lack of any clear set of political ideas of his successor, Isabel Perón. The view taken here is basically different. It is held that the typical and intrinsic disorder of a populist coalition is of a different and much less intense kind. The extremely chaotic performance of these years is the consequence of the two attempts to take control of the government made from opposite sides by groups relatively marginal to the popular coalition. The first attempt, made from the left, was a most unnatural step for this particular party in this particular country. As could be expected, the attempt failed; however, it damaged the whole fabric of the Government coalition as well as its credibility. The second attempt was made immediately after the death of Perón by the extreme right, led by the President and her Minister of Welfare, an attempt that failed after producing a deep convulsion among the leaders of the party and the rank and file. Again this was a very unnatural step. It was imposed on a trade-union based party; it had but a slim – if any –

chance of success, and failed miserably after a head-on collision with the trade unions in mid-1975. This analysis attributes to Isabel Perón qualities of determination and political will, however much one may or may not dislike what she did, or whatever one may think of her other personal qualities.

What seems clear is that hers was not a government going adrift, as many commentators of the period described it. On the contrary, the essence of the 'finale' was the revolt of the party against the swing to the right that the President and her entourage were trying to impose. This revolt – and not the ineptitude of the President – created the deadlock which lies at the base of the final chaotic situation; her ineptitude and lack of qualifications were indeed factors, but were not the main cause. Most commentators would probably take issue with me on this point, but it is indeed one of the main contentions of this book. This collision lay behind the extraordinary price explosion and the ensuing high level of inflation; both are problems whose intensity cannot be explained on purely economic grounds.

The period between the lurches to the left and to the right was far from being peaceful and straightforward. Nevertheless, despite the incoherences on the economic front, the disagreements between the remaining members of the populist coalition and the tense relationship with the unions, this was the period when the Government enjoyed the greatest consensus. There were even some novel developments which softened some of the hard edges – most notably the better relationship, at times even excellent, with the main opposition party, the Unión Cívica Radical (UCR), which made an equivalent effort to overcome its old factionalism. As Perón put it in his own peculiar way: 'Instead of our old slogan which said that for a Peronist there is nothing better than another Peronist, we will have a new one [which will say that] for an Argentine there is nothing better than another Argentine.' The press remained independent, really all of it strongly anti-government. Allies were sought, and a sprinkling of non-Peronist candidates were included on the party slate. This is not to say that some of the old abusive behaviour did not appear, as in the handling of the radio and television stations and in the settling of disputes within the party. This last aspect, however, is mixed up with an absolutely new element, the appearance of subversion, which increased the general level of violence throughout Argentine society.

During this intervening period, then, things proceeded much as might be expected and even showed certain improvements. By contrast, the attempted takeovers from the left and from the right came as a great surprise. The existence of ambitious groups on the left and right wings was natural and to be expected, but not that either of them could gain control of the centre of the stage. That the Government was susceptible to such rash takeovers was not a chance happening and evidenced a weakness characteristic of parties with a strong personalised leadership and a weak organisational structure. Both attempts failed as a consequence of the rallying of the more middle-of-the-road forces of the party, including (prominently) the trade unions. This anchorage in the middle of the political spectrum seems intrinsic to the Argentine populist coalition and was, it is claimed, part of its strength. It was the tension caused by these turn-abouts, particularly the second, which created the chaotic climate that coloured the last stages of the Peronist regime. This basically political chapter should help us to understand the economic developments of the period, which are described later.

Chapter 4 deals with the package of structural long-range economic reforms attempted during the initial months of the new government. It was a very ambitious package of reforms, which were radically to change the economic face of the country. Not much of the programme was implemented, and under the pressure of more day-to-day problems it was soon forgotten, but during and just after the election it had a great significance, pervading the whole campaign and determining to a great extent the final alignment of many groups either for or against the new government.

A distinction has to be made, however, between the rhetorical boasts made during and after the campaign and what the programme actually said. It is the rhetoric which is better remembered, by supporters and critics alike. The promises were much more radical and drastic than the actual programme, even more than one would expect in an electoral campaign. The economic programme was mildly left of centre and mildly nationalistic, though strongly interventionist. It reflected most the views of the business sectors within the alliance, which accepted some 'progressive' measures concerning taxation and a polemical agricultural law; these business sectors were not much interested in agriculture. In return for these measures a set of policies favourable to local capitalists was put forward. These concerned foreign investment, industrial protection and, a significant novelty, the promotion of industrial exports, including exports to countries of the Soviet bloc. They thus had at the time – extraordinarily enough – a suspiciously leftish ring.

Moreover, all the policies had a strong interventionist bias. This was noticeable in foreign trade, mainly in agricultural exports, which were to be managed by State companies. It was also noticeable in the banking sector, which was to be centralised through a financial reform leaving the banks as mere agents of the credit allotted to them by the Central Bank. Characteristically, these measures were presented as much more drastic than they really were, i.e. as nationalisation of trade and nationalisation of bank deposits. They were so trumpeted in order to satisfy the demands of the rank and file of the party at the price of antagonising the business community more than was necessary and making implementation more difficult. The role of the State was also noticeable in the so-called 'social pact', a kind of general price and wage freeze; this became, as we shall see, one of the central and most intensely implemented sets of measures.

The programme was full of unrealistic targets and Utopian aspirations. But it was relatively mild, even if one may disagree with its aims, and not so different in spirit (*mutatis mutandis*) from the programmes of some of the European socialist parties. It was more interventionist but also more distinctively pro-business. In itself it did not justify the reaction nor the excitement with which it was received. However, people's perception of the programme was influenced not so much by what was said as by the circumstances in which it was said. Secondary and minor statements gave rise to all kinds of suspicions; they seemed to confirm the most terrible apprehensions. The times were such as to make this reaction understandable; one should not forget that this was the time when the Montonero organisation was playing a leading role in the campaign.

Chapter 5 is mainly devoted to an analysis of the economic developments of the period. This may be divided into six different periods, each of which may be easily characterised:

June December 1973 — Initial economic policies; stabilisation programme; social pact and price and wage freeze; reformist measures.

January–September 1974 — Mounting problems with the price freeze and the contradictory expansionist policies; problems in the foreign sector.

September 1974–May 1975 — Partial 'flexibilisation' of policies; introduction of financial restraint; crisis in the foreign sector.

June–July 1975   Drastic readjustment; political conflict;
                              beginning of a recession.

August 1975–January 1976   A gradualist approach, rebalancing of
                              relative prices, partial indexation of the
                              economy; anti-recession measures and
                              balance-of-payments crisis.

January–March 1976   An attempt to 'cool' the economy and
                              the effects of the oncoming revolution.

While the initial swing to the left had serious political consequences, to the point of forcing a change of President, it did not affect the economic scene too seriously. In fact, the initial economic programme launched in June 1973 was carried out somewhat independently of the general policies of the Cámpora period and was regarded at the time as a concession to the middle-class sections of the party. The first Minister of Economy, a member of the Confederación General Económica (CGE), the small-business organisation, lasted seventeen months, serving under all four presidents, and followed basically the same economic policy. This was made up of the stabilisation pro- gramme and the set of reformist measures mentioned in Chapter 4. The stabilisation scheme, as we shall see, had two characteristic stages. The first had some success as it was based on a 'social pact' which tried to enforce a certain distribution of income. It was also based on a price freeze and the lowering – in real terms – of certain prices, which in turn gave rise to some of the tensions that contributed to the destruction of the whole scheme later on. The success of the initial stage, from June to December 1973, was to some extent the con- sequence of the authority exercised by a popularly elected government led by a strong leader. This gave credibility to the programme and brought down inflationary expectations. Another equally important factor was the improvement in the international situation, which provided a windfall gain. It helped the initial distributionist policies, although it hindered the stabilisation programme through its effect on the prices of imports. The end of this stage was heralded by the deterioration in the terms of trade which took place from the end of 1973, and was brought about by even greater increases in import prices, the very significant external inflationary pressures and the in- creasing incongruity of a price freeze accompanied by expansionist monetary and fiscal policies. All these gave rise to increasing economic difficulties, internal shortages, reduction of investment and a loss of reserves; there was a situation of repressed inflation.

By the death of Perón in July 1974 the middle-of-the road economic programme was showing obvious strains. While a significant change was necessary, that it was made after the loss of a forceful leader and accompanied by a drastic political move to the right created additional strains and opened a period of unprecedented instability.

Isabel Perón had five Ministers of Economy, who lasted six, three, one, six and two months, respectively. In economic policy she started in September 1974 with a mild movement towards the right. From May to July 1975 an all-out move to the right was made. But it required a degree of allegiance from the Justicialista party which was just not there. On the contrary, the trade unions staged an open rebellion which nearly brought down the Government. This conflict was at the root of the extraordinary intensity of the price explosion of the middle of the year. A rebalancing of the economy was to be expected, but in this case what was abnormal was its intensity.

The price mechanism had become the battleground for the distribution of income, and these fights became in turn one of the roots of the inflationary process. What was noticeable was the great degree of oscillation of relative prices and the parallel changes in distribution associated with the oligopolistic behaviour of important groups.

The price explosion was accompanied by a reduction in real terms in the amount of money in circulation, owing to the tremendous price increases and the strong flight from money. The explosion was to a great extent the consequence of the political struggles. At the same time, it helped to increase the intensity of these struggles and to create a chaotic climate. By August 1975 the President had lost all of her arbitrating power; she barely retained her position, becoming only a figurehead. The Government was taken over by the moderate middle-of-the-road groups, strongly supported by the unions; they were able to remain in control until January of the following year.

The economic situation was coloured by the aftermath of the price explosion, while some gross distortions in relative prices were gradually redressed. An attempted come-back by the right wing of the party produced a stalemate by the end of the year. By that time it had become obvious that a military coup was about to take place. It was expected by the business and agricultural sectors and by a good part of the intelligentsia.

The President regained full control of the Government, and attempted a more moderate right-wing programme, but the imminence of the coup took away all credibility from the Government. When a new price explosion took place, the Government retreated into impotence. The price explosion this time was connected with the Government's loss of any kind of authority and, above all, with the extremely destabilising influence of the expected military coup, which took place on 24 March 1976.

Without a grasp of the political developments, these years cannot be understood, as the intensity of the conflicts within the Government coalition and its loss of arbitrating power were crucial to the economic process. Nevertheless, some of the most purely economic dilemmas, although not their intensity, have a suspiciously typical character; this can be seen in the early stabilisation programmes.

Argentina's evolution during these years was after all not that original. There was an auspicious beginning while she rode the tail end of world prosperity; then there was a serious balance-of-payments problem at the time of the oil crisis, which adversely affected her terms of trade, and subsequently stepped up inflation. What can be seen is that Argentina was not only unable to cushion the effects of the world crisis but managed to compound them to an exceptionally high degree. In this lies her unfortunate originality.

Chapters 6 and 7 try to go over some of the major economic issues posed by the 1973–6 experience. In Chapter 6 we tackle three major issues, beginning with the investment performance, public and private, of this period, compared with previous ones. We here become involved in the controversy, which has been intense in Argentina, over whether popular governments are less or more investment-oriented.

Although instinctively one may be tempted to think that popular governments tend to invest less in order to distribute, the fact is that during this period total (particularly public) investment was much higher than in any previous period, including the apparently pro-investment 'right-wing liberal' years from 1966 to 1970. This apparent contradiction has to be analysed, taking into account the growth trend of investment over at least the last twenty years. Investment shows a quite persistent positive trend, independently of the type of government. A comparison with any earlier period shows a significant growth in investment. It is as if the whole socio-economic mechanism, in responding to a set of diverse pressures, tends to 'solve' the social equation through more investment, the opposite of what one might expect. A proper analysis should be focused on deviations from the trend. With this stricter view, there is not much that can be concluded that is statistically significant. However, the little that can be said gives some support to the first instinctive reaction about the investment behaviour of popular governments, but to a much lesser extent than expected.

The second issue has to do with the poor performance of sectoral profits, a much discussed complaint of businessmen during the period, particularly when compared with the growth of wages. Although the picture is far from bright, it is not so bad as one would expect. Nevertheless, the uncertainty and the wide differences within the main sectors may go part of the way to reconciling the figures with the attitudes of the period.

The third issue has to do with the impact on the foreign sector of the international crisis of 1973, and of the internal measures, mainly devaluation, taken in response to it. The international crisis explains a large proportion of the initial prosperity and the ensuing external disequilibria. More controversial is the analysis of the extent of the external redress and, if accepted as a fact, whether the mid-1975 devaluation, maintained until March of the following year, was effective, and whether the price paid was the maintenance of a strong cost-push throughout the period.

Chapter 7 deals with several issues even more directly connected with the inflationary process. Problems that do not show themselves so clearly in less prolonged or milder inflations become more clearly observable when inflation becomes extremely intense or variable. Not only are we able to see certain problems, but, in addition, new phenomena appear that do not exist at lower inflationary rates. There is no doubt that high and persistent inflations have an interest of their own.

The first issue which arises from the experience of this period is whether inflationary processes can be interpreted in terms of warring factions. Analysing the Argentine case, it would seem that inflation is in good measure the consequence of fights between oligopolistic sectors. It would also seem that their fighting spirit is in turn increased by inflation, and thus a most disgraceful vicious circle is created.

The second and connected topic is the oscillatory character of Argentina's inflation, i.e. the oscillation of relative prices. This oscillation may be associated with the behaviour of the oligopolistic sectors, and their attempts to manipulate prices. At one time they might succeed, only to see other sectors (including their suppliers) do the same thing, cancelling out what thus prove to be short-lived gains. In the end nobody is able to gain any permanent advantage, but those who are weak or unable to fight for their prices are washed out in the process. A correlation is attempted between the rate of inflation and the degree of price oscillation (duly defined), and proves to be surprisingly high. In addition, it is implied that similar inflations, if judged by their rate of price variation, may be differentiated by their diverse oscillatory patterns. In Argentina, a significant increase in the oscillatory character of inflation took place after the 1975 explosion. The further implication is that, the severer its oscillatory character, the more difficult it will be to control the inflationary process, a problem which may lie behind the extraordinary resilience of Argentina's post-1975 inflation.

The third topic concerns the existence of a kind of inflationary cycle. This phenomenon is connected with what has been described as the stop–go character of the Argentine economy, but it is not the same. The correlation between the inflation cycle and the standard income cycle is rather weak. The inflationary cycles are associated with a certain pattern whereby periods of declining inflation are usually the consequence of the 'repression' of some particular price, compared with its equilibrium value. This price repression tends to create an imbalance which cannot be sustained indefinitely. Finally, the freeing of the repressed price becomes inevitable, to avoid the economic consequences. Oddly enough, we can see that, when relative prices become distorted, inflation falls, and that, when they are redressed (in line with some presumed long-term relative price equilibrium), inflation rises. It is as if policies oriented towards efficiency are, in the short term, inflationary, while other kinds of policy can, for a while, work better.

The chapter concludes with an analysis of indexation, one of the few ways in which inflation can be made less harmful, given the unfortunate fact that it cannot be brought under control quickly. An analysis of the effects of indexation on the money market, on the variability and predictability of the rate of inflation, and finally on relative price movements, both of the oscillatory and of the more long-term structural type, is followed by a summary of the planned and actual steps taken towards the indexation of the economy during the second half of 1975. The emphasis here is on the greater positive impact of indexation in maintaining the efficiency of the economy in the long term than in toning down inflationary pressures in the short term.

Chapter 8 is a kind of epilogue. It is not really an analysis of the social and political issues raised by the period, which would require a separate study. An attempt is made, however, to pull together some of the political issues referred to in the course of the work as a whole. The political instability that has characterised Argentina for more than fifty years is very briefly reviewed, in an effort to show that a system of sorts has emerged which has allowed all major groups to take their turn in government, but with very little power-sharing. This has been Argentina's peculiar way of accommodating the various social groups. The main reasons behind the chaotic finale are also analysed, stressing that the death of Perón was neither the sole nor even the most important factor. Emphasis is rather on the importance and the shattering consequences of the two sharp changes in policies, the first towards the left and the second very much towards the right. The open struggle between the President, supported by the extreme right wing, and the bulk of the party, supported by the trade unions, is what in my view explains the chaotic conditions of 1975 and the passive attitude of the trade unions to the military coup of March 1976.

We conclude with a short comment on the much discussed matter of the intensity of the reformist aims of Peronism, and whether it was a lack or excess of zeal that determined the outcome of this period.

BIBLIOGRAPHY

di Tella, G., with the collaboration of B. Fernández and C. San Román (1981) *Los Diarios 1972–1976* (Buenos Aires).

BCRA (1979–80) Serie de trabajos metodológicos y sectoriales (Buenos Aires: Gerencia de Investigaciones y Estadísticas Económicas, BCRA).

Germani, G. (1962) *Política y sociedad en una época de transición* (Buenos Aires).

Halperín, T. (1964) *Argentina en el callejón* (Montevideo).

Romero, J. L. (1946) *Las ideas políticas en Argentina* (Buenos Aires and Mexico). (There is a later expanded edition published in 1975.)

2 The Long Wait

While the study of any process requires an understanding of previous developments, here it is all the more necessary, as we are trying to analyse the return of a regime which had been in power nearly three decades before, from 1946 to 1955. Perón's first stay in power left a most significant imprint both upon followers and upon opponents. His traumatic downfall was followed by his long exile and an equally long electoral ban on his partisans. This wait of more than seventeen years introduced several changes in the significance and role of Peronism; these were even greater than those normally involved in moving from government to opposition.

It is not intended here to give a detailed account of those years. This has been done elsewhere, either for the whole period or for some aspects of it (Halperín, 1964, 1972; Romero, 1975; O'Donnell, 1976; Portantiero, 1978). All that is intended, particularly for the non-Argentine reader, is to review some of the main issues, especially those which had a greater bearing on later developments and on Perón's unexpected comeback.

THE INITIAL DIVIDE

Over the last forty years Argentina has experienced a bitter fight between Peronist and anti-Peronist forces which has poisoned its social, political and intellectual life. If one takes a broad view, one could say that Argentina is suffering the birth-pangs of a new social system which would include not only the middle classes, who became part of it during the first half of the century, but also the working classes, and that this will take most of the second half. One may even be tempted to conclude that, after all, a span of less than a century for such a far-reaching process is no longer than was required by the countries of the Northern hemisphere, where the process was at least as troublesome and protracted. Easy transitions are very few and unfortunately do not set a pattern. The first appearance of Peronism,

16

from 1946 to 1955, introduced many new elements into the social and economic scene. These mainly concerned the greater mobilisation of workers, the central role given to trade unions, and the nationalistic economic policies of an industrialisation effort based on the home market, local capital and State intervention, and they were accompanied by an increased pace of urbanisation.

> The social aspects were probably the more important. Thanks to Peronism the popular masses acquired a consciousness of their own significance. They became a category of great significance in national life, a force capable of exerting power. ... [Peronism] gave them the sensation of power, of meaning and of active participation in the country's political changes. (Germani, 1978).

However, these changes could not be made in a painless way, as it meant 'destroying or neutralising the ... web of structural relationships in existence up to that moment' (Mora, 1980). The social changes were intimately connected with the transfer of more than 10 per cent of GNP from landowners and capitalists to wage-earners, a process that was initiated at the beginning of the period.

This was not a 'structural' reform, nor is it something that social revolutionaries, particularly of the Latin American variety, get very excited about. Still, it is the kind of change that significantly affects very important groups. After all, much of the discussion in everyday political life has to do with where the money goes. Even smaller shifts than this produce intense discussions in other, more mature countries. Revolutions, at least in Argentina, have seldom taken place in the face of tremendous social dangers, but more often when shares in the national income have been altered one way or the other. Peronism's initial nationalistic slant hurt British interests and the Argentine groups connected with them; their loss of power was painful and created resentment, despite the fact that it was inevitable. What was more important was that native entrepreneurs, although favoured by the new economic outlook, were aware that the changes were part of a less well known and less predictable set of policies. In a way they felt the loss of the protection provided by a set of established even if less favourable traditions. A pro-foreign-capital policy creates some resentment among local entrepreneurs, but at the same time implies a guarantee that no strange experiments will be tried and that private capital, both foreign *and* domestic, will be protected. An anti-foreign-capital policy, by contrast, may be suspected of being one step away from a policy inimical to all private capital.

At times the problem was not so much the consequences of the new policies as the mere fact that they were being introduced by new social and economic groups. These had not been expected to exercise positions of power and wealth; suddenly they were seen, and saw themselves, in such positions. The newcomers had competed directly for positions of political and economic power; now they were ostentatiously maintaining their individuality, their different values and mores. This was not restricted to the trade unions but was extended to the new economic groups favoured by the regime, bringing complaints about 'the submission of the national economy to the dictatorship of an industrial oligarchy close to [the present Government's circles]' (UCR, *La Prensa*, 17 Dec 1948). A number of expropriations of land and local businesses were made in a most haphazard way. Even if quantitatively they were not significant, they created a deep distrust and a sense of legal insecurity. In business circles it was felt that 'nobody can work in peace under the threat that any morning one may wake up to the news that one is no longer the owner of one's property' (*La Nación*, 1 Mar 1950). The State increased its role substantially; it now ranged from the purchase of most of the basic staples by federal agencies, to the granting of credit at negative rates through the semi-nationalised banking system, and the granting of import licences – significant favours in times of multiple exchange rates. A small circle of Government protégés made themselves extremely rich through official favours; this created a climate of business immorality which by far exceeded that which normally accompanies social and economic changes of this kind. The increased role of the State created a whole new set of antagonisms, which were aggravated by the way in which the new interventions were handled. The impression was given that the State was not bound by any set of rules, old or new.

Throughout, one has to distinguish between the intrinsic resistance that some of the far-ranging structural changes would have created in any case, and the varieties which appeared as a consequence of the particular ways in which these changes were carried out. Changes are seldom made in a 'pure' or 'perfect' way, but there is little doubt that some of the peculiarities of Peronism added fuel to the antagonism, and lost the Government the support of middle-class groups, professionals and intellectuals who did not disagree with its ultimate objectives.

On the political front, the behaviour of the Government contributed also to the impression that the regime was not bound by any set of pre-existing rules. Political opponents were harassed and in some notorious, though exceptional, instances jailed for short periods. The only opposition party of any significance, the UCR, vigorously criticised a situation in which 'the Government has taken over full political, economic and cultural control, wiping out the freedom of the press and of the radio, reducing the [Justicialista] party to an autocratic group led in an autocratic manner by the Government itself' (*La Prensa*, 17 Dec 1948). While these high handed policies were not new to the country – and continued after 1955 – they were conducted in a different style. Previously, constitutional governments had been deposed, candidates had been banned, elections had been annulled or rigged, but the press had been free and education, while obviously reflecting the views of the establishment, had been basically autonomous. Now, the electoral process was free, no candidates were banned, but the press was brought under control and education was formally regulated.

Most newspapers and radios were either bought, one by one, or closed down – as in the notorious case of *La Prensa* – while others had to maintain a semi-official line in order to survive. The impression given to the press was that 'the precept for all the inhabitants of the country, as well as for its political parties and newspapers, was to see, to hear, and to shut up' (*La Prensa*, 18 Nov 1948). Compulsory affiliation to the Peronist Justicialista party was instituted for Government employees, despite the fact that most of them were in any case already enthusiastic supporters. As one can imagine, the Government was soon accused of having fascist leanings. However, despite the fascist origins of a proportion of its leadership and the initial ideological preferences of its leader, the urban and the working masses succeeded in instilling a popular character into the movement and to a large extent into the entire regime. What is puzzling is that non-democratic practices are usually implemented by minority parties which cannot win in any other way; the Peronists were able to win elections by substantial margins but also thought it necessary to take coercive measures quite unnecessary for electoral success. The democratic values which they mistrusted would have given them a much greater legitimacy; the authoritarian or Fascist ideologies with which they toyed worked against their acceptance.

In cultural matters the Government met significant obstacles. The universities in particular became the centre of intellectual resistance. Traumatic intervention soon occurred; there were many dismissals, though not so many if they are judged by later standards. The

Government claimed that the universities represented an elitist and reactionary view of society and that it was necessary to open them to
new groups. This allegation was not completely unfounded, but the
way in which the attempt to open them was made was extremely awkward and contributed to a lowering of academic standards. Besides
this political interference, a significant increase in student enrolment
took place, particularly at the secondary and university levels. To
some extent this was a consequence of the better distribution of
income. Even people who have little sympathy for Peronism have considered that 'Peronism promoted .... a genuine and important
educational growth' (Mora, 1980), something that fortunately was to
continue. At all levels, even at the primary one, a policy of political in-
doctrination was attempted, though of an elementary sort. The
Government was culturally nationalistic. This nationalism ranged
from an attempt to emphasise some presumably forgotten values of
Argentina's cultural tradition to a merely anti-foreign attitude.
Indeed, some of the questions posed by this attempt to revive a
'national and a popular culture' were more interesting than the jejune
results, limited to the picturesque. In any case, most intellectuals, with
the initial exception of the Catholic nationalistic minority, were
strongly antagonised by the new cultural policies and by the way in
which they were 'imposed upon the intellectual production of the
country, as well as upon its transmission, something ... which runs
counter to the guarantees given in the Constitution, not being
condoned by any of the existing laws' (*La Nación*, 12 Sep 1949).

Some aspects of the final performance of the Peronist government –
for example, the conflict with the Church and aspects of Perón's own
behaviour, that were considered extravagant – also contributed to the
impression that the Government was unreliable and capable of
dangerous and unpredictable actions. However, it would seem that the
reformist but limited character of the Peronist regime should have
been clear enough to dissipate any dangers of a social convulsion. In
several ways it represented a much milder 'danger' than the Eurocommunist challenge of our days, or even of a British-style labour
party. The fantasies about the revolutionary potential of Peronism
seem quite far-fetched.

Nevertheless, what Peronism wanted to achieve was within the
range of changes which normally excite, if not the imagination, at
least the political will of large sectors of the population, particularly
of the lower classes. It is difficult to determine to what extent the
antagonism and bitterness created by the initial Peronist governments

was a consequence of the structural changes that took place, or of the peculiar ways in which they were carried out. It is obvious that both played an important role. While some of the peculiarities border on the *petite histoire*, they would appear to throw a lot of light on the events of the time.

DOWNFALL, REDRESS AND PERSECUTION

If the years of Peronist dominance were a traumatic experience for many important groups, Perón's downfall in 1955, 'the many casualties caused by the bombing' (*The Times*, 17 June 1955) by the rebel forces – many at least by previous standards – and the immediate repression that followed left an equally strong and bitter impression on the Peronist following, intensifying feelings already high. A thorough purge of everyone tainted with any kind of association with the previous regime was made in the armed forces, the Government and the universities. The army intervened in the trade unions, and many of the leaders, as well as many of those of the Justicialista party, were imprisoned, while a public campaign through the press, radio and television tried to discredit the previous regime. In many ways it was the exacerbated reverse of what had happened during the previous period – a statement which would certainly be contested by many in Argentina. The Government thought that, instead of repeating past excesses, it was at last redressing them. However, the Peronist fold took what happened as a severe and very harsh political persecution. And persecution it was, differently applied to different social groups, but no less intense than the Peronists had carried out before. The climax of the new period, before things began to calm down in 1958, was an attempted coup staged by Peronist groups in 1956. The uprising was easily brought under control, but for the first time in this century the punishment included the shooting of the leaders and a score of the more ardent followers.

The more bellicose Peronist resistance groups sprang up as a consequence of these killings. Even some of the Peronist subversive movements of the early 1970s can be linked to these beginnings, although the bulk sprang up quite independently, even if they used this uprising as a symbol. What is clear is that the division of Argentine society into Peronist and anti-Peronist groups was extremely sharp by the late 1950s; both were able to display real and serious grievances, and both had their mythology and their martyrs.

MODERNISATION AND DEVELOPMENT

One of the most important developments during the first decade after Perón's downfall was the reopening of the country to foreign contacts, both cultural and economic. This accelerated the process of modernisation. The previous inward-looking phase had started involuntarily in the 1930s with the world crisis and had been accentuated during the years of the world conflict. After the war, and for the first time quite voluntarily, Argentina had embarked on a nationalistic course which had kept the country outside the mainstream of world economic and cultural developments. In a way it was a belated reaction to the previously high level of foreign influence. While the 1920s were the apex of the internationalist attitude, the early 1950s were the high-point of the inward-looking trend. As these things go it was quite to be expected that the country would again veer towards a more internationalist attitude. An interruption of more than twenty years in contacts with the world was, however, bound to create quite a few strains when normal contacts were resumed, and some of the problems of the period can be associated with this accelerated 'updating' in cultural and economic matters. To begin with, a complete change took place at the universities. Besides the inevitable vendettas against the people who had collaborated with Perón, a modernisation process took place. The social sciences, which are a good example of this transition, were for the first time opened to American influence. New disciplines such as sociology were introduced, and others, such as economics and psychology, were developed to new levels – the last recognising European influences as well (Halperín, 1972).

The media had previously laboured under a whole set of restrictions regarding foreign coverage of news and the introduction of books and films. Now, all of a sudden, the country again obtained access to foreign material of all kinds. In the economy, foreign capital, which had been restricted during the previous period, was lured back and, although it did not move in in the expected amounts, it had an effect. A foreign business community was built up again, this time very much under American influence. The urbanisation process which had picked up during the previous period continued, even if at a slighter slower pace, increasing up to the middle 1960s the size of the shanty towns that had sprung up in all big cities. Migrants moved from relatively structured social habitats into the depersonalisation typical of the big cities, an ideal situation for the maintenance of a personalised political loyalty to a leader of the Perón type. This social and cultural modernisation created a particularly strained situation for the young people coming into the labour force and into the universities, exacerbating their normal degree of confusion and anxiety and increasing the usual gap between the *Weltanschauung* of the young and that of their elders. Whether a link may be found here with the behaviour of youth groups in the early 1970s is impossible to determine, although it has been argued with some force (Torre, 1980). What is clear is that there was an 'across the board modernisation of Argentine society, observable in the type of consumption ... of the middle classes, in the anti-traditional structure given to the dominant ideologies from a university in full scientificist expansion, and in the mass media' (Portantiero, 1978). All these were typical traits of the Frondizi government which came to power in 1958 as a consequence of an electoral deal with Perón, who had been banned by the military. It became usual for political parties of all shades to criticise the military for these discriminations, but to take full advantage of their consequences.

In exchange for electoral support, the new government granted an amnesty to political prisoners, recognised the trade unions and allowed them to elect their officials, which in practice meant handing over the leadership of the Confederación General del Trabajo (CGT) to the Peronists. As it turned out, few of the old leaders survived. A new generation emerged; they were equally identified with Peronism, but had not been appointed by Perón himself, and had gained their new positions as a consequence of their own efforts.

The election of Frondizi came as a surprise, and was much against military expectations and wishes, a fact which tended to create an underlying instability. Although Frondizi was elected on a left-of-centre programme and was able to count on the support of middle class and intellectual groups, once in power he made a complete about-face, pursuing instead a modern right-of-centre programme. The new government started by signing an agreement with the IMF, thus opening the door to foreign investors, in particular to American capital. While the country during the Perón years had emphasised light import substitution and local capital, it was now to develop heavy import substitution and foreign direct investment. The new attitude was that 'it does not matter where capital originates, only its functions matter. If it serves national objectives, it is welcomed and it is useful' (Arturo Frondizi, *La Nación*, 2 July 1961). The originality of the economic programme was the mixing of an extreme import-substitution scheme – that of the Economic Community of Latin

America (ECLA) – with a pro-foreign investment policy abhorred both by the ECLA people and by nationalists of all shades. The strategy was to encourage foreign capital in the high-priority areas, steel, petro-chemicals, paper and oil. The big successes took place in oil, where production boomed, and in the car industry, the latter having a significant impact on industry as a whole, in particular technological externalities. The emphasis was clearly on the new capital-intensive industries rather than on the updating of the older, established industries which were using backward technologies. This tended to create a dual situation, a modern, foreign-owned, capital-intensive, high-priority and growing sector and an old-fashioned sector, mostly locally owned, with a low priority and relatively stagnant. No wonder that the local industrialists who had been so favourable to Frondizi began to veer away, looking back with nostalgia to the old days prior to 1955 when no foreign capital had competed with them. Frondizi's turn-around was too drastic, exceeding by far the usual difference between an electoral platform and an effective programme. It created tremendous ideological and semantic confusion and introduced a degree of cynicism and political double talk that had serious consequences for the future political life of the country (Corradi and Torre, 1978).

The bitter reaction of the trade unions to this new turn of government was soon felt in a wave of strikes of unexpected strength which took place at the beginning of 1959. The Government launched an emergency plan known as CONINTES (Conmoción Interior del Estado), imprisoning some of the labour leaders and cancelling some of the privileges recently granted. The strikes collapsed, leaving bitter resentment among the union leadership who only one year before had been instrumental in having the Government elected. However, even in this confrontation a conflict that was to prove characteristic of future events could be seen within Peronist ranks. The Peronist National Command, which was subordinated to Perón and made up mostly of politicians, criticised the trade-union leadership for being too hesitant in its anti-Government attitude and for 'not having instilled in the rank and file sufficient revolutionary fervour' (*Militancia*, 19 July 1973). The difference did not go unnoticed; the Government soon tried to co-opt some of the union leaders through offering special benefits to one union after another, but with limited success. It inaugurated, however, the practice of negotiations with the union leadership, in particular with the so-called *participacionista* group. This was to continue, and, despite the failed strikes and the anti-labour economic policies, this represented a big change for the unions. Instead of being ostracised, they began to be accepted as an integral part of the system. It was clear that despite 'the deep disagreement between their points of view . . . a dialogue is going on between the Government and the CGT, a dialogue which has a political implication' (*La Nación*, 2 July 1961). During Frondizi's period there was a recognition of the role of the trade unions – the CGT being 'normalised' in 1961 – and a certain legitimation of the Peronist movement as a *de facto* power, although it always remained on the fringe.

In 1961, the Government tried its hand in several provincial by-elections. It no longer had the support of Perón and was now opposed by the bulk of the labour leadership. However, it fared surprisingly well in these by-elections, held, it is true, in areas where there was a small degree of industrialisation and a small work-force. In one of the industrialised provinces, Santa Fé, the Government was able to win through the strong popularity of the local leader of the party. At this stage Frondizi was able to attract much of the anti-Peronist vote, including that of the right. Encouraged by these results, the Government went ahead with the national elections of 1962, which included all the larger provinces, among them the crucial province of Buenos Aires. Peronism was harassed but, even so, Peronist candidates were allowed to run under a variety of different party labels. The very odd ticket for the province of Buenos Aires was made up of Andrés Framini, a labour leader, as governor and Perón as deputy governor. Peronism carried the province and also the city of Buenos Aires, while the Radicals carried the province of Córdoba. Nationwide, Peronism got 30.9 per cent of the vote, the Government 26.2 per cent and the Radicals (UCR del Pueblo) 19.9 per cent. The results created a state of shock, which blurred the excellent performance of the Government and the poor performances of the other two major parties.

Although the Government was willing to annul the elections, it could not get support from the armed forces. Moreover, its political turn-around had lost it the allegiance of its former supporters without gaining it the sympathy of the groups at which the policies were aimed. Despite initial successes, Frondizi could not become a credible representative of these groups and ended without significant support. This reversal was paralleled later on by Isabel Perón's, which similarly broke the original alliance without creating a workable alternative. It is this which was at the root of the downfall of both Frondizi and Isabel Perón. Independently of what one may think of their respective objectives, both were able to muster transitory support, a fact which their failures have tended to blur. It is not so easy to show that their failures were inherent in their policies; one can only say that their success was improbable but not necessarily impossible. The military coup against Frondizi, one of the most unwarranted of a long list of quite unwarranted coups, was part of a most serious internal crisis in the army which nearly brought the country to the point of civil war. The illusions of the 1955 anti-Peronist groups had been shattered. Democracy, in which they formally believed, had given the Government to their despised foe.

> The spirit of legality is hurt and in disarray, because it is perplexed. Its essential driving force, ... its faith in the law and the Constitution has been affected by the 18 March elections, by the annulment, and, even more so, by the downfall of Dr Frondizi. (*La Nación*, 1 Apr 1962)

After an armed confrontation in which some people were killed, the *azul* military group emerged triumphant. They were more open to a degree of accommodation with the Peronists and were committed to a return to civilian government, while the defeated *colorado* group contained the more intransigent hardliners.

CHANGES WITHIN THE TRADE UNIONS

As a result of the Frondizi government, the Peronist movement and in particular the trade unions emerged with a greater degree of legitimacy. They had learnt about their importance, even if they had been unable to gain power. They had also learnt that, to the extent that they had tried for power, they had been brushed aside. As a pressure group they knew that they had sufficient weight and were reckoned with by the military, who now courted them. The union movement was split, from the very start, between a more militant and somewhat left-inclined group – at times known as the *combativos* – and another, less ideological, more pragmatic group – at times known as the *participacionistas*. At the beginning, particularly after the November 1955 coup staged by the military hardliners and led by Aramburu, the militant reaction was the one which came more naturally. When governments tried a soft line, they found in general an adequate response, but when they tried a harder line, as after the downfall of Frondizi, the trade union answer was a radical stand, as expressed in the Huerta Grande programme of 1962. It was a way of pointing out their capacity to become dangerous if persecuted and set aside.

A turning-point of particular interest to our story was the contained but intense conflict between Perón and the unions. This had already come into the open during the 1961 strikes and gained in intensity from 1963 onwards with the ascendancy of Augusto Vandor both in the '62 Organisations' – the Peronist trade-union group – and in the CGT (the workers' federation). The conflict was not diminished by the assassination of Vandor in 1969, and has been simmering ever since, being a most important ingredient of the problems of the 1973–6 period. The conflict goes back to the formation of Peronism. While it is true that the trade unions had been helped, one could even say fostered, by Perón's government, from 1945 to 1955 they had gradually acquired their own momentum. The typical anti-Peronist criticism had been that the new unions were so much a Government creation that they would collapse after the downfall of Perón. It is not impossible that Perón himself believe that he had 'created' the unions, so to speak. After the 1955 coup, the unions suffered several military interventions of varying intensity. By the late 1950s, however, the military and the business sectors had come to appreciate the importance of being able to deal with an organised representation of labour as a better alternative to the spontaneous movements which were bound to occur in its absence. At the same time, Vandor and his group preferred to negotiate with the military, which made no pretence of bypassing the trade-union leaders and appealing directly to the rank and file; the leaders were needed by the military and were considered as legitimate – but subordinate – members of the system. The unions, while maintaining their allegiance to Perón and to Peronism, suffered some significant changes related to their obvious need to accommodate themselves to the existing conditions; it was this which was at the basis of the Perón–Vandor rift. It is one thing to take a militant position when you are far away from a country and from its risks, and another to be equally militant when living in the country. Moreover, the unions had many practical problems to solve on behalf of the rank and file; they had to maintain a relatively large bureaucratic organisation, with lawyers, accountants, doctors, and employees of various kinds managing important social services. They had a significant vested interest (legitimate, but none the less vested) in maintaining a functioning apparatus. While it was useful for them to keep up an identification with Peronism which contributed to the communication of the leaders with the rank and file and was a symbol of protest, they did not want this to hamper the maintenance of permanently open channels of communication with successive governments and with pressure groups. There is a similarity with the evolution of some of the European trade union movements: these have maintained their allegiance to the traditional socialist or communist ideology – which has had a useful rallying function – while at the same time stressing the practical functions of everyday union life. The Eurocommunist development is a complex phenomenon, but to a great extent reflects the importance of down-to-earth trade union demands; these have forced the disposal of that part of the ideology which hindered progress and the substitution of a 'modernised' version serving the new needs. 'Modernisation' has meant a loss of much of the former content, particularly of revolutionary zeal, a change disguised in complex phraseology so as to make it universally acceptable to the old-timers. At a much lower level of ideologisation, the conflict within the Justicialista party to which we are referring developed very much along the same lines. With Vandor, the Peronist trade unions reached one of their peaks of self-assertion and also one of their peaks of lack of interest in structural changes.

From Perón's point of view, one of the greatest nuisances created by Vandor's trade union-centred strategy was that, by having clearer bounds, the unions could not so easily be used as a tool of his political manipulations and threats. In several instances Perón tried to create competing groups, generally to the left of the bulk of the trade union movement. The first attempt was the creation in 1966 of the oddly named '62 organizaciones de pie junto a Perón', which lasted until 1967. The second and more significant one was the creation in 1968 of the splinter CGT de los Argentinos, led by Raimundo Ongaro, which lasted until 1970. While Perón had a total command of the political expression of the movement, easily defeating the trade unions – as in the Mendoza elections of 1964 – he had no more than nuisance value to the autonomous labour movement, which was basically able to follow its own pragmatic line. A more important threat to the Vandor line was the appearance of some left-of-centre – or at least more militant – trade union groups. This was probably the consequence of the fact that the nationwide, centralised and necessarily bureaucratic trade union organisations had been increasing their distance from the rank and file, becoming less sensitive to labour demands at the factory level (Torre, 1978). Compared with the short distance and easy access prevailing earlier, union members felt less well represented by the trade union hierarchy and looked for alternative and more direct channels. These developments meant an increase in the diffusion of power within the trade union structure, an increase in the degree of militancy, and a reduction in the power of the national leadership. Some of these more militant and ideological labour groups appeared in Córdoba, as in the case of the *clasista* unions which gained ground in the new, large and automated factories which had sprung up in the early 1960s. For a while it was not clear whether this indicated a new radical trend among the working classes or merely an increase in their militancy. Although of a localised character, they were able to pose what seemed a real threat, carrying weight till 1974, when the intervention by the authorities of the national union, with the support of the Government, stopped the left-wing drift. The abrupt disappearance of the trend does not allow us to reach any clear-cut conclusions. The main issue is whether these left-wing 'deviations' were normal but limited movements, or were the beginning of a significant, long-term development which might have changed the character of the labour movement. Although the answer to this question is ideologically loaded, one may dare to say that it is more probable that the bourgeois character of most of the Argentine labour movement, in accord with the relatively high income and consumption level of its rank and file, created a clear boundary between what was possible and what was not.

THE RADICAL INTERLUDE

After the downfall of Frondizi the military stopped short of a takeover, mainly because of their deep internal divisions, but remained indeed the power behind the throne. After an interim period, restricted elections were called in 1963, this time won by the more traditional radical group, the UCR del Pueblo, running against a loose alliance led by the former head of the military government from 1955 to 1958, General Aramburu. Both were acceptable to the military but Aramburu's right-of-centre coalition was the more favoured, a fact that recreated a basic underlying tension between it and the new Radical government. Both, however, were very cool towards any *rapprochement* with Peronism or with the trade unions, which had been banned during the electoral process, something which prompted them to an immediate and active opposition. The Radicals got just over 25 per cent of the vote, Aramburu 13.9 per cent, while, significantly, more than 19 per cent were blank votes, representing the hard core of the Peronist vote which had no other electoral outlet. This division of the vote was considered to place the legitimacy of the election in question. Once in office the new government followed a slightly left-of-centre policy which soon made both the propertied and the Peronist groups uneasy, although obviously for very different reasons. The allegation from the right was that the Government did not have an adequate understanding of the needs of the business sector. Rather than being against business it was considered to be indifferent. The Government's mild but clearly anti-foreign attitude, best exemplified in the annulment of the oil contracts with foreign companies signed by Frondizi's government, created additional disquiet. It was also considered, and with some reason, that the Radical approach was impervious to the modernisation needs of the country, as if the clock could be turned back. Quite a few of the post-1955 changes were reversed. The groups which had been associated with the previous modernisation attempt reacted vigorously, considering that 'We will now shut the doors of the country ... returning to economic isolation with its sinister follow-up of frustrations, shrouding ourselves in the thousand times repeated concepts about national treason and imperialism that Argentines have overcome long ago' (*Clarín*, 6 Nov 1963).

The Radicals were ridiculed in a vicious way by the press as extremely old fashioned, timid and inefficient, in what can now be seen as a concerted campaign. Nevertheless, they made up one of the most principled, democratic and tolerant political groups in the country. This was even admitted by some of the opposition parties. 'The Government's performance is full of dignity and probity, as the institutions function normally and the rights and guarantees envisaged by the Constitution are assured' (Federación de Partidos de Centro, *La Nación*, 26 Jan 1964). However, this tolerant behaviour and this belief in democratic procedures, with the ominous expectation of free elections – and the eventual return of Peronism – not only failed to prevent their downfall but in fact contributed to it. The business sector in turn was apprehensive, and was not reassured by a satisfactory economic performance. The increases in GNP during 1964 and 1965 were 10.3 and 9.1 per cent respectively, but this was considered a mere recuperation from the 1962 crisis. It was based more on an increase of consumption than on an increase in investment. The revival created inflationary pressures and some balance-of-payments problems, which were, however, mild compared with previous and later difficulties (Mallon and Sourrouille, 1973). The performance of those years, particularly when taking into account conditions prevailing in 1963, was not at all bad. They were good years and when viewed from a distance they look even better.

The main attack from the right, however, was based on the presumed fact that the Government lacked a minimum degree of authority. The way it handled some of the strikes and particularly some of the sit-ins was considered as evidence of lax behaviour. These factory occupations, which took place in May 1964 as part of a general plan, were of a particular strong-arm character and in many cases included the taking of hostages. Such situations lasted for a few days and were potentially explosive; for a while they gave the impression of getting out of hand. The business sector considered the occupations 'threatening and subversive' (*Polémica*, 22 Feb 1964) and demanded 'strong action', something which would have worsened things to a dangerous degree. The sit-ins could not be kept up and so they dissolved. This was partly owing to the Government's 'do-nothing' attitude, which by not creating an opposition gave the strikers the appearance of indulging in a pointless exercise. While the policy of the Government was probably the wisest possible under the circumstances, it still gave the business sector the impression of a serious lack of authority and seemed to mark the beginning of social chaos.

Whilst these were the main allegations from one side of the political spectrum, on the other side the Peronist groups were unhappy at the attempts of the Radical government to foster some of the internal feuds in the party as well as in some of the major unions. This was part of a strategy to get some kind of popular support beyond its traditional lower middle and middle-class groups. The Government and the Labour Ministry tried to interfere in the life of the trade unions, taking sides in some internal disputes, and followed an explicit policy of dividing the Peronist leadership. An example of this was the admittance of Isabel Perón into the country with the expectation that she would divide and hamper the political efforts of the labour leadership. The occasion was the election in the province of Mendoza in 1964 in which two Peronist candidates were running. One was supported by Perón and with the help of Isabel's presence he got two-thirds of the Peronist vote, while the other, who also invoked his support but only had trade-union backing, got the balance. The antagonism between Isabel Perón and the labour leadership was to have its importance later on during her government. Vandor, who had engineered the attempt at autonomy, retreated after the defeat to

his purely trade union position, where Perón did not dare to challenge
him, but not without a further – but indirect confrontation – at the
end of 1964. In a confusing episode, Perón attempted – and failed – to
return to the country. What had happened was that Vandor had tried
to challenge Perón's leadership by exposing his reluctance to run the
risks of a return to the country. Great pressure was put on Perón to
convince him of the need for his return. He was in a delicate position
and – finding no way out – had to make an attempt, even if half-
heartedly. He began a trip to Argentina, but was stopped in Brazil at
the request of the Argentine authorities and had to return to Spain.
Apparently the faithful had tried to bring back their courageous
leader; a serious confrontation had taken place. However, it did not
have any of the expected consequences – one way or the other – in
shifting the internal balance of power. By 1965 the Peronist groups
had become suspicious of the various attempts made by the Radicals
to divide them. Quite understandably, the reaction of the leadership,
and of Vandor in particular, was extremely negative. They even began
to support, in a none-too-veiled manner, a military coup. The
Radicals, who had a somewhat similar social base, were in a sense
more dangerous to the Peronist leadership than the military, who had
no popular support whatsoever and had no alternative but to
negotiate with the unions. This new line was supported among
Peronists by imputing to the military 'nationalist' and even 'populist'
attitudes, a survival from the 1944–55 period.

At the end, the Radicals had the opposition of labour and the
opposition of the business and propertied groups, and of quite a few
intellectuals, particularly of the 'developmentalist' school. When the
Radicals were finally brought down in June 1966 they were extremely
isolated. A typical right-of-centre comment made at the time of their
downfall heavily criticised the Government's 'administrative
paralysis, its inability to take measures and to understand the magni-
tude of the problems which it faced . . . and its unshakeable confidence
that time alone could bring about the needed solutions' (*La Nación*, 3
July 1966).

What finally brought the downfall of the Radical government, however, was its allegiance to liberal democratic values. In fact it became
clear that it had been firm in its intention to go ahead with fair
elections in 1969, which meant an inevitable Peronist victory. The
military, which had half-heartedly stopped short of a full coup in
1962, moved again in 1966.

THE MILITARY COMEBACK AND KRIEGER VASENA'S ECONOMICS

The 1966 coup was made on the assumption that a different political system was necessary to prevent once and for all the advent of Peronism, and even of the middle class UCR. Only once in the past, in 1930, a non-liberal autocratic regime had been attempted and this had met strong resistance even among the established groups. The new attempt by Onganía to set up a non-liberal system of government met with the same distrust, even from groups that fully agreed with the new economic policies. These groups were prepared 'to consider Onganía's political set up only as a temporary stage, no matter what faults may have been exhibited in the past by the political parties' (*La Nación*, 10 July 1966).

They may have considered a lengthy transition necessary, but they rejected an alternative political system. The importance of the widely shared democratic values inherited from the modernising elite that had 'created' the country at the turn of the century was again evident. The new government was the consequence of an uneasy alliance between military groups with clearly non-liberal values and business sectors with strong international ties, counting on labour acquiescence. The initial period from September to December 1966 had a marked nationalistic slant. In the crucial Ministry of Government (the Interior) a politician well known for his nationalistic leanings was appointed, while Néstor Salimei, a militant of the Catholic right with vague nationalistic leanings who was not a full member of the business establishment, was appointed to the Ministry of Economics. The more nationalistic authoritarian line clashed with the more liberal pro-business groups, creating a delicate situation for the government. It had to yield, and appointed Adalbert Krieger Vasena as the new Minister of Economy, an outstanding and true representative of the industrial and financial groups. He was also welcomed by the agricultural sector, something which was to change later on. From January 1967 onwards, Onganía followed a less pretentious and somewhat milder authoritarian political line, together with a substantially liberal economic programme. It was a 'neat division between the economic and political spheres of influence [as] can be more clearly seen every day' (*La Nación*, 22 Jan 1967). The novelty of the economic strategy was that it soon showed a clear industrial and financial bias, instead of the one traditional to these type of policies, in favour of the agricultural sector. A significant and presumably once-and-for-all devaluation was made, increasing the price of the dollar by 40 per cent with the idea of maintaining thereafter a fixed rate of exchange, something which was to become one of the stumbling-blocks of the whole programme. The novelty was that the devaluation was accompanied by *ad valorem* taxes on agricultural exports, thus avoiding the initial abrupt transfer of income to the agricultural sector. These were eliminated gradually, barely compensating for the increase in domestic prices, given the fixed exchange rate. Another novel element was an expansionist monetary policy based on a tight fiscal programme and a generous credit policy particularly towards the private sector (van Rijckeghem, 1972). This was made compatible by the drastic reduction of inflationary expectations and the increase in the demand for cash and monetary assets. A sort of incomes policy was imposed through the freezing of wages at 95 per cent of their historical real values, which allowed wages to maintain their share of the GNP at around 44 per cent. At the same time a flexible price agreement with the 500 leading firms was made. After nearly two years the programme achieved a reduction in the rate of inflation to less than 10 per cent per year (something that was to be short-lived) without a reduction in the level of economic activity. It was by no means a classically orthodox policy as initially interpreted by supporters and foes alike (Braun, 1970). It departed from previous orthodoxy on three main counts: first, in its attempt to avoid a transfer of income from the industrial to the agricultural sector; secondly, in its attempt to impose some kind of price control on the leading business firms; thirdly, in its expansionary monetary and credit policy. In this programme one can detect a clear emphasis on expectations and the cost side of the inflationary process, which set it apart from more characteristic monetary solutions; it even had some similarities with aspects of the 1973–4 stabilisation programme. On the other hand the programme was traditionally *liberal* in its emphasis on foreign capital and in the role given to private enterprise. The economic situation improved substantially, making 1969 an excellent economic year in terms of production, balance of payments and inflation, and not so bad for real wages and income distribution.

This successful initial stage was, however, much affected by the change in expectations resulting from the depression of particular sectors, which built up pressures. There followed the inevitable second stage, in which relative prices bounced back and the full circle of economic policies was completed. Unfortunately the reliance of the programme on fixed exchange rate, while contributing substantially to the initial reduction in the rate of inflation, depressed the agricultural and the new industrial export sectors; it reduced the net effective protection to industry while bolstering imports. The combination of a fixed exchange rate and a strong, though declining, internal inflation tended to overvalue the rate of exchange once more, a situation which was reflected in the poor performance of the external sector. Reserves were bolstered, however, by significant foreign borrowing, which compensated for the small amount of direct investment. In the agricultural sector, this situation was barely compensated for by the reduction in export taxes on agricultural exports, while agricultural prices fell to some of the lowest levels of the decade. The situation was aggravated by the fall in the international price of meat. This lowered internal prices, and gave rise to a serious cattle crisis which finally turned the whole agricultural sector against the Government. In the short run, the cattle crisis and the low price of beef, so important in Argentina's diet, contributed to the anti-inflationary programme, as it helped to keep down nominal wages without depressing too much the level of wages.

Over industry some clouds began to gather. The problems were partly a consequence of the increase in foreign participation in the industrial sector and the reduction in the level of the net effective protection of industry, brought about by the reduction in the nominal level of the tariff and by the increase in the overvaluation of the rate of exchange. The smaller and more locally owned businesses resented the preference exhibited by the Government for the larger, more modern and more foreign-owned firms. These were to a great extent one and the same, a consequence of the Government's desire to modernise the economy and increase the general level of efficiency (Gerchunoff and Llach, 1975). Krieger Vasena's was indeed a major attempt to modernise the economic structure of the country. It echoed the view that the country was 'at least three decades behind with respect to other nations, and catching up on the time which has been lost will require increased efforts in the immediate future. ... 'Much has been done, but not at the pace required by the world in which we live' (*Clarín*, 14 Nov 1966). It is still open to question whether the Krieger Vasena programme could have continued with minor adjustments if political troubles had not appeared. A devaluation of the peso, an increase in beef prices in particular and a new round of inflation were inevitable. Probably the 1971–2 developments would have taken place in any case, but not necessarily on the same scale.

The argument that the political troubles were a direct consequence of Krieger Vasena's economic policies cannot really be upheld.

The illusions of the labour leaders when the new government came in proved to be short-lived. What is surprising is not so much that this was so, but that they could have had any illusions at all. Some of them were counting on recreating an alliance between the military and labour, an illusion that has been shared by quite different circles since 1955. The unions found themselves faced with a government which initially offered economic policies even less palatable than the previous ones, and which used the same strong negotiating techniques, or even harsher ones. The only consolation was that no attempt was made to bypass the labour leaders. Whatever support was given to the new government in its initial stages was soon withdrawn, while the labour movement became divided over the degree of confrontation it should pursue.

THE THREAT OF SUBVERSION

We now have to go back to the downfall of Perón in September 1955, and in particular to the 'coup within a coup' which two months later opened the way to the hardliners led by General Aramburu. This created even more intense resentment among the Peronists, whose natural reaction was to veer towards an equally hard line and indulge in more radical attitudes, or at least in more radical rhetoric. The harshly repressed Peronist uprising of 1956 can be identified as the starting-point of armed resistance. However, for many years it was more of the type waged by a defeated and persecuted party, and it did not have a social revolutionary character.

Perón at that time also indulged in radical rhetoric, but at the same time was willing to negotiate when he could, for example with Frondizi. His initial political appointment of John William Cooke as head of the movement, a position that he held until 1969, was an indication of this leftish attitude. It is true to say that Cooke, who was to become the leader of the pro-Guevarist faction after the Cuban revolution, had at that time a milder outlook, but radical he certainly was. The Perón–Cooke letters (1973) are a fascinating account of the latter's attempt to pin Perón down to a revolutionary line. However, Perón always tried to keep open as many different options as he could, broadening his appeal to encompass as wide an ideological range as possible. He simultaneously supported contradictory policies, a tactic which gave rise to the most disparate interpretations. This strategy won him substantial benefits, though at the expense of a confused image.

In 1960 there was a timid attempt to start a guerrilla base (*foco*) in Tucumán; at the time it seemed odd and extravagant. By small steps, subversion became one of the most significant new factors, with far-reaching consequences in politics and for the general fabric of society. It is difficult to understand how this kind of violence came about, and how it took root in so many young people. It is one of the tragedies of Argentina in recent times. Nothing of this kind had been known in the country at least since the anarchist upsurge of the first two decades of this century. In the background were the continuous revolutions, repressions and violations of the rule of law which had taken place. These had created an obnoxious climate where the idea of limits, rules and tolerance had been weakened. This, however, cannot be construed as a cause. Another contributory factor was the general political mood prevalent in Latin America in the late 1960s and early 1970s, a mood which permeated most institutions, including the Church and the military. This was the time of Velasco Alvarado in Peru, Torre in Bolivia, both prominent members of the armed forces, and Allende in Chile. However, a left-wing attitude has to be distinguished from a subversive and violent one. There is a qualitative difference between them, even if at times the alleged ultimate objectives may not look too dissimilar. When judging political movements, the means are at least as important as the ends; it is the means which people will experience, while most of the ends will remain on paper.

Another and more specific factor which was part of the left-wing mood was the progressive line taken by the Church, heralded by the Third World movement (*Tercermundismo*). The Medellín Episcopal Conference of 1969 was a landmark in this progressive evolution, which condemned economic and political oppression and encouraged the participation of the laity in political reform.

No specific encouragement was given to violent means, even less to subversion as such, but in the particular Latin American context of the 1960s and early 1970s the jump was not difficult to make. Some priests and members of the laity made it, justifying and practising violence. More significant than these extreme cases were the speeches and pastoral letters of some of the more influential and higher-ranking prelates. Without condoning violence, they took what today can be seen as a lenient attitude towards it.

The theology of liberation – one step further along this road – in the minds of many equated injustice with violence and, even more extraordinarily, justified the return of kind for kind. Its preachings fell upon responsive ears. Injustice can be worse than violence, but it is a problem of a different kind.

What were the social origins of the young people attracted to the subversive movements? Most of them came from middle and upper middle-class groups. They had been born in and lived through the impact of the accelerated modernisation of Argentina's society during the 1960s. Some of them came from families who had lost positions of relative prestige or power which they had held in the past. Many came from a Catholic background and had formerly been associated with nationalistic and right-wing groups. Some of the older ones came from the Peronist resistance which had developed since 1956 and which had been intermittently active.

Nevertheless, the combination of all these circumstances does not come near to explaining the extraordinary upsurge of violent subversion, extraordinary because of its pervasiveness among the young and the viciousness of its actions. After all, many of these circumstances prevailed in other countries of Latin America but have not produced similar consequences. In Chile, for example, the radicalisation of political groups was much more intense than in Argentina, but subversive groups of the Movimiento de Izquierda Revolucionario (MIR) type played little part in the process.

The most violent disturbance took place in 1969 in Córdoba. For a few days Córdoba saw violence in its streets, sniper shooting, rioting and physical destruction. Although there was a background of resentment and dissatisfaction among many people, there was no relation between the degree of dissatisfaction and the kind of violence which took place. What is clear today is that it was not the spontaneous phenomenon which many people at the time, and some political scientists (Delich, 1974), believed it to be. It was one of the first occasions on which the subversive organisations had an active political impact on Argentine society (Hodges, 1976).

A surprising aspect of the *cordobazo* was the weak reaction of the Government. The allegation that the military repression was intentionally delayed in order to create an awkward situation for the Government is quite unproved and seems at least an oversimplification. A reason which goes much deeper is that the hesitant reaction was evidence that the military still did not think that it had a primary role in the repression of popular uprisings. Many still held the view that an alliance between the army and the people was possible; this may have influenced the paradoxical attitude of the Government, which, despite its hard image, took a temporising line. The governor of the province was sacked and the newly appointed military governor declared that 'instead of talking about a rebellious attitude it is better to talk about the energy [*pujanza*] of a strong people' (Commodore Huerta, *Análisis*, 5 July 1969). The same kind of line was also taken by the military commander of the province, General Carcagno, and Colonel Harguindeguy, who was to become the first commander-in-chief of the Cámpora regime. Soon after, the Minister of Economy, whose policies were vaguely considered to be responsible for most of the problems, was replaced by José María Dagnino Pastore. He followed the same basic economic policies but was less linked, at least in the public mind, with the establishment.

The final blow for the Onganía government was the kidnapping and murder of former president Aramburu by the subversive Montonero organisation, which was making its first bloody debut. Public opinion was shocked. Some blamed the Government for its lenient handling of the investigation; others maintained that the Government had connived with the kidnappers.

The government of General Onganía is responsible of Aramburu's kidnapping; even if it is not the material author, it has at least looked on with a complacent attitude [Héctor Sandler, leading member of Aramburu's coalition].

There are some facts, which make it difficult to discard the possibility of a sinister plan [self-titled group of Friends of Aramburu].

(*Análisis*, 16 June 1970)

Aramburu, who had veered towards a more liberal attitude, was beginning to appear as a potential replacement for Onganía, should the military opt for a government along less authoritarian lines with conservative civilian support, and this was the basis of these extraordinarily far-fetched accusations. However, that they were made at all is a good indication of the shocked state of public opinion. This kind of accusation, accompanied by a demand for strong, though ill-defined, action has not been uncommon in other countries when subversion has started its acts of violence; it is an irrational reaction to an unknown but seriously felt new danger. Onganía was left with scanty support. He was not in favour with the bulk of the liberal conservative groups, who were annoyed by 'the notorious disagreements between those who want a democratic outcome in line with our democratic traditions, and those who want to impose forms of governments alien to our Argentine traditions' (*La Nación*, 7 July 1968). Radicals, who shared these apprehensions, and Peronists, who did not, were also sternly opposed, as were the trade union groups who had acquiesced at the beginning. The agricultural sector was nearly in a state of rebellion, while the more locally owned and smaller enterprises had been antagonised by the modernisation programme. The Government retained only the support of the larger and more international business sector, an economically significant but politically insufficient base of support.

MILITARY CRISIS AND DEVELOPMENTALIST ECONOMICS

Onganía was finally replaced in a movement headed by the commander-in-chief of the army, General Alejandro Agustín Lanusse, who, however, stopped short of taking full power. A compromise candidate was named, Roberto Marcelo Levingston, a general without any military base. It was a most unstable situation and could not last. The change of presidents, Levingston for Onganía, showed quite openly the wide divisions among the military and destroyed the credibility of a period of long and solid military rule. Levingston had to preside over the dissolution of the stabilisation scheme and the loss of foreign support for the economic programme. While up to 1968–9 the Government had given the impression of a successful performance, by 1971 it was breaking up both on the political and on the economic front.

The most immediate economic effect was to impair the foreign-borrowing potential, which had been one of the bases of the 1967–9 stabilisation programme. The new Minister of Economy, Aldo Ferrer, attempted a 'developmentalist' policy with a moderate but clear nationalistic slant. A preference for purchases of local origin was legally imposed on State agencies. Local credit on foreign capital was restricted and there was discrimination according to the nationality of capital. At the same time an attempt was made to increase the level of investment by the State sector; this was not financed by an increase in taxes, but rather by increasing the Government deficit; the previous administration had reduced the level of the deficit to an all-time low

(1.7 per cent of GNP in 1971) and a moderate increase was compatible with the expected level of inflation. The investment target of the National Plan was increased, as if this was an important step; it did not mean much more than a declaration of intent, as no meaningful actions were taken in that direction. These measures created a deep resentment in the foreign community and also alarmed local capitalists, who were wary of the new interventionism and suspicious about the ultimate objectives of the new policies. Other actions were the inevitable consequence of the previous programme. As mentioned earlier, the previous economic policies had left a 'repressed' situation, and a certain 'unloosening' was to be expected (see Chapter 7, section on inflationary cycles, and Appendix). It could have been done in several different ways, but all of them would have meant a renewal of the inflationary process. As usual, the imbalance in the foreign sector was the one to set the pace of the readjustment process. A significant devaluation became necessary and was put into practice in a succession of small steps along the lines of the crawling peg of the 1964–6 period. Although this new policy was considered by many people to have destroyed the previous stabilisation, it was to a great extent its inevitable consequence, aggravated by the beginning of the political troubles. The expansionary and more nationalistic economic policies satisfied to a larger extent some of the diffuse aspirations of the military but antagonised the business sectors. Curiously, the cattle-raising sector, which benefited so much from the restoration of its relative prices, was not won over by the new policies. Cattlemen had a deep distrust of the Levingston–Ferrer group, which they considered unreliable, among other things because of their attitude towards foreign capital. This distrust was compounded by the increasing economic troubles, particularly the renewal of inflation.

THE MILITARY WITHDRAWAL

The substitution of Levingston for Lanusse was the final blow to any remaining expectations of a long stay by the military. The lack of confidence in the durability of the Government aggravated some of the problems in the economic sphere. The Ministry of Economy was dissolved, leading to a serious lack of co-ordination. This problem was compounded by the new open-handed and incoherent economic policy of the Treasury, headed by Juan Quilici, which tripled the fiscal deficit from the low levels reached previously – 2 per cent in 1968–70 –

to about 6 per cent. The rate of inflation, which during the two previous years had already risen to nearly 40 and 65 per cent per year, moved, after a temporary slowdown during the second half of 1972, to an annual rate of more than 100 per cent during the first months of 1973. This reflected the uncertainty of the political situation and the inevitable anticipatory price increases. The external situation was extremely delicate, the Government being forced to sign a tough agreement with the IMF in mid-1972 in order to overcome the stringency in the foreign exchanges. However, this took place just at the time when the country began to feel the effects of a dramatic improvement in its terms of trade, export and import prices increasing by 40 and 10 per cent respectively. Even so, the beneficial effects were not felt immediately, while the inflationary impact was.

The mounting economic problems in turn began to affect the political situation and this was one of the reasons which impressed on the military the possible advantages of a withdrawal. Its belief was that 'there will not be a final solution to our economic problems until a political solution is reached' (Lanusse, *La Nación*, 12 Mar 1972). There were more important, specifically political, developments which pointed in this direction; these were partly a consequence of the increasing disagreement within the military regarding their long-term institutional participation in government. Some kind of return of the Peronist party began to be considered as a possible alternative. This was a surprising conclusion, in view of the firm determination which had kept the party banned for more than seventeen years.

The declared attempt of the Government to end the military regime and the possibility of elections galvanised public opinion and stirred the political groups. The Lanusse project, while looking like a dangerous gamble, was the only one to emerge with force, being, moreover, in line with the traditional liberal values still strong in the country. His belief was that 'whether liked or not Perón is a fact of life' (27 Aug 1972); and that, 'To the extent that we can go ahead with the normalisation of the institutional set-up together with Perón and with the Justicialista party, the more solid and lasting will be the consequences' (9 Oct 1972).

The Government envisaged a moderate programme aimed at electing a 'reliable' candidate, probably President Lanusse himself. This was to be the consequence of a modification of the electoral system coupled with negotiation with Perón. The electoral reforms were basically aimed at minimising the possible representation of the Justicialista party, reducing at the same time the stay in office of the elected candidates. These objectives were to be achieved through the introduction of 'ballotage', so as to help the coalition of anti-Peronist candidates in the second round while not requiring complicated alliances in the first. The tenure of office was to be a maximum of four years in order to reduce the strong pressures that built up during longer periods. It was arranged to have elections simultaneously at the national, provincial and city levels at four-yearly intervals, eliminating the continuous upheavals caused by the almost yearly elections.

The negotiations were the most essential part of the political project. Their basis was the growing belief that the Justicialista party was not after all such a terribly dangerous animal. The labour movement was clearly reformist at most, very much in line with the North American type of union, and the more Peronist unions were the less ideological. What was unsettling, however, was the allegiance given to Peronism by the subversive groups, giving it an aura of terror. At the time, however, this was thought to be a consequence of the blocking of normal electoral channels. Although negotiations with the subversive groups were never entertained, it was believed that the readmittance of Peronism into the political system would take away their main justification. A political solution would be found to the threat of violence. A typical attitude was that 'the isolation and final suppression of the guerrilla will only be possible if a political and social context capable of taking away the essential reasons for this kind of conflict is created' (Tcherkeski, *La Opinión*, 12 Jan 1972).

The readmission of Peronism was the consequence of conflicting aims among the military, which was also permeated by the conflicts of civilian society – at least the conflicts within the middle classes – and by the growing awareness of the merely reformist character of Peronism and of the need to take away the alleged basis of subversion through the election of a legitimately chosen government. It was thought that, if Peronism was accepted, it would be less open to revolutionary influence and more inclined to support the system as such. It is not absurd to compare this situation with the one which took place during the first and second decades of this century, when the Radical party (UCR) was finally allowed to participate in national elections on the grounds that it would be less dangerous to have it within the system than to keep it outside where it would be open to revolutionary temptations. Similarly this time, the change was also prompted by the conviction that, although the Justicialista party represented a different social group, it too was more liable to be integrated into the existing social fabric if allotted a share of the 'spoils'.

Both attempts were made with the intention of allowing only a minority participation; the newly admitted party would become a 'loyal opposition' which would support the system. In both cases the process got out of control, and ended with the handing over of the government to the new opposition. The strains so introduced contributed to the failure of both experiments, the first after fourteen years and the second after less than four.

The Government attempted a national-unity programme, the Gran Acuerdo Nacional. It was meant to be an agreement with Perón for the election of Lanusse in exchange for a legalisation of Peronism at most other levels – a deal which had precedents. Antagonisms, however, ran too deep. More importantly, there were doubts that the military would be willing to make such a significant accommodation without being forced. Perón thought that 'all these tricks made by the military dictatorship tend either towards a badly disguised process of electoral fraud, or towards finding a more or less acceptable way... of leaving everything as it is' (*Clarín*, 3 June 1972). The Government tried direct negotiations through the Argentine ambassador in Madrid and through a special envoy, Colonel Cornicelli, but these came to nothing. It then tried to bully him into deciding to come to Argentina before August 1972; if not, he would be banned from the presidential race. This also was believed to be a strategem:

> Nobody can consider seriously that the Justicialista leader will come back, become a candidate and, as is obvious, take power and finally be allowed to govern. It is evident that the present military set-up would not allow such an experiment.
>
> (Eichelbaum, *La Opinión*, 2 Aug 1972)

In fact Perón followed an ambivalent course, as he, like everyone else, was not clear about the future outcome. He tried to leave the door open to the different alternatives, i.e. more or less free elections, or a continuation of military rule, appearing at times 'in the position of welcoming or hindering the elections' (*La Prensa*, 25 Mar 1972). The political section of the party pressed Perón to make concessions, as any political solution would favour their position. The unions were ambivalent, as they had learned to lobby successfully under military governments and were afraid of what seemed a political gamble. The youth groups were even less interested, being already committed to a more direct and drastic strategy.

The Government, and more so the military, tried to extract from

Perón an open and clear-cut condemnation of the subversive groups and of their notorious killings of military leaders. Perón was unwilling to do so, as this was precisely what he was implicitly promising if he was accepted and he was not willing to make the repudiation in advance. This made some go so far as to think that 'violence, rather than being condemned [by Perón], has been stimulated. A condemnation has been sought [by the government] in vain' (*La Prensa*, 22 Apr 1972).

The Government had to follow the dynamics of the process it had unleashed. By the end of the year even significant sectors of the establishment felt that 'the elections are absolutely necessary because without them there is no stable solution. ... The strong government that the country needs will come about through the extraordinary strength generated by elections and [by the ensuing] democracy' (*La Nación*, 23 Nov 1972).

The big development at the end of the year was Perón's decision to come back, not with the intention of becoming a candidate, (which, according to the electoral rules, he could not) but to appraise the situation, rouse the enthusiasm of the faithful, and select the candidate of the Popular Front (the Frecilina, later to be named the Frejuli). His arrival in November 1972 against all expectations was not marked by disturbances, partly owing to the exceptional security measures taken by the Government. Everybody was surprised by the turn of events. Even President Lanusse declared that 'the country has lived through an experience that, until a very short time ago, seemed impossible' (*La Nación*, 23 Nov 1972). From some quarters, Lanusse was accused of having 'recklessly stimulated ... this journey ... which has [caused] a state of alarm and uncertainty' (*La Prensa*, 28 Nov 1972), while others from opposing quarters thought, on the contrary, that as a consequence of the visit 'a general conciliatory climate has prevailed' (*Mayoría*, 22 Nov 1972). The relationship between Perón and the Radicals was excellent, starting what was to be described as a 'flirtation' and a 'near idyllic dialogue' (*Clarín*, 18 Feb 1973).

Perón's main decision, taken just after his return to Spain immediately before the end of the year, was his nomination of Héctor Cámpora as the presidential candidate. This was a strange decision; he was an old politician of the party, held in low esteem by almost everybody in the party and elsewhere and abhorred by the military because of his links with the Peronist left. The selection was considered both by some political commentators and by some of the leaders of the Justicialista party to be an indication that Perón did not want to go to the polls, and that he preferred to have his candidate banned by the military. This would have shown that they were not playing fair, and would have given Perón a lot of negotiating power without forcing him to tackle some of the difficult decisions that a complete comeback would pose.

Perón probably considered two prospects. On the one hand he was following an improbable electoral strategy, forcing the situation so that, if elections came at all, they would come after the military had yielded completely. Alternatively, if he was banned it would enhance his moral position and improve his bargaining strength. Some thought that he preferred the latter outcome and that 'as he has lost his hopes in a military coup interrupting the path to elections, ... he is accumulating obstacles' (*La Nación*, 14 Jan 1973).

The Government was outraged, but by now it could do nothing. Electoral momentum was already high and military disarray was also at its peak. Even so, 'the decision of the Government not to veto ... the presidential candidacy of Cámpora surprised a large number of political leaders, including Perón himself' (*La Nación*, 5 Apr 1973).

When the dissolution of the military regime and the possibility of a return of Peronism began to be entertained, the inevitable jockeying for position within and around the Peronist movement began. The small-business association, the CGE, which in the past had been favourable to Peronism, was very hesitant in its support, as it did not believe that Perón was really planning to participate in the elections. Initially it veered towards the Radicals and only after the electoral result did it throw its support behind Perón. The labour movement demanded a paramount role, something which Perón was keen not to give it, since by now its expectations were even higher than at the time of Vandor.

The conflict between Perón and the unions was predictable, but the intensity of the fight and some of the methods used were not. The extraordinary emphasis given to the youth groups and the way they were used to check the power of the unions were quite new. Perón spoke of the 'need to change the leaders [of the unions] for young people; those who have been in power until now have had their day, to replace them is not a lack of justice' (*La Nación*, 2 Apr 1973). Up to that time party candidacies were divided between politicians, women and trade unionists, each having a third; now they were to be divided by quarters, so that 25 per cent would come from the youth groups. These groups had become more vocal and emotional. They had developed an extremely romantic version of Peronism, idealising its past and producing a sceptical reaction even among old-timers. They were very much against the unions, considering them as bureaucratic inter- mediaries and distorters of the 'true will' of the rank and file. They longed for spontaneous communication between the people and the leader, even rejecting the idea of a party in favour of the vague notion of a *Movimiento* in which there would be no bureaucracy, no affilia- tion and no elections, and where leaders would appear by natural con- sensus. They hoped to 'transfer the level of political decisions from the State bureaucracy to the popular base' (Peronist Youth, *La Opinión*, 22 Apr 1973).

The anarchist overtones were coupled in some groups with a ruthless approval of violent methods. These groups attained import- ance in the universities, competing successfully with the traditionally anti-Peronist groups, which were by now outflanked by the Peronist left. They also had some appeal in intellectual circles, where this new radical version of Peronism became fashionable.

Other intellectuals, however sympathetic, did not agree. 'We cannot believe for a moment that the Peronist movement will be trans- formed into a revolutionary leftist force. ... [it is to be expected that] it will be moderate and nationalistic, with a strong bias towards social welfare and a more equitable distribution of wealth' (di Tella, *New York Times*, 25 Apr 1973).

Many members of the more purely political branch of Peronism sided with the youth movement. They had lost significance after 1955 and had to look for trade union patronage, in many cases suffering humiliating experiences. Although each had different reasons, they found in the Peronist Youth a group that shared their anti-union feelings. The Cámpora–Abal Medina coalition (the latter was General Secretary of the party and a member of the youth movement) re- presented very well this anti-union alliance. It was dominated from the start by the youth elements. They were able to develop an organi- sational strength which the feeble political sector did not have, except in some provinces which were not at all sympathetic to the left. The Cámpora–Abal Medina alliance gave power to the Peronist Youth and to the radical elements within it to a much greater degree than Perón himself had envisaged. Although there can be no precise measure of the extent of the 'overshoot' compared with Perón's inten- tions, it certainly pushed issues further to the left than a multi-class alliance of the Peronist type could withstand. The campaign for the return of Perón and to an even greater degree the electoral campaign were dominated by the new alliance. The degree of control by radicals and contacts with subversive elements were greater than the majority of the public were aware of.

The military, despite all the frustrations and the obvious dangers involved, against all expectations went ahead with calling the elections.

BIBLIOGRAPHY

Braun, O. (1970) 'Desarrollo del capital monopolista en la Argentina', in Braun (ed.), *El Capitalismo argentino en crisis* (Buenos Aires).

Cantón, D. (1971) *La Política de los militares argentinos, 1900–71* (Buenos Aires).

Corradi, J. and Torre, J. C. (1978) Introduction to Corradi and Torre (eds), *The Return and Fall of Peronism, Argentina 1973–6* (Philadelphia: Institute for the Study of Human Issues, forthcoming).

Delich, F. (1974) *Crisis y protesta social: Córdoba 1969–73* (Buenos Aires).

de Pablo, J. C. (1972) *Política anti-inflacionaria en la Argentina, 1967–70* (Buenos Aires).

Diéguez, H. and Petrecolla, A. (1974) 'La distribución funcional del ingreso y el sistema previsional argentino, 1950–69', *Desarrollo Económico*, no. 55 (Oct–Dec).

Diéguez, H. (1976) 'Crecimiento, distribución y bienestar: Una nota sobre el caso argentino', *Desarrollo Económico*, no. 61 (Apr–June).

Gerchunoff, P. and Llach, J. (1975) 'Capitalismo industrial, desarrollo asociado y distribución del ingreso entre los dos gobiernos peronistas, 1950–72', *Desarrollo Económico*, no. 57 (Apr–June).

Germani, G. (1978) *Authoritarianism, Fascism and National Populism* (New Brunswick, NJ).

Gillespie, R. (1979) 'Peronism and Left Militarism: the Montoneros', *Bulletin of the Society for Latin American Studies*, no. 30 (Apr).

Graham-Yooll, A. (1981) 'Chronology 1955–76' (London, mimeo).

Halperín, T. (1964) *Argentina en el callejón* (Montevideo).

Halperín, T. (1972) *Argentina: La democracia de masas* (Buenos Aires).

Hodges, D. (1976) *Argentina: 1943–76: National Revolution and Resistance* (Albuquerque, NM).

James, D. (1978) 'The Peronist Left 1955–75', *Journal of Latin American Studies*, vol. 8, pt 2.

James, D. (1978) 'Power and Politics in Peronist Trade Unions', *Journal of Inter-American Studies and World Affairs*, vol. 20, no. 1 (Feb).

Kirkpatrick, J. (1971) *Leader and Vanguard in a Mass Society: A Study of Peronist Argentina* (Cambridge, Mass.).

Little, W. (1973) 'Party and State in Peronist Argentina 1945–55', *Hispanic American Historical Review*, no. 53 (Nov).

Little, W. (1975) 'The Popular Origins of Peronism', in D. Rock (ed.), *Argentina in the Twentieth Century* (Pittsburgh).

Mallon, D. and Sourrouille, J. (1973) *La política económica en una sociedad conflictiva: el caso argentino* (Buenos Aires).

Mora, M. (1980) 'El Estatismo y los problemas políticos del desarrollo argentino' (Buenos Aires, mimeo).

Mora, M. and Llorente, I. (eds) (1980), *El Voto peronista: ensayos de sociología electoral* (Buenos Aires).

Moreno, O. (1980) 'El Peronismo 1955–70' (Oxford: Centre for Latin American Studies, St Antony's College, mimeo).

O'Donnell, G. (1976) 'Estado y alianzas en la Argentina 1956–76', *Documento Centro de Estudios de Estado y Sociedad*, no. 5 (Buenos Aires).

Peralta Ramos, M. (1978) *Acumulación de capital y crisis políticas en Argentina (1930–74)* (Mexico).

Perón, J. and Cooke, J.W. (1973) *Correspondencia* (Buenos Aires).

Portantiero, J. C. (1978) 'Economía y política en la crisis Argentina, 1958–73', *Zona abierta*, no. 14–15.

Potash, R. (1980) *The Army and Politics in Argentina, 1945–62: Perón to Frondizi* (Stanford, Calif.).

Romero, J. L. (1975) *Las ideas políticas en Argentina*, expanded edn (Buenos Aires and Mexico).

Rouquié, A. (1978) *Pouvoir militaire et société politique en République Argentine* (Paris).

Torre, J. C. (1978) 'Workers and Unions under the Last Peronist Government, 1973–76', in J. Corradi and J. C. Torre (eds), *The Return and Fall of Peronism, Argentina 1973–76* (Philadelphia: Institute for the Study of Human Issues, forthcoming).

Torre, J. C. (1980) 'El sinolicalismo entre la reivindicación y la participación' (Buenos Aires, mimeo).

van Rijckeghem, W. (1972) 'Política de estabilización en una economía inflacionaria', *Desarrollo Económico*, no. 46 (July–Sep).

Villanueva, J. (1966) *The Inflationary Process in Argentina 1943–60*, Documento de Trabajo no. 7 (Buenos Aires: CIE, Instituto Torcuato di Tella).

Villanueva, J. (1973) 'Peronismo: el exilio 1955–75', *Cuadernos de Marcha* (Montevideo) no. 71.

3 The Peronist Presidencies

THE ELECTION OF PERÓN'S CANDIDATE, CÁMPORA

A few months before the end of 1973 a return of Perón was unthinkable. Nevertheless, a short succession of steps lifted nearly all restrictions and allowed an incredibly free election – incredibly free in view of the risks involved. The elections were won by the Justicialista coalition with nearly 50 per cent of the votes. This was not surprising, but it exceeded what the Government and even the leaders of the coalition had expected, particularly since Perón had not been allowed to run and his candidate was very weak. It seemed that, no matter what was done, electoral results for the Peronists would always be exceedingly good, a fact which reduced the influence of the moderates in the Front. In nine of the twenty-four electoral districts, its candidates exceeded the 50 per cent mark (Table 3.1) thus avoiding a second round, which was won in all but two districts. In these the official candidates named by the Cámpora group were at odds with the local Peronist caudillos, and they were lost to splinter Peronist parties fostered by them.

It could be seen that the Peronist vote was again made up of two dissimilar groups (Mora, 1975; Mora and Smith, 1980). In the urbanised centres the working electorate prevailed; here it did not have a personalised leadership and the unions were the organisational backbone. On the other hand, in the less urbanised provinces the unions were not influential; the personalised leadership of a local caudillo was paramount, making possible a degree of manipulation not so different from that of the old conservative caudillos of the past. This dichotomy was a reflection of the initial development of Peronism, which drew on, among others, both the urban socialist and the rural conservative electorates.

The elections were celebrated as a big step in the achievement of a political solution. Some of the doubts that had existed about the willingness of the military to hand over power were dispelled, for the Government had launched a process which had gone beyond the point

TABLE 3.1   Presidential Elections, 11 March 1973

	Frejuli (Cámpora)		UCR (Balbin)		Alianza Popular Federalista (Manrique)		Alianza Popular Revolucionaria (Alende)	
	'000	%	'000	%	'000	%	'000	%
City of Buenos Aires	664	37.0	427	23.8	332	18.5	259	14.4
Province of Buenos Aires	2306	52.3	870	19.7	566	12.9	450	10.2
Catamarca	45	53.8	16	19.5	17	20.15	1	1.8
Chaco	132	58.1	66	29.0	20	8.6	4	1.9
Chubut	32	52.2	16	26.4	8	12.9	2	3.7
Córdoba	517	44.9	410	36.4	115	9.9	38	3.3
Corrientes	126	46.5	32	11.9	—	—	11	4.1
Entre Ríos	231	52.8	133	30.3	22	5.1	16	3.7
Formosa	52	67.9	20	26.6	1	1.1	2	2.3
Jujuy	104	88.4	7	5.7	4	3.2	—	—
La Pampa	44	45.6	15	15.2	31	31.8	4	3.7
La Rioja	41	60.4	19	28.2	2	2.9	1	1.3
Mendoza	250	49.2	93	18.3	76	14.9	10	1.9
Misiones	72	54.8	35	27.0	10	7.6	3	2.0
Neuquén	22	51.0	9	21.6	8	17.7	3	6.0
Rio Negro	47	47.1	21	21.5	8	7.9	3	3.1
Salta	127	61.8	31	14.9	39	18.8	3	1.3
San Juan	94	46.9	23	11.1	4	2.2	4	1.8
San Luis	56	56.7	14	14.5	10	10.2	3	3.4
Santa Cruz	12	51.1	8	33.1	2	9.5	0.6	2.7
Santa Fé	604	49.2	189	15.4	357	29.1	40	3.3
Santiago del Estero	135	65.4	35	16.8	21	10.1	12	5.9
Tierra del Fuego	1.3	44.8	0.8	26.5	0.5	17.4	—	—
Tucumán	217	59.1	37	10.1	85	23.2	14	3.9
Total	5908	49.6	2537	21.3	1775	14.9	885	7.4

Alianza Republicana Popular (Martínez)	2.91%
Nueva Fuerza (Chamizo)	1.97%
Socialista Democrático (Ghioldi)	0.91%
Socialista de los Trabajadores (Coral)	0.82%
Frente de Izquierda Popular (Ramos)	0.41%
Did not vote (percentage of valid votes)	15.39%
Blank votes and annulled	2.12%

Source: Ministerio del Interior, Dirección Nacional Electoral.

of no return. The general mood was that of national reconciliation.
The day before handing over the Government the commander-in-chief
of the air-force spoke of

> the need to rise above hate and vengeance, aware that national
> unity is a precondition, [and the need] of restating the role of the
> armed forces within the new aims of the country, so as to place
> them at the service of their people's objectives and aspirations. In-
> stead of isolating themselves in a professional non-committed
> attitude they have to collaborate in the definitions of those
> objectives and in ... their achievement.

Reconciliation and a new commitment were promised, but some say
in affairs was also clearly demanded. It was felt that, while the
dangers were clear, it was at last possible to attempt a period of
normal political life. The mass mobilisation which accompanied the
electoral process moved the whole spectrum of opinion, within the
Justicialista party and outside, towards the left, creating an
exhilarating climate. It was like a sudden explosion of pent-up
demands. All kinds of projects were put forward; there was a general
idea that now the popular forces were in power anything was possible
and any obstacles could be overcome. A mood developed which at
times was festive, reckless, irresponsible or directly provocative. On
inauguration day the traditional ceremonies were intermixed with
popular outbursts, troops were derided in public and public buildings
were occupied by members of the Peronist Youth, who assumed that
new authorities were to be elected by popular vote. Although this idea
never materialised, it contributed to the impression that things were
getting out of control and to an enormous uneasiness. As it was put at
the time, 'The wave of occupations [sit-ins] that have become general
... is both confusing and unacceptable and may create a chaotic
climate and a power vacuum' (*La Opinión*, 15 June 1973). However,
the main prevailing mood was that at last a political solution had been
found and that it was worth a trial. A general shift towards the left, or
at least an extremely understanding view of its aspirations was taken
by most sectors. A new commander-in-chief of the army was named.
The more radical groups wanted to leapfrog over all the generals and
name one of the colonels, supposedly sympathetic to the new government, something which would have meant the early retirement of the
whole top brass. However, military precedence was followed, the
appointment falling on General Carcagno, a leading member of the

azul cavalry group – which had been running the army since the 1962
revolt. It was clear from the beginning that the new commander-in-
chief was trying to patch up the former rift between the army and the
new political currents. At the Caracas Inter-American Military
Conference he declared,

> The army of my country comes here, ... recognising the basic
> principles of non-intervention [and] of the free determination of all
> peoples, ... in a context where ideological differences lose all
> meaning. Either we renew ourselves and understand our final
> objectives in accordance with what our countries require ... or we
> condemn them to become victims of aggressions which are moving
> them away from their avowed destinies. The image of our armies, as
> praetorian guards of an unjust political economic and social order,
> is extremely pernicious to the health of our countries.
> (General Carcagno, *La Opinión*, 6 Sep 1973)

It is clear that the army thought that subversion had taken root as a
consequence of the lack of legitimacy of previous governments and of
the existence of injustices.

> By identifying subversion as a response to the unjust social order,
> the armed forces ... warn that the elimination of subversion by
> sheer force becomes impossible and that the use of military power
> against subversion creates an ever greater distance between the
> armed forces and the people to whom they belong. (*La Opinión*, 6
> July 1973)

The army launched the so-called Dorrego operation, whereby con-
scripts co-operated with the Peronist Youth and members of the
Montonero organisation in civic-action programmes. It was hailed as
an expression of the 'degree of understanding ... reached among all
groups of Argentine society [and of the] favourable disposition to
tackle common tasks ... superseding individual, social, political, and
philosophical attitudes' (*Clarín*, 8 Oct 1973). The Church too was
permeated by the same mood, taking the line that injustice was the
breeding ground of violence and that, rather than seeking to remove
the consequences of injustice, it was more important to attack its very
roots. If this was not done, 'a peaceful revolution would not come off,
and legal and illegal manifestations of hate and violence will be intensified' (Archbishop of Santa Fé, *La Nación*, 3 Jan 1974). But, while

the general line was clearly progressive, the Church was not particularly sympathetic to the new government. Their relationship was much more distant than had been the case in 1946. What became important, colouring the whole process, was the active participation of young people of Catholic upbringing in the extreme left-wing youth groups and in the Montonero organisation.

Many intellectuals were taking a similarly progressive line. The upsurge in political activity, the main trends of the Government and the prevailing level of violence were considered an inevitable historical development; they were the consequence of the modernisation process, of the evolution of income differentials, of the struggle between classes or within classes, of social mobilisation, of downward social mobility, of frustrated aspirations, and so on.

While at the beginning some of these explanations were – as they still are – quite valid, the point had been reached where the bulk of violence was the work of groups which had become autonomous factors in the Argentine scene and which require less broad and more specific interpretations. However, not many people in the country were aware of the widespread activity and importance of these subversive organisations, and the fact that a head-on confrontation was taking place. The freeing of political prisoners arrested for acts of violence, kidnappings and murders was one of the crucial initial-issues. The military had warned before the elections in a five-point programme (7 Jan 1973) signed by nearly all the generals that they would not accept 'an indiscriminate amnesty to all those subject to judicial process or condemned because of violations associated with subversion and terrorism'. However, subversion had been instrumental in the military withdrawal and in the call for elections, and had many allies in top Government positions. Equally important was the spirit of national reconciliation and the belief, shared by many people on the right, that the amnesty 'could be the starting point for dismantling the vicious circle of conflict, and an indispensable basis on which to build ... peace, [which would be] one element in a global pacification scheme' (*Clarín*, 12 May 1973). The left-wing groups staged a menacing rally outside the main Buenos Aires prison, bringing an irresistible pressure to bear. Probably the Government would have gone ahead in any case, but 'in an extremely risky situation it decided to bring forward its decision to pardon the prisoners, ... trying to avoid even worse events' (*Clarín*, 22 May 1973). The decision was passed by Congress, which met specially for that purpose, with the support of the Radicals. No discrimination was exercised, and probably it would have been difficult to exercise any. But the decision was to be paid for dearly. At least some military sources consider this a major setback in the fight against the subversive groups, as many of the past and future leaders were freed that day. This concern was shared in many quarters; many doubted, quite rightly as it turned out, whether this measure would lead to the pacification of the country. It was thought, however, that at least the Montonero organisation would renounce violence and that the Ejército Revolucionario del Pueblo (ERP) group, finding itself isolated, would follow suit. In fact the Montonero organisation, differentiating itself from the ERP group, declared a temporary suspension of its violent activities. However, it kept its arms and implied that its future behaviour depended on the fulfilment of a revolutionary programme.

The situation was not really clarified. The initial disorderly occupations, the numerous kidnappings of executives and the assaults made by the ERP on military targets were not denounced by the Montoneros. They made statements declaring that 'Our strategy is still that of total war: that is, that which is waged everywhere and by all kind of means, with the participation of all the people, using the most varied methods, from civil resistance to [mass] mobilisations [and] even the use of arms' (Fuerzas Armadas Revolucionarias (FAR)– Montoneros, 9 June 1973). Even more bluntly, but somewhat later, the head of the Montoneros, Mario Firmenich, when asked whether they were abandoning the use of force, answered,

By no means; political power comes out of the mouth of the rifle. If we have come up to this point, it is because we had rifles and we used them. If we abandoned them, we would suffer a setback in our political position. In war there are moments of confrontation, such as those which we have gone through, and there are moments of truce, in which preparations are made for the next confrontation. (*El Descamisado*, 11 Sep 1973)

No wonder that there was an early impression that the political solution to the subversion problem, even in the case of the Montoneros, where there had been more hope, was not working. The commonly voiced reaction was that 'The advent of constitutional authorities and the [passing of] the amnesty law does not seem to have restrained [violence], but, on the contrary, seems to have contributed to its intensification' (*La Prensa*, 5 June 1973). In its disappointment, this clearly indicates the kind of expectations that had existed.

The Cámpora government, on account of its short stay in power, took few measures. Among the more important of these were the appointments of many public officials with strong left-wing leanings. These were not at all obvious in the case of many candidates, who had rather right-wing backgrounds. Probably few people thought at the time that people such as Raúl Bidegain, Ricardo Obregón Cano and Vaca Narvaja, the governors of the provinces of Buenos Aires, Córdoba and Mendoza, had any leanings towards the left; the same could be said of Jorge Taiana, the Minister of Education. They were in fact members of those upper-class groups within the party which had connections with the bourgeoisie. Some came from families who had lost positions of power and wealth within their groups. They had conservative political backgrounds and their moves towards the left had been made rather recently. The case of Rodolfo Puiggrós, who was appointed to the controversial post of Rector of the University of Buenos Aires and had a clearly defined left-wing background, was rather an exception, considered necessary in order to avoid the traditional opposition against Peronism from that quarter. On the other hand, the positions in the Government dealing with economic matters were placed in the hands of the confederation of small businesses, the CGE. Its economic programme could not be described as left-wing at all; it was mildly nationalistic and mildly distributionist. It was not a socialist programme, as it did not envisage an increase in the extent of public property, but on the other hand it was clearly interventionist and relied on State action, having in general little confidence in the workings of the market.

One of the essential elements in this plan was the so called 'social pact'. This was central to Peronist ideology. The 'pact' in fact implied an agreement on how, under the aegis of the Government, to split the national income between the workers, represented by the trade unions, and the various business sectors, represented by a single voice. This idea had some corporate overtones, particularly in the need to force a unique representation on each sector. What was most essential from a Peronist point of view was the implication that the various sectors of society, or, to put it in a different way, the various classes, or at least some significant fractions of them, could be brought together in a harmonious solution. Government encouragement was viewed as an essential function of the State; if a coalition with the characteristics of the Justicialista party was in charge, then success was considered possible.

The pact (which we will analyse in more detail in Chapters 4 and 5) required a lot of prodding from the Government. To get the support of the trade unions, Perón himself had to win over the General Secretary of the CGT, José Rucci. The unions were concerned not only with the economic consequences (which proved not to be negative) but also with the suspension of collective bargaining – one of their more important activities. The General Secretary of the CGT was instrumental in arriving at a solution, something which might be connected with his assassination at the hands of the subversive organisations in September of the same year. The programme was in fact interpreted, within the Front, as a concession towards its middle-class and business sectors. Criticisms from the right were mostly directed against its interventionist nature, on the unenforceability of a price freeze and on its implicit disregard of the market. However, the business sector had expected worse kinds of solution from the Cámpora government and was suffering an inflation that had reached more than 100 per cent during the last months of the previous government; it therefore reacted in a rather positive mood. *La Nación* (10 June 1973) said, 'The social pact [seems] reasonable enough to meet with the approval of the business organisations . . . which can find within their general lines of policy a way to coexist' (*La Nación*, 10 June 1973). On the other hand, the expectations of mildly reformist sectors were that 'many will feel disillusioned as the wage rise has been smaller than anticipated and has been followed by an increase in public rates and taxes and by the suspension of sectoral wage negotiations', conceding however that other aspects of the pact meant 'a change in the structure of power . . . an important step in the pacific revolution' (*La Opinión*, 12 Dec 1973). This ambivalent attitude could also be seen in the attitudes of the Communist Party and the Montoneros. The first declared that 'the bourgeoisie takes some positive measures of an anti-monopolistic character, but imposes the major burden of the sacrifices on the working classes' (31 June 1973), while the second stated that they were 'against the social pact in the terms in which it has been conceived but not against class collaboration' (*La Nación*, 9 Sep 1973). The ERP had fewer hesitations and condemned the pact in unequivocal terms. The main spotlight of attention however, was focused not on the economic but on the political front, where a serious confrontation between the opposing groups within the Peronist movement was taking place. This conflict came drastically to a head on the occasion of the second and final return of Perón to the country, on 2 June. At the huge rally organised for his reception in Ezeiza, a savage gun-fight between the

Montonero and ERP groups and the López Rega thugs broke out. As the partisan press described it,

> Perón met with the discord of his followers. [Violence] was to be expected as all these people have lived clandestinely for too many years and have been accustomed to a climate full of danger, too near to their own or to somebody else's death. The heroes of war often become the troublemakers of peace. (*Mayoría*, 21 June 1973).

This was the first appearance of the right-wing action groups. These were the forerunners of the so-called 'Triple A' groups organised to fight subversion through illegal methods. Although it is not clear which group was the initial aggressor, the right-wing groups are in general considered the more responsible. The fact that both groups were heavily armed is, however, the best indication of how precarious was the truce which had been reached. In any case, the Montonero organisation thenceforth resumed its acts of violence.

The Cámpora experiment was doomed from the start, as it only represented the views and interests of a minority of the movement which had had little influence in the past and, as it was shown later on, had scant electoral support. The natural friction between a leader such as Perón and a Peronist president was enhanced by the new political orientation taken by Cámpora. Conflict now became inevitable, helped on by the coalition of small businesses, the labour unions and the right wing represented by the inner circle around Perón. This was a much more typical Peronist alliance, the same as characterised the first two Peronist governments; even the university youth groups pursued their traditional opposition. Perón endorsed the efforts of this coalition and forced the resignation of Cámpora on 12 July 1973.

THE FALL OF CÁMPORA AND THE NEW ELECTORAL CALL

The presidency was handed over to Raúl Lastiri, head of the Chamber of Deputies and a member of the right-wing group, by-passing, through a legal artifice, the suspect head of the Senate. That despite the questionable legitimacy of the process so few voices were raised – oddly enough, *La Prensa* was one of those – is a good indication of how the exclusion of anybody suspected of associations with the Cámpora regime was received.

Following the Constitution, new elections were scheduled for September. In these Perón could at last be a candidate. The crucial decision before the election was Perón's choice of his wife Isabel as the vice-presidential candidate. Very different alternatives had been entertained, even the possibility of choosing the leader of the opposition and head of the UCR, Ricardo Balbín. Although it never reached the stage of negotiation, the fact that it was considered at all is an indication of the conciliatory image projected by Perón, very different from the one projected in his first two presidencies.

Since his return, Perón had been trying to appear as an elder statesman who was above petty problems; he talked about national reconciliation and pressed his supporters to yield to the requests of their political allies. The naming of Isabel, however, though not completely unexpected, gave the impression that he was returning to some of the personal and arbitrary practices which had previously been so costly in terms of respectability and public acceptance. In the generally favourable political climate, an effort was made to interpret this nomination as an attempt to avoid an internal confrontation, or, less favourably, as the inevitable behaviour of a charismatic leader who could not stand any kind of competition.

> The obvious meaning of the candidacy of Señora Perón is the need to assure the unity [of the movement, which] would have been unable to absorb a sectoral candidate. [However,] the possibility of an effective presidency by Isabel Perón in the case of a succession meets today with scepticism from all quarters. (*La Opinión*, 10 Aug 1973)

While Isabel's good relations with López Rega were known, her nomination seemed not to favour any particular group within the Front. Nothing was further from the truth than this appearance of neutrality. She wholeheartedly sided with the right-wing group, and this was to colour all the later conflicts of her presidency. This time the result of the elections was a foregone conclusion. 'While the March elections determined the future path of the Nation, [the September elections] are summoned to confirm a solution already reached among the leaders' (Mariano Grondona, *La Opinión*, 20 Sep 1973). Perón got 65.1 per cent of the votes, far exceeding the previous results of the Front (Table 3.2). This time the 50 per cent mark was surpassed in all but one of the electoral districts, the exception being the city of Buenos Aires. Perón could be voted for through the official Frente

TABLE 3.2   Presidential Elections, 23 September 1973

	Frejuli (J. Perón, I. Perón)		FIP (J. Perón, A. Ramos)		UCR (R. Balbín, F. de la Rúa)		Alianza Federalista (F. Manrique, M. Raymonda)		Socialista de los Trabajadores (C. Coral)	
	'000	%	'000	%	'000	%	'000	%	'000	%
City of Buenos Aires	755	47.2	127	7.1	558	31.2	303	16.9	45	2.5
Province of Buenos Aires	2435	55.6	382	8.7	993	22.7	484	11.1	83	1.9
Catamarca	55	66.3	5	5.5	17	21.0	6	7.2	–	–
Chaco	134	59.2	17	7.3	64	28.4	11	4.8	1	0.3
Chubut	37	53.7	6	8.0	18	26.6	7	10.4	1	1.3
Córdoba	571	50.7	61	5.4	377	33.5	104	9.2	14	1.2
Corrientes	141	53.0	14	5.3	100	37.7	10	3.8	–	0.1
Entre Ríos	239	54.7	23	5.3	135	30.8	37	8.4	4	0.8
Formosa	45	58.7	6	7.6	22	29.0	2	2.9	1	1.7
Jujuy	85	70.5	7	5.5	14	11.8	15	12.3	–	–
La Pampa	50	52.1	7	7.7	26	26.8	12	12.1	–	–
La Rioja	42	63.8	4	6.6	18	27.0	2	2.6	–	–
Mendoza	290	56.5	42	8.1	83	16.2	94	18.3	–	–
Misiones	79	56.3	13	9.2	38	27.0	9	6.2	–	–
Neuquén	36	59.3	6	10.1	12	20.0	5	8.6	–	–
Rio Negro	53	53.5	9	9.6	27	25.9	9	9.3	–	–
Salta	144	67.7	12	5.8	32	15.0	24	11.4	–	–
San Juan	119	59.1	13	6.6	54	27.0	13	6.3	–	–

Santa Fé	660	53.7	■	97	7.9	202	16.4	254	20.6	16	1.3
Santiago del Estero	123	65.6	—	—	—	—	—	—	—	—	—
Tierra del Fuego	1	47.2	—	7.8	1	22.8	1	22.2	—	—
Tucumán	274	72.7	16	4.5	57	15.2	25	6.8	3	0.8
Total	6439	57.3	878	7.8	2880	26.3	1439	12.8	184	1.7

Blank votes 1.2%
Annulled 0.5%

Source: Ministerio del Interior, Dirección Nacional Electoral.

Justicialista de Liberación (Frejuli) or through a dissident, blatantly left-wing Frente de Izquierda Popular (FIP). Both had Perón as the presidential candidate, but while Frejuli had Isabel as vice-presidential candidate, the FIP had Jorge Abelardo Ramos, a well-known left-winger. These received respectively 59 and 8 per cent of the vote, in all 17 more percentage points than in the March elections (Cantón and Jorrat, 1980). Although there were, as usual, a few grumblings from *La Prensa*, the election campaign was hailed as 'one of the most civilised that can be remembered' and as having created a new situation where 'violence, if not wiped out, has been made illegitimate and has been morally destroyed' (Grondona, *La Opinión*, 25 Sep 1973).

PERÓN AS PRESIDENT

This time Perón appeared as a staunch defender of the system. He was being elected to do away with the previous progressive experiment and with a clear mandate to wipe out subversion. After the accession of Lastiri, and even more so after the election of Perón, the previous radicalisation was drastically reversed. In the provinces of Córdoba, Salta, Mendoza and Santa Cruz, the left-leaning governors were removed – basically in accordance with 'rights of intervention' granted by the Constitution to the Federal Government – being replaced by appointed *interventores*. In the case of the province of Buenos Aires the governor was forced to resign, and was replaced by the deputy governor, of trade-union extraction. The ease with which these changes were made was in part owing to the fact that none of these governors had any local following, their candidacies having been decided by the Cámpora entourage with little backing from the major party groups. At the same time many high- and medium-ranking officials with similar left-wing views were dismissed from the provincial and from the national government. In the University of Buenos Aires, the appointed rector was dismissed, and the former vice-president, Vicente Solano Lima, known for his right-of-centre attitudes, was installed instead; he was instructed to bring the situation under control, but without a head-on collision. In all this a certain care was taken, apparently by Perón himself, not to deepen the rift excessively, something which was not done after his death. Perón's move from opposition to government and to a position of responsibility had narrowed tremendously the broad range of support which he had been able to attract during his long exile. The alarm at the speed of the erosion of his previous following is quite understandable: government responsibilities proved costly to such a multitudinous mass of disparate supporters. Having shown what by now seemed an exaggerated complacency over the Peronist Youth groups, the commander-in-chief of the army and some of the members of his group were removed, 'due to the fact that their move had carried them too far away from significant sectors of the army' (*La Opinión*, 20 Dec 1973). A non-political appointment was made instead, respecting the traditional military hierarchy. The left-wing tide that had swept the country was now being reversed everywhere.

The youth groups oscillated between some semblance of playing according to the new rules of the game and an open confrontation and support of subversive activities. Their idea of maintaining a legal branch, first called the Juventud Peronista and later on the Partido Peronista Auténtico (PPA), and at the same time maintaining some allegiance to the subversive Montonero organisation, was completely unacceptable to the Government, as it would have been to any government of any political shade. The subversive organisations had been legalised since the political amnesty of 1973. While the allegedly Marxist-oriented ERP never stopped its violent activities, the Montonero group had first declared a kind of temporary truce, but had resumed its violent activities after the Ezeiza confrontation. Just before the assumption of the presidency by Perón, the Montonero group killed the General Secretary of the CGT, one of the foremost union leaders and one of the more influential in obtaining their support for the economic policies of the government. It was a clear affront to the President, who, while still showing some restraint, angrily declared that 'The killing of Rucci ... is the culmination of political degeneration, a consequence ... of a long and bitter fight which has had its influence on our youth, at times justified but which today is in danger of diverging completely from the essential interests of the Republic' (*La Nación*, 4 Oct 1973). The other act of violence that shocked the country was the assault on the army barracks at Azul in January 1974 by the ERP, one of the more audacious attacks made by the subversive organisations. It was considered as an intended affront not only to the Government but to the military as well. Perón gave exceptional importance to it, although the measures taken, as often in these cases, did not match up to the excited demands for action made at the time. One of the measures, however, was a drastic reform of the penal code, which produced the resignation of eight dissenting Peronist members of Congress, most of them associated with the youth groups. An agitated controversy among the Peronist leadership went on over whether or when to ban the Montonero organisation. While it was a great nuisance and was putting the Government in an awkward position, the ban would have meant the end of any hope of bringing its members back into the fold by persuasion, and the beginning of a bloody repression. The ERP was banned in September 1973 but the Montonero organisation not until one year later. The youth groups tried to avoid an open confrontation with Perón, in view of his enormous popularity with the working people. They pretended formal allegiance while trying to continue their attacks on many of his policies, attributing them to the right-wing groups and to the labour leaders. After various ups and downs they were finally spectacularly ejected from the party by Perón himself during the public rally of 1 May 1974. These groups then tried a new strategy through the creation of the PPA, which apparently dissociated itself from violence and from subversive organisations. The dissociation was dubious but was believed by some people. The party was, however, allowed to organise, and even to participate in the only provincial elections held during this period, in Misiones in April 1974; it got 5.5 per cent of the votes, against 46 per cent for the Front and 39 per cent for the Radicals. It was argued that its members were a lesser danger recognised than banned, and that, recognised, it was easier to identify them.

This period saw the ascendancy of the right wing represented by Isabel Perón and particularly by the Minister of Welfare, José López Rega; they became increasingly influential, although they did not get the upper hand until the death of Perón. Nevertheless they were able to use strong-arm methods, as on the occasion of the return of Perón. These were effective in wiping out some of the opposition but incensed the left-wing groups and gave them excuses for their very similar attitudes. This was another occasion where the use of force accomplished some short-term objectives at the risk of compromising more important long-term ones. One of the important elements still missing within the party was an organic political sector, a vacuum which was filled by a precarious alliance between the right wing, the small business sector and the labour unions, the same as had brought the downfall of Cámpora and the election of Perón. Instead of an organic political branch the movement had to rely on such an alliance, and while this helped to maintain a plural power structure, it made it unstable. Each of these groups was strong, and they were sharply divided among themselves. The lack of a smoothly running machine which could arbitrate between them was keenly felt.

The general evolution of the Government was proceeding along expected lines. 'Perón has placed his movement in the centre . . . opting for a coalition of forces, . . . rather than choosing a single movement, exclusive and authoritarian'; 'A pluralistic system of political parties has been consolidated creating an extended sense of compromise absolutely new in Argentine politics' (*La Nación*, 3 Aug and 18 Nov 1973). At this juncture the hypothesis behind the initial approach to Perón by Lanusse seemed to be vindicated. Perón and his movement were behaving in the expected way as a true part of the system. They represented quite a different social alliance from the one represented by the opposition, but it was one that could not endanger the functioning of the system as such. The Government seemed on the way to a more peaceful and predictable future. In economic policies it continued a middle-of-the-road course. The problems and inconsistencies which began to build up were an inherent part of their populist approach, characteristically trying to improve distribution and investment at the same time, and trying to check inflation through price controls while pushing demand to new high levels. Equally predictable were some of the initial tensions between Perón, Gelbard and the labour leaders on account of the social pact; it was very much a repetition of 1945–55. The loss of the youth and the left-inclined groups reduced the range of support for the Government, but, on the other hand, it also reduced the disparity of interests represented and the antagonisms and the fears of other groups.

This is not to say that the Government was without problems, and serious ones. Like most middle-of-the-road movements it had problems on both sides of the political spectrum. On the labour front the activities of the subversive groups increased the normal strains between the leadership and the rank and file. It is also quite probable that the leadership, being centralised and national in scope, was more adept at representing the workers at the older and smaller factories, with their familiar problems, and less capable at handling the peculiar characteristics of the newer and larger mass-production factories established in the late 1950s and 1960s, which required closer contact between leadership and rank and file. Moreover, a struggle for power was going on between the older leadership and that emerging in the increasingly important new sectors. This development more than anything else may have been at the root of the unrest in the large factories, particularly in Córdoba, during this period; it is at least a suggestive possibility which has been pointed out by some authors (Torre, 1978). The Government had a deteriorating relationship with the agricultural sector; farmers were incensed by a reduction of their

relative prices, although these were still above those of the Krieger
Vasena period, and particularly by the progressive character of the
agricultural law referred to previously. The situation was better but
not too clear in industry. The old Unión Industrial group had merged
with its former arch-rival, the CGE, actually forming the
Confederación de la Industria Nacional (CINA); this was viewed as in
favour of the Government. A fair accommodation was reached by
these two groups, but at a price; the CGE groups in the CINA moved
ideologically towards the position of the Unión Industrial, veering
away from their previous support of the new government. In a way the
CGE obtained a pyrrhic victory. Nevertheless, the grumblings from
the industrial sector were not serious until the middle of 1974.

The Government was suffering from what could be described as
normal strains. It had cut itself off from the left, to a greater degree
than would have been the case but for the initial 'abnormal' swing to
the left which had so shaken the party and the country. It had very bad
relations with the agricultural sector and a difficult but not impossible
relationship with the business sector. It had the wholehearted support
of the labour leadership, with some unrest among the rank and file,
very much as might be expected. Subversion was the new unexpected
factor and was increasing, although it was not yet the central problem
it became later on. It was clear here that a political solution had failed
and that the subversive movements had not abandoned their fight just
because the Government had been democratically elected and had
strong popular support.

Two very significant events took place at the end of Perón's
presidency. The first was on the occasion of the big rally organised for
the 1 May celebrations in 1974. The youth and the Montonero
organisations formed up in special columns in the Plaza de Mayo,
chanting slogans against Isabel. Perón reacted violently and
condemned them in the strongest terms, lauding instead the trade
unions and the CGT.

> The Government is committed to the liberation [of the country], not
> only from colonialism ... but also from these treacherous
> infiltrators who work from within, and who are more dangerous
> than those who work from the outside. ... It would seem that some
> make the pretence of having more merit than those who have fought
> for more than twenty years. ... I have made no mistake ... on the
> appraisal of the quality of the trade union organisations, despite
> these stupid people who shout. ... These organisations have been

wise and prudent ... despite the fact that they have seen their leaders assassinated, while still the time of punishment has rot arrived.

This was a most serious and a most public row. The youth groups marched away from the Plaza, leaving it half empty; this was the first public rebuke to the leader. Later in the day, at the inauguration of Congress, Perón declared,

We will overcome violence, no matter what its origin. We will overcome subversion. We will isolate those who are violent and maladjusted. We will fight against them with all our forces ... within the Constitution and the law. No victory which is not also political is valid in these matters. And we will succeed.

From then on, the Peronist leadership abandoned all hope of winning these groups back into the fold. The political solution to subversion had failed, and Perón and his party had come squarely up against it. The established groups were elated, considering that 'The forces which had traditionally criticised Peronism should now make an act of faith ... in a government of national concord. ... This Peronism is indeed different from that of 1946' (*La Nación*, 5 May 1974). However, the figure of the popular leader had emerged somewhat scarred and a new rally was organised for 12 June; this time it was basically organised by the trade unions, who tried to demonstrate their capacity for mobilising people, which had been considered second to that of the youth. The rally, the last in which Perón was able to take part, was successful, measured by the degree of participation. It gave Perón the opportunity to repeat his appeal for order, lauding the opposition, but sharply criticising his followers for their lack of discipline and accusing some of them of 'doing nothing to secure peace and allowing themselves to become fellow travellers of disruption'.

Immediately afterwards, Perón fell seriously ill. This gave rise to all kinds of rumours, including that of a return of the military. The more prevalent mood was that of a spirit of 'solidarity which has not only moral but also political significance. A country that has for so many decades seen blatant collisions has been able to exhibit a solid cohesion, and an understanding ..., without exceptions, that national unity has to be set above any ideology or interest' (*Clarín*, 30 June 1974). From then on, both the politicians and the military contemplated the possibility of a viable government headed by Isabel Perón or another intervention by the armed forces.

THE DEATH OF PERÓN AND THE ACCESSION OF ISABEL

The death of Perón on 1 July 1974, after a short illness, was a shock to an already delicate political situation. He had been following a predictable course, even if not one that appealed to certain sections, and his death was bound to increase the uncertainty of the future. The speeches made about Perón on the occasion of his death were surprisingly laudatory. Representatives of the main institutions, the armed forces, the Church and the political parties, competed in eulogy. The commander-in chief of the army, General Anaya, said,

> The nation mourns the death of one in whom was summed up all the resolve of a people. He has served our Fatherland, which he loved so dearly, for more than half a century. He had two passions, the army and the people, ... He leaves us, in active service, with the highest military rank, having offered himself until the very last for the happiness of his people. The Argentine Army is in a state of mourning, but it is not alone, ... it is accompanied by the immense sorrow of the nation before the death of its leader. ... The commanders-in-chief of the navy and air-force expressly join in this emotional farewell to the one who had been its highest commander. The armed forces of the nation, within the prescriptions of the law, will seek ... to reach his ultimate objective: the unity of the nation.

The head of the Church, Cardinal Caggiano, remembered

> The clairvoyance of General Perón in having sought, ... with the political leaders of the country, a fruitful dialogue aimed at the union necessary for the reconstruction of our land. He recognised ... the autonomy of political parties, accepted opposition and asked for constructive criticism. He reconciled businessmen and organised labour ... never accepted violence ... which was his enemy in the ... terrorist wave that tried to kill republican institutions.

The head of the UCR, Ricardo Balbín, representing the other political parties, said,

He has put his seal to this definitive confluence, and to this new consciousness that has put all of us to work ... to the common cause. It would not be fair if I did not admit that I am here as a representative of old struggles, but because they were open and clear they have allowed this new understanding ...; a surprising new relationship has been born ... let us make good his last will ... to bequeath peace to the future generations of Argentines.

Even if one takes into consideration the shock produced by the death and the special circumstances in which these eulogies were made, which tended to exaggerate more normal attitudes, it would be fair to say that Perón died at a point of relative concord, having been accepted by a wide range of public opinion.

The mounting problems of the Government could be explained by invoking purely 'structural' factors, but it is impossible not to make an explanation in personal terms when the leadership (maybe for 'structural' reasons) had exercised such a significant arbitrating role, keeping together an exceptionally broad coalition representing disparate interests. The death of Perón not only allowed tensions which had been repressed to surface again, but prompted the appearance of others peculiar to this leaderless situation. Isabel Perón managed to retain, however, more authority and more arbitrating capacity than might have been expected. This was partly owing to the traditional power of the presidency no matter who exercised it, and partly owing to the fact that, in a party where emotions usually ran high, Isabel's name was a symbol of the unity of the movement. Many leading members of the party and of the trade unions thought, even though they disliked her, that, without a comprehensive ideology or a structured party, the risks of dissolution without her were too great. When Isabel was named as vice-presidential candidate, many people assumed that, while this would avoid an internal jockeying for position, hers was not a serious nomination which would provide a viable succession.

The assumption, even within the party, was that, if Perón died during his presidential term, a military coup would become unavoidable. Isabel was not considered as having the minimum personal qualifications for the presidency and it was assumed that she would not be able to remain, even as a figurehead. The story developed in a different way. Though many within the military had already begun to consider the coup as inevitable, there was now a consensus that she should be allowed a fair try. The big surprise was that Isabel did not assume either the position of a figurehead or one above the contending factions. On the contrary, with the full support and under the strong influence of López Rega – she tried to run the show, vigorously pushing forward a right-wing programme along authoritarian lines, alarming even the traditional establishment:

> The apparent political move towards the right has its dangers as the reaction to subversion may become unreasonable and a certain sense of equilibrium [may be] lost. ... It was said that fascists are frightened liberals ... in fact a right-wing dictatorship can be the consequence of conceptual theorisations, or the consequence of despair, something which is much more common than ideology. (*La Nación*, 10 Nov 1974)

This change in policy was as decisive in intensifying the conflicts of the ensuing period as the loss of the leader; it placed in question the authority of the President to a much greater degree than would otherwise have been the case. As the new programme implied a new social alliance, it was bound to break the precarious equilibrium between the various sectors which were still supporting the Government and force a new realignment. The trade unions, the small business groups and the small parties which had supported the Government stepped back and relations with the Radicals cooled. New lines were thrown out towards the military and the more established business sector. The new programme, even if distasteful to many, was not incoherent; in fact it was quite audacious, as it implied a drastic departure from a long Peronist tradition, and was aimed at groups such as the military and large and foreign businesses, which had previously been at odds with Peronism.

It contained five basic aims. The first was a new and determined effort to wipe out subversion, with civilian paramilitary groups, later to be known as the Triple A, doing the dirty work instead of involving the military in any direct way. The groups which had been used sporadically within the party to 'solve' some internal feuds – as in the Ezeiza shooting – were now to be enlarged and used methodically to control the subversive organisations.

The second aim was the elimination of left-wing infiltration in education in general and in the University of Buenos Aires in particular. Although Perón had already gone back on his previous support of the Puiggrós group, a solution had been attempted which tried to avoid open confrontation. Now the reversal was to be completed. The

Minister of Education was dismissed and replaced by a relatively right-wing member of the old guard, Oscar Ivanissevich, a former Minister of Education in the second presidency of Perón. A new rector was named at the University of Buenos Aires – a well known right-winger and tough nationalist.

The third aim was an end to the relatively nationalistic and reformist anti-business economic policies. There was to be a move towards foreign capital, a market economy and reliance on private capital for investment and growth. Wages were to be reduced and industrial discipline was to be imposed. There was still stress on the need for low-cost housing and a rise in the minimum wage; this meant a reduction in wage differentials and was particularly hard on organised labour and its more highly paid members. The main characteristic of the programme, however, the feature that was to give it its essential flavour, was its intensity, which surpassed anything that had been tried in the past along these lines, even by Frondizi or Krieger Vasena.

The fourth aim was to bring the labour leadership under control, by dismissing some of the more militant and independently minded officials, some of whom were vulnerable to corruption charges, and naming a new subservient union leadership. This is the main reason for the later intensity of the economic measures and for the intensity of the reaction to them as well. The programme was seen as a means of creating an impossible situation for the labour leadership in relation to their rank and file, so forcing a change. What really was at issue was not only a higher or lower level of wages and a better or worse distribution of income, but also the political survival of the trade-union leadership and the continuance of the labour movement as an independent source of power.

Fifthly and most essentially, the military were requested, as a *quid pro quo*, to abandon the political neutrality which they had maintained since the resignation of General Carcagno, and move to a position of tacit support, assuming that the set of policies that were put forward justified such a request. This was achieved in May 1975 – even if only for a few months – when a new commander-in-chief was named, General Numa Laplane, who advocated a policy of *profesionalismo integrado*, which implied precisely this tacit support.

Probably the foregoing description of the programme does not transmit its full flavour. With slight variations here and there this programme could be one of a traditional conservative or an authoritarian right-wing group. The objectives in themselves could have been shared by most right-of-centre groups. However, the methods used, the fascist overtones and the intensity of the measures raised objections even from some of these. The lack of understanding between the Isabel Perón–López Rega group and the Argentine right deserves a more detailed study than the one made here. It may be typical of such turn-arounds that, when the leadership of a party tries to depart sharply from its traditional policies, it loses the support of the faithful without gaining that of the group which would benefit from the new line. In a way it was similar to Frondizi's sharp turn to the right in late 1958 after a few months of his presidency, which was never believed in and taken for what it was by the right.

It is not easy to determine the reasons for the particular position taken by the Isabel Perón–López Rega group. They may have had a feeling that the party would veer too much towards the unions, leaving them powerless instruments of its wishes. Isabel Perón and López Rega needed a cause in order to emerge as distinctively as possible from the other main contending groups. The course chosen could also bring them some new, external allies in exchange for that internal support they would lose. The antecedents of Isabel Perón and López Rega, as well as of some of their close allies, did not help build up confidence in them. Isabel's position was too much a unique consequence of Perón's decision, and, while this may have helped avoid the risk of an internal rift when she was nominated, under the new circumstances it was detrimental to her being considered a credible leader. Some personal eccentricities of López Rega, his allegedly occultist inclinations and his patronage of dissident Catholic groups, contributed to a general image of unreliability. Isabel's group was, moreover, associated with a disorderly and arbitrary management of its own areas of influence. A case in point is the personal charity organised for Isabel, the Cruzada de Solidaridad Justicialista, which, although receiving State funds, was at times used for the personal expenditure of the President. One of these instances gave rise to a legal action which went on through most of her presidency, poisoning the general climate towards her and her group and surrounding them with an aura of corruption. Even without a drastic right-wing programme such as the one chosen by Isabel and López Rega a new realignment was bound to take place, as the previous equilibrium was already under strain. With a programme such as this, however, the scope of the realignments and the oppositions which were aroused were increased enormously. In September 1974 the Montoneros publicly declared that they would 'resume the popular armed struggle ... against the oligarchic and imperialist forces' (*La Opinión*, 7 Sep

1974). It had been obvious since the death of Rucci that this was already the case, but the fact that it now became explicit added a new dimension to the conflict. This decision was not shared by all left-wing groups, as some thought that violence was a dead end, a view that lay behind the organisation at the end of the year of the PPA. The Government allowed its organisation on the grounds 'of not playing into the hands of open subversion, in the hope that the maintenance of a legal outlet would finally create a crisis between the more legalistic left groups and those who insist on armed confrontation' (*La Opinión*, 2 Mar 1975).

This subtlety was not at all characteristic of the fight against the left. Intervention in the University of Buenos Aires took place in a most severe fashion, meeting little resistance from the previously militant student groups. Despite the general agreement from most middle-of-the-road and right-of-centre groups on the need to redress the situation in the university, the way in which the intervention was handled and the pretence made by Alberto Ottalagano, the newly appointed Rector, that the option 'was one between *justicialismo* and Marxism ... with Christ or against Christ' prompted a reaction from many people who were frightened that 'Nationalist fascism is ... repeating with its excesses the same violations and blunders characteristic of the previous [left-wing] government of the University' (*La Prensa*, 6 Oct 1974). After nearly three months the Government dismissed Ottalagano, giving the impression that the university, 'after having been [originally] in the hands of the left, had moved towards the right and was now [ready] to take its [middle] course' (*La Nación*, 28 Dec 1974).

The anti-subversive portion of the Isabel–López Rega programme created bitter ill feeling and opposition. Even if ethical considerations are set aside, its results were ambiguous and difficult to ascertain; terrorist attacks increased, 1975 being one of the two worst years in the whole period; nobody can tell whether they would have been fewer or not had the Triple A not been in existence. Most people were frightened by the development of what looked like open gang warfare.

It is clear that when subversion reaches a certain point counter-insurgency becomes unavoidable, leaving aside the question of measures aimed at its deep-rooted causes. Even when this counter-insurgency is carried out by the military and according to the law, it creates much uneasiness, as many traditional civil liberties may be endangered. Nevertheless it can be understood and accepted, as in the case of the repression of the Tucumán *foco*, which had the approval not only of the Government but also of the head of the opposition, who thought that 'The intervention of the armed forces has to be respected; it is subject to civilian authority. ... They act on our behalf, and do not affect the [democratic] process' (*La Nación*, 10 Feb 1975). If, on the other hand, counter-insurgency operations are carried out in violation of the law, the situation becomes very much worse. Worse still was the case here, when the task was done illegally and by a fraction of the Government's party working through anonymous bands who acted according to unknown rules.

The implementation of the economic and labour policies proved to be more difficult and was delayed until March 1975. However, soon after the death of Perón, the Minister of Economy was dismissed and in a compromise was replaced by one of the members of the so-called 'historic group', Alfredo Gómez Morales, who had had an important role in the 1952–5 stabilisation policies. His appointment had significant political implications: it meant a serious setback for the CGE, which in due time complained of the 'dangers of an IMF-style stabilisation policy'. On the other side of the political spectrum, the reaction was quite positive, 'the impression ... being that the Government has begun a correction of its course that will mean, after the excesses and mistakes that we have experienced, a return to common sense' (*La Prensa*, 24 Oct 1974). The agricultural sector expressed its 'complaisance', pointing out that 'Now that subversion is being attacked as never before [and] the university has been straightened out ... if the Government modifies its economic policy it will get ample support' (Celedonio Pereda, President of the Sociedad Rural Argentina, *La Opinión*, 26 Oct 1974).

The essential problem, however, was the fight within the ruling coalition between the unions and the right wing headed by the President. The last months of 1974 and the first of 1975 saw a growing confrontation between them. The unions saw themselves as the only real source of power and wanted 'a greater active role and a real share in the strategic planning and in the tactical execution of important national policies' (*La Nación*, 27 Mar 1975). The President did not want to give them any significant say and a most ambiguous relationship developed; declarations of trust and loyalty were made which were not sufficient to disguise the mutual distrust. It was not only the President who was afraid of the power of the unions; the traditional right thought, quite characteristically, that 'The activity of the trade-union groups no longer recognises any limit' (*La Prensa*, 9 Sep 1974). This antagonism surfaced once more on the occasion of the return of the body of Eva Perón to the country. This event was full of strong symbolic meaning, but, instead of being a unifying occasion, it was handled by López Rega in a secretive way which specifically excluded trade union participation. In such an emotional affair, the affront to the unions was extreme. The displeasure of the unions was also shown in their increasing criticism of the economic policies, which was centred around the increase in the cost of living; they pressed for a return to stricter price controls. The CGT declared its 'profound disagreement with the unilateral and autocratic methods used by the Minister of Commerce in the fixing of prices' (*La Nación*, 25 Jan 1975). More than just attacking this specific problem, they were expressing the awkwardness of their position in supporting a government with which they were increasingly at odds.

The Government was, however, advancing with its programme. It was meeting increasing opposition, while results were still elusive. This situation caused it to harden its attitude; it became much less open, both with its smaller political allies and with the Radical opposition. This high-handed attitude was shared by both the right wing and the unions, in contrast with what had been the attitude of Perón or, for that matter, of the political wing of the party. At the same time, the smaller members of the government alliance became more critical. The Frondizi group, the Movimiento de Integración y Desarrollo (MID), began to distance itself, beginning in October with a scathing criticism restricted, however, to the economic policies of Gómez Morales, while in December it practically broke away from the Government coalition altogether. The stance of the Radicals was more in line with their past attitude, but strains showed. They accused the Government of 'cutting off the dialogue, of taking decisions without consultation, of allowing the creation of an artificial micro-climate capable of disturbing the running of government ... creating factionalism' (*La Opinión*, 10 Oct 1974).

By the beginning of 1975 the external economic situation had worsened, compounding the problems derived from the political isolation of the Government. In March a devaluation precipitated wage demands, which gave the impression that the social pact had already run its course. The right wing now thought that the time had at last come to go all the way with the original economic programme, and installed Celestino Rodrigo as the new Minister of Economy. While the right had previously hindered in a contradictory way some of the moderate policies advanced by Gómez Morales, it now proceeded to support an extremely drastic programme. The change of policy was considered 'an absolute novelty, a challenge to [the former] ideology, habits and political emotions ... a spectacular warning from an unequivocally popular government [which offers] the promise of a general political realignment' (*La Nación*, 7 June 1975).

The measures included a devaluation of more than 100 per cent and an increase of public-sector prices of up to 200 per cent. The seriousness of the previous economic situation should not be played down; a significant change was necessary. However, the calm and rapidity with which the programme was imposed were really extraordinary, and can only be explained as an attempt to create an impossible situation for the labour leadership. If the programme had been successful a change in the labour leadership would have become a possibility and the five-point programme would have been, if not completed, substantially advanced. In any case, it was 'clear evidence of the move of López Rega towards the centre of political power' (*La Opinión*, 3 June 1975).

However, the right wing had overreached itself. The leaders of the trade unions were outraged and shocked; they realised that they had to fight for their survival. It was now not only a matter of stopping an adverse policy, but also a question of surviving as credible autonomous leaders or of being replaced by leaders named by Government circles, as in the state-controlled unions of Spain and Italy during the Franco and Mussolini regimes. The unions vacillated between an attempt to bring down Rodrigo and López Rega and the more drastic plan of bringing down the whole Government. It was not easy to distinguish between the ministers and the President, who had given them explicit and public support.

But the political cost of the wider strategy, and the risks involved, were too great. Isabel Perón still had some symbolic value as leader of the Justicialista party. While she did not have personal charisma, as President she was still a rallying symbol for the Peronist rank and file. Toppling her might have divided the party; it might have brought a new election in a delicate situation and with a split party or, more probably, a military coup. For the Peronist leaders these were not very appealing alternatives. The attempt was made to make the impossible, or, at least, obviously unconvincing, distinction between her and her ministers.

The CGT called for a national strike, to be held on 7 and 8 July, 'rejecting the arbitrary measures of the Government, which have brought about a collision unprecedented in the history of Peronism between its leader and her workers' (5 July 1975). The trade union strategy was to organise mass mobilisations while they pressed for an exorbitant wage increase of about 160 per cent, which created an impossible position for the Government. Their actions were, as intended, politically explosive and ended with the dismissal of López Rega and Rodrigo, the first – possibly – with some kind of army participation and the second after some weeks of terrible labour unrest and public demonstrations staged by the unions. This was at the time considered 'the deepest crisis that can be remembered in the contemporary life of the Republic' (*La Nación*, 20 June 1975).

As if this was not enough, the crisis spilled over and gave rise to an internal feud within the top army command. The commander-in-chief, General Numa Laplane, who had supported the Government during the López Rega period, was under strong pressure from the more professional (and the more anti-Government) groups. The unions tried to keep out of it, as Numa Laplane had not been too sympathetic to them either. Some union leaders, for example Lorenzo Miguel, tried to rally some popular support for him, but they were completely rejected by the bulk of the leadership. The situation was resolved, for the time being, with the naming of General Videla as the new commander-in-chief in late August.

The Government was by this time losing most of its support. The elimination of Gelbard had cut its ties with the CGE and now the elimination of the right wing left the unions with most of the power, checked only, and that to a small degree, by the very weak political branch of the party. The trade unions were surprised by their new commanding role, which exceeded their traditional expectations. Vandor, the initiator of this policy, had merely wanted to share power within the party, and had at no time entertained the idea of an exclusively working-class party, not even of a worker-dominated party.

Although the President had not been removed, her authority now disappeared altogether. Angel Robledo was named as Minister of the Interior and Antonio Cafiero as Minister of Economy, an obvious choice in view of his traditional links with the trade unions and his reputation, together with Gómez Morales, as one of the party's chief economists. Cafiero had been involved with Vandor ten years before in the Mendoza elections which had prompted the intervention of Isabel Perón, and had not been on good terms with her or with López Rega. The reactions to his appointment and to his first measures were favourable, even from groups which by now were overtly critical of the Government.

It has to be admitted that, under the circumstances, Cafiero has behaved in a pragmatic and responsible manner. He has had to adjust to the sharp limits imposed by reality, having to perform the disagreeable role of administering a crisis which certainly is not of his making.   (*Clarín*, 8 Nov 1975)

The President was by now just a figurehead but still retained the formal position of power. She had a cabinet that had been imposed on her, and, while the labour leaders needed and used the name of the President, they resented her attitudes and inclinations. Soon after this the President was given a leave of absence which lasted for nearly five weeks; the presidency was assumed by Italo Luder, the head of the Senate, another outstanding representative of the moderate political wing. The image of the Government improved significantly even among groups which ought to have preferred the previous right-wing policies: 'Luder's first measures as interim president created a sense of euphoria in political circles, having opened new contacts and let fresh air into the relations of the Government with the armed forces and the opposition' (*La Opinión*, 11 and 20 Sep 1975). The performance of the new men in power 'was a stimulating example ... which can modify positively the general course of the Government' (*La Nación*, 18 Oct 1975). These laudatory remarks were made despite the new union-based realignment. This apparent inconsistency was connected with the fact that the new group was more reliable, as it was made up of some of the more reputable politicians of the Justicialista party. Their policies might have been less palatable, but on the other hand they were more credible, they had more 'known boundaries' and were less unpredictable. Their more democratic leanings and the fact that they were not tainted with allegations of corruption created new hopes, even if only for a short while.

The new group's chances of carrying on the middle-of-the-road policies were not great. In the economy, although the inflationary outburst of the middle of the year had begun to subside, the intensity of the relative price variations created tremendous anxiety, having a negative effect on the political climate. Still, the prospects were not too bad until mid-October. At the end of that month a new round of wage increases was agreed at a moderate level of 15 per cent. What was serious was the series of differential rises, some overt, others under the table, that the various unions tried to obtain over and above the general level. It was clear that, as a result of the distortions in relative wages brought about by the mid-year turmoil, the unions were behaving in a moderate manner when acting collectively but not so when putting forward their special cases.

The increasing power of the unions alarmed many groups. Some said that

> they are about to attempt a big jump in their road to power. [While before] they were the backbone of Peronism, . . . they now want to become the head, . . . occupying the centre of the stage, rather than its periphery. (*La Prensa*, 25 Oct 1975).

> The big question is whether, as part of the increased trade-union power, Justicialism will go ahead in trying to become a true labour party. (*La Nación*, 11 Dec 1975)

> The unions are trying to take over, unilaterally, the whole representation of Peronism . . . moving away from the basic role given to them [by Perón]. (*La Opinión*, 23 Oct 1975)

The unchecked power of the unions, their exaggerated demands and irresponsible behaviour made a significant contribution to the pre-coup climate. At this stage the Government was being harmed as much by its allies as by its foes. At the beginning of October however, Isabel Perón returned, rejecting a second leave of absence that was being engineered by the Minister of the Interior, Robledo. After having agreed in principle to the scheme, she changed her mind at the last minute, and in a fighting speech made on 5 November, she stated that she would continue in her job to the very end.

From then on the Government was divided; an impasse was reached and an anarchic situation slowly took hold. The possibility of revolution began to be publicly voiced and some economic groups began to prepare public opinion for this development. Two lock-outs by the agricultural sector helped to create a pre-revolutionary climate. A new business association, the APEGE, openly assumed a rebellious attitude. By the end of the year some financial groups which had been mildly co-operating with the new set-up (for instance, the Asociación de Bancos Argentinos (ADEBA) – the association of national owned banks) started to drag their feet in view of the general deterioration of the political situation. Many groups began to act as if a coup were in prospect, becoming extremely rigid and aggressive in their requests. While this was partly the consequence of current problems, it created new and increased difficulties and set the scene for the end.

It was said that the military were delaying the coup until the situation became impossible, in order to make their decision welcome to the large majority of the population. This was called at the time the strategy of the 'rotten apple' – let it rot until public demand to do something becomes unanimous. This strategy was successful, and it naturally contributed to the further rotting of the apple. The open discussion of the coup and the activities of some business sectors in trying to create favourable conditions for it significantly contributed to the chaotic situation at the end of the year.

The Government was caught in an increasingly difficult position. At the top it was utterly divided between the more middle-of-the-road group and the right wing. The unions were at odds with the President and their extreme ambitions were undermining the middle-of-the-road alliance. The initial hopes raised by the new economic programme changed to disappointment. An increasing number of formerly friendly groups began to criticise it on the grounds that it was not clear which of its measures 'would allow redress in the critical situation. Those that have been taken have been partial and disconnected. Although they can be the answer to political pressures, they do not take into consideration economic reality,... and will have the opposite consequences to those desired' (CGE, 11 Oct 1975). The CGE and the CINA, its industrial branch, began to move away. The Frondizi group formally disowned the Justicialista Front, declaring that 'rather than moving out of the Front we simply take note that it does not exist any more ... the hopes of millions of Argentines have faded away ... the State, morals, the economy, culture are in crisis' (MID, 18 Dec 1975). In a more constructive but equally critical tone, the Radicals began to give up hope of any improvement, condemning 'the tendency of the President to follow the arbitrary guidelines of secret groups led from a distance [by López Rega]' (*La Opinión*, 21 Oct 1975). The governor of the province of Buenos Aires came out in what practically amounted to an open revolt; he sharply criticised the President, saying that 'If things continue like they are today, we will not reach the elections of 1977' (30 Sep 1975). The Government was divided between those who wanted to intervene in the province, led by Lorenzo Miguel, and the more moderate and more democratic line, led by the Minister of the Interior. The matter was then settled by the commander-in-chief of the army, General Videla, who came out in support of the governor, one of the first of the few public indications that the military were making contacts with civilian groups.

As if all these problems were not enough, the Government had to tackle the allegations of corruption levied against the President by

Parliament. The moderate group wanted to satisfy public opinion and allow an investigation that would indict many members of the López Rega entourage, and possibly end up by indicting the President as well. A parliamentary investigation was rejected but a judicial one was allowed (17 Nov 1975), a solution that left everybody dissatisfied.

The military decided on the coup some time during the second half of 1975, probably in late October or early November. It showed, however, signs of not being eager to go ahead and gave several warnings to the Government; of course, heeding these warnings would have meant paying a high price for temporary survival. In any case, various statements by the top military contributed to the pre-coup climate. In a sombre speech General Catán, head of the crucial Campo de Mayo garrison, declared that 'It is sad to see that every day moral values are attacked and that this is consciously and unconsciously tolerated, ... we do not react, as a people or as a nation' (4 Oct 1975). General Boasso, commander of the Neuquén division, stated that the armed forces were not supposed to be 'the custodians of an order whose legitimacy is based on numbers and not on law, that upsets reason and is blind to facts, ... that fosters speculation, persecutes work, suffocates progress, does not recognise a hierarchical order, and is based on lies' (*La Opinión*, 16 Oct 1975).

Monseñor Bonamín, the military chaplain, stated in a similar mood that 'There are many sins, many crimes, much cowardice, much treason, much shamelessness, at every level, even in the higher ones; one wonders whether God will not demand something more of our armed forces, something which would set an example to the whole nation' (28 Sep 1975). The main request, although not the most openly voiced, was for the dismissal of the President and the more right-wing elements of the Government. Initially the critics seemed to be willing to allow the resumption of the presidency by Luder, not caring or realising that it meant a move toward a more union-based alliance. They blamed many of the problems on the person of the President, whom they considered to lack the minimum requirements for authority, tarnished by allegations of corruption and surrounded by a strange and disreputable inner circle including some former associates of López Rega. In December there was an abortive air-force coup; this was controlled but, as it now seems, at the price of a definite agreement on the coup that was to follow.

In January the President tried to regain her lost authority, at least within the party, attempting to obtain full military support by suggesting something along the lines of what was called the

Bordaberrización of the Government: that meant presenting a civilian legalistic façade which allowed direct military intervention in the naming of most significant positions, including most cabinet posts, as had been done in Uruguay under President Bordaberry. This kind of offer showed a perception that the views of the right wing were not much different from those of the military. In some ways it followed naturally from the five-point programme of López Rega. At this juncture the offer had little appeal. The President's group had become too disreputable; it had a record of failure and a contested position even within the party, although the President herself still enjoyed a degree of popularity.

After the rejection of this offer, the President tried to carry out a similar programme on her own. She started by dismissing the prominent leaders of the centrist alliance, Robledo and Cafiero, replacing them by personal appointees. The influence of some former associates of López Rega was here again evident, particularly that of former President Lastiri. The new economic policy was more moderate than Rodrigo's had been, but was significantly tighter than that of Cafiero. It was appropriately called a National Emergency Plan. The unions reacted sharply, considering that 'It will reduce real wages, reduce consumption, reduce investment and dismantle the role of the State'; they requested a new plan which 'should reject the reactionary liberal recipes' (quoted in *La Opinión*, 11 Mar 1976).

For the first time a Peronist economic programme had as an explicit and public aim a reduction in the level of real wages. The labour leaders stopped the wage negotiations which had been going on since the beginning of January, and for a fortnight it seemed as if an open confrontation, similar to that which had taken place in June 1975, would surface again. A wave of very similar stoppages began to paralyse the factories as a protest against the new economic measures. However, the leadership was hesitant. A direct confrontation seemed pointless when everyone was expecting a coup. Submission to the President and to the right-wing policies seemed a very bad choice, but under the circumstances the only one. In Parliament some sections of the party hesitated in their plan to impeach the President. Some had thought that this could avoid a coup, but the more general opinion was that the coup was inevitable and that under such circumstances impeachment was an unnecessary show which would divide the party to no avail. Other last-minute attempts were made to redress the situation, but the President wanted to continue with her programme; she even succeeded in imposing her candidates on a party congress on

6 March 1976, defeating the moderate Robledo line. By now all sectors expected the coup. The Radicals, one of the few groups that did not push for it, could put forward no solution. The speech by their leader on 16 March was dramatic and touching, but did not point to any way out. At this juncture there was none.

The military coup found the party divided and at odds with its leadership, unable and unwilling to put up a fight. 'Yesterday morning the Government finally crumbled. ... This was not a surprise ... as the Government had been dead long before' (*La Nación*, 25 Mar 1976). The military coup met no opposition, and ended the three and a half years of Argentina's second populist experience. It had indeed been an unhappy one.

BIBLIOGRAPHY

Cantón, D. and Jorrat, J. (1978) 'Occupation and Vote in Urban Argentina: the March 1973 Presidential Elections', *Latin American Research Review*, vol. XIII, no. 1.

Cantón, D. and Jorrat, J. R. (1980) 'El Voto peronista en 1973: distribución, crecimiento marzo-septiembre y bases ocupacionales', *Desarrollo Económico*, no. 77 (Apr–June).

Corradi, J. and Torre, J. C. (eds), forthcoming, *The Return and Fall of Peronism, Argentina 1973–76* (Philadelphia: Institute for the Study of Human Issues).

Graham-Yooll, A. (1979) 'The Press in Argentina: 1973–1978', *Index on Censorship* (London) May.

Jelin, E. (1977) *Conflictos laborales en la Argentina 1973–76*, Documento CEDES no. 5 (Buenos Aires).

Landi, O. (1978) *La tercera presidencia de Perón: gobierno de emergencia y crisis política*, Documento CEDES–CLACSO no. 10 (Buenos Aires).

Mora, M. (1975) 'La estructura social del peronismo', *Desarrollo Económico*, no. 59 (Oct–Dec).

Mora, M. and Smith, P. (1980) 'Peronismo y desarrollo: las elecciones de 1973', in M. Mora and I. Llorente (eds), *El Voto peronista: ensayos de sociología electoral* (Buenos Aires).

Rock, D. (1975) 'The Survival and Restoration of Peronism', in Rock (ed.), *Argentina in the Twentieth Century* (Pittsburgh).

Torre, J. C. (1978) 'Workers and Unions under the Last Peronist Government, 1973–76', in Corradi and Torre (eds), *The Return and Fall of Peronism*.

Wynia, Gary (1974) *Economic Policy Making under Stress: Conflict and Exchange in Argentina*, Latin American Administration Committee ser. 2, Occasional Paper no. 11 (London: Institute of Latin American Studies).

4 The Structural Reform Programme

After these mainly political chapters we can now move ahead with the analysis of economic developments. As a consequence of the electoral campaign and the radicalisation of the political spectrum great expectations were created about the nature of the future economic programme and the identity of the specific group who would carry it out. The programme that had been used during the campaign was understandably diffuse, being patterned on the multi-party agreement (the *coincidencias programáticas*) reached at the end of the previous year (7 December 1972) between the Peronists, the Radicals, the small-business union, the CGE, and the workers' confederation, the CGT.

After the elections, the first notice of the future intentions of the Government in the economic field was the appointment, at the suggestion of Perón, of José Gelbard, head of the CGE, as Minister of Economy. This came as a minor surprise, as the CGE and Gelbard had been lukewarm towards Cámpora; they thought that his candidature was an indication that Perón was not really keen on going ahead with the elections, and so they had been in closer touch with the Radicals. After the election result was known, they were able to manoeuvre successfully (with the help of the anti-Cámpora groups) to regain the favours of Perón. When Gelbard was appointed it was explicitly announced that they, as a group, were to be given a free hand over the whole of the economy. This decision bypassed the Cámpora candidates and some of the leading economists of the party, the latter mildly supported by the party's politicians.

The economic programme was launched with great trumpetings and was presented as a revolutionary one, partly in an attempt to avoid a confrontation with the left-wing groups who had been left out of this most fundamental area. It was presented as a programme capable of transforming the social outlook of the country, placing the economy 'at the service of popular causes, turning it into an adequate tool for the anti-imperialist struggle' (Gelbard, 1 May 1974, made on the submission of the law to Congress). The new programme, a 'code for the reconstruction and liberation policies' (ibid.), was based on the National Pledge Act (Acta de Compromiso Nacional) that had been agreed between the CGE, the CGT and the Minister of Economy at the beginning of the new government (30 May 1973). It was based on the one hand on a set of structural reform measures – the subject of this chapter – and on the other on a stabilisation scheme.

The reformist programme was launched at the time when political radicalisation was reaching its climax. Although it was the responsibility of a group which was at odds with Cámpora and his followers – and was already trying to depose him – it was seen as another sign of the same political climate. It was received by the established sectors with suspicion, more because of the general political setting and the timing of its launch than because of the programme itself. The Radicals, on the other hand, thought that the programme fulfilled their previous December agreement with the Peronists, and 'shared its general outlines' (Juan Carlos Pugliese, former Radical Minister of Economy, *Clarín*, 12 Aug 1973). It could be said that the prevailing 'image was one of economic and social reformism' (Grondona, *La Opinión*, 12 July 1973).

The general outline of the programme was strongly interventionist, mildly nationalist, and distributionist. The programme considered that 'The State has to become the principal agent for the transformation and change of the ... development of the Nation' (ibid.). The State was to advance on a wide front. In the case of the export trade, it was to take over the handling of cereals and meat; in the case of credit it was drastically to increase its traditional control, and in the case of the wholesale and retail trade it was to fix maximum prices and retailers' margins. A three-year plan, and a good one at that, was made and presented as a major tool of the new policies. However, as in previous experiences, it was not much more than a declaration of intent and bore little relationship to what the Government ended up by doing. The plan, following the pattern of previous ones made under the Radical and the military governments, made sectoral projections based on the use of input–output techniques. These projections were construed as being in themselves 'the policies', while in fact no indication was given of how the various sectors were to reach these targets (di Tella, 1971). At the same time, the plan said very little about the role of the price mechanism or the level of relative prices. These characteristics were not specific to Peronism; they reflected a tradition of planning among 'progressive' economists which tied in very well with the Peronist distrust of market forces. However, it is one thing to think that the price mechanism is non-optimal and another to think that it can be ignored. Another essential element of the economic programme was its nationalist leanings. In contrast to the 1946–55 experience, very few expropriations were contemplated. A clear preference was established for local capital; this matched the interests of the CGE, but not those of the trade unions, which despite their rhetoric remained basically aloof on this point and offered no resistance when this policy was reversed. Besides these interventionist and nationalist objectives, the other fundamental trait of the programme was its emphasis on distribution. Its avowed objective was to improve the share of wage-earners so that, 'in a spirit of absolute fairness, 50 per cent of the national income should accrue to capital and 50 per cent to workers, instead of two-thirds and one-third, respectively, as has been the case since 1956' (Perón, 25 Oct 1973). More important than this was the way in which this was to be achieved through an explicit incomes policy. This was supposed to bring together opposing social and economic groups and supersede class conflicts, an idea central to the Peronist ideology and in line with its social composition. The incomes policy took the form of a specific three-way agreement, the so-called 'social pact' between the CGT, the CGE and the State, through its Ministry of Economy. Although the social pact had its greatest impact on the short-term stabilisation policies which we analyse in the following chapter, it was conceived as a fundamental solution to the previous antagonistic situation and a big step towards an 'organised community'. In this sense it could be considered as a policy of fundamental structural change.

We now move from the general outline of the programme to the particular measures and laws, even if a good part of them were never implemented. Nevertheless, they coloured the initial period and an analysis of them helps us to understand some of the initial hopes and aspirations and the resistances to them. About forty laws and agreements (see Table 4.1) embodied the most significant aspects of the programme. Those that were specifically economic dealt with the agricultural sector (land use and State intervention in agricultural exports), with the industrial sector (industrial protection, development of small business, industrial promotion and foreign investment), with industrial exports and trade with the socialist bloc, with financial and fiscal reforms, with the organisation of the State sector and, finally, with price and profit controls. The laws which had social implications were those dealing with the organisation of trade unions, with the regulation of labour contracts, with social security and with health.

TABLE 4.1   Significant Laws and Agreements Connected with the
Reform Programme

---

(1) *Measures affecting the agricultural sector*

22 538/73: Tax on the expected normal productivity of land
20 535/73: New powers for the Meat Board, particularly in the export
  trade
20 573/73: New powers for the Grain Board in the export trade
Sep 1973: Concerted Policy Agreement with the agrarian sector
[Not passed by Congress] Agrarian Law

(2) *Measures affecting the industrial sector*

20 545/73: Protection of labour and national production (*Protección al
  trabajo y la producción nacional*)
20 560/73: Promotion of specific new industries
20 568/73: Creation of a corporation for the development of medium-
  sized and small enterprises (Corporación para el Desarrollo de la
  Pequeña y Mediana Empresa)
20 557/73: Foreign investment
Concerted Policy Agreement with the automobile sector

(3) *Agreements affecting trade with the Socialist bloc*

Trade agreement with Cuba, 27 Feb 1974
Trade agreement with the USSR, 7 May 1974
Trade agreement with Poland, 9 May 1974

(4) *Financial reform*

20 520/73: Nationalisation of bank deposits
20 521/73: Decentralisation of the boards of the Banco de la Nación and
  Banco Nacional de Desarrollo
20 522/73: Expropriation of (specific) private banks
20 523/73: Measures affecting financial intermediaries owned by banks
20 530/73: Changes in the charter of the BCRA
20 574/73: Rules and regulations affecting financial intermediaries
20 663/73: Regulations affecting transferable time deposits

(5) *Tax reform*

20 532/73: Acceptance of payment for formerly undeclared taxes
20 537/73: Waiving of penalties for undeclared taxes
20 538/73: See under (1)
20 628/73: Profit tax
20 629/73: Tax on capital and wealth
20 631/73: Value-added tax (IVA)
20 634/73: Sharing of taxes between the national and provincial governments
20 643/73: Tax concessions for investments on the stock exchange
20 644/73: Creation of the National Fiscal Federal Police Agency

(6) *Organisation of the State*

> 20 549/73: Waiving of the seniority rights of civil servants, permitting their dismissal
> 20 558/73: Creation of the Corporation of National State Enterprises (CNEE)
> 20 680/73: Empowering of the State to fix maximum prices
> Concerted Policy Agreement between the State and the provinces

(7) *The State and the market*

> 20 680/73: Empowering of the State to fix maximum prices, force productivity, etc.
> 20 535/73: See under (1)
> 20 573/73: See under (1)

(8) *Labour legislation*

> 20 615/73: Trade Union Law (*Ley de Asociaciones Profesionales*)
> 20 744/74: Work Contract Law

(9) *Social security and health*

> 20 748/74: Integral Health System
> 20 118/75: New pensions law

It was in fact an ambitious programme and a comprehensive one, even allowing for some inconsistencies. It was received by most of the left as falling short of a true change, embodying very few if any of their ideas; it was considered a concession to the middle-class sectors of the Government coalition.

MEASURES CONCERNING THE AGRICULTURAL SECTOR

The agricultural sector soon became one of the more controversial. Héctor Giberti was appointed as the Secretary of Agriculture; he was not connected with the agricultural establishment and was considered a technician – a derogatory connotation in the eyes of the sector – with left-wing leanings. This apprehension was not dispelled when he was joined by a progressive group of Catholic technocrats of traditional extraction.

The agricultural policies were embodied in the so-called Agrarian Law – proposed but never passed by Congress – which provided for the expropriation of unproductive land; in a special tax law (20 538/73) which instituted a levy on the 'normal' estimated productivity of land; and in two laws (20 573/73 and 20 535/73) which enlarged the trading functions of the National Grain Board and National Meat Trade Board. These laws, particularly the last two, implied an advance in the role of the State at a time when part of it was in the hands of radicalised groups; this created an immediate opposition from the established sectors over and above what would have been expected in response to the measures themselves.

The proposed Agrarian Law was in the tradition that land, being a 'God-given asset', was in a different category from other capital assets. It assumed that 'Agricultural land has to fulfil its social purpose ... and should be considered a working asset and not a profit-making one.' The law proposed the expropriation of unproductive land, defining it as land which had not been in production for the last ten years, or had produced less than 30 per cent of the estimated 'normal yield'. The price was to be fixed in accordance with past productivity and was to be paid in special Government bonds with maturities of twenty, twenty-five and thirty years and yearly rates of 5, 4 and 3 per cent, adjustable to the rate of inflation and saleable at any time. The existing Consejo Agrario Nacional was empowered to proceed with the expropriations. A special proviso of the law established the possibility of organising large units along the lines of workers' management sharing schemes, something which, even if never implemented, helped to antagonise the whole sector and distract attention from more immediate and realistic matters.

The tax law was a repetition of attempts that had already been made during the Illia and Onganía periods. The idea of a tax not on actual production, but on an estimated 'normal' production, had been growing among tax experts of all shades of opinion. By being a fixed tax, it was supposed to penalise those who produced less than the average, while benefiting those who had higher-than-average yields. Its emphasis was on efficiency and it did not have distribution as an objective. Under the new law, a Government agency was to estimate the normal production of all units, thus giving the State a new function in a very sensitive area. An excessively high appraisal of potential productivity could become – intentionally or not – equivalent to the expropriation of the land, i.e. through the expropriation of its rent. This could not have taken place under the old tax on produce, since, if the rate became too high, the producer could choose not to produce. Under the new circumstances there was no way out. This was precisely the purpose of the law and the reason for the resistance to it. Resistance was, however, very much enhanced by suspicions about the final intentions of the Government; under previous right-wing governments, such as Onganía's, even the landowning groups had partially accepted this tax system.

The new law differed from the previous projects in that it provided that the tax rate should increase with the size of the landholding, so that the larger ones should pay higher rates. This introduced a distributionist element, and required the identification of ownership of limited liability companies. This levy did not replace income tax, but was considered a part payment to be deducted from the final income-tax assessment. While this was deeply resented, all tax experts, then and now, have been very uneasy about a dual tax system – one sector's tax based on wealth and another's based on income – since there arises the possibility of gross evasion based on overpricing by the first sector to the second.

Despite the great suspicion that these laws created, some degree of co-operation was obtained from the small-farmers' association, the Federación Agraria, from the co-operative movement, Confederación Intercooperativa Agropecuaria (Coninagro), from the big-landowners' association, the Sociedad Rural Argentina, and from quite a few of the smaller rural societies, but never from the strongest federation, the diehard Corporacion de Asociaciones Rurales de Buenos Aires y La Pampa (CARBAP). The first three institutions signed the Agrarian Concerted Policy Agreement (Acta de Política Concertada con el Agro, Sep 1973) and were represented in the special commission that was set up. This agreement established mutual commitments; producers were to increase their productivity and total volume, acquiescing in the specific taxation laws, and were promised in exchange stable and satisfactory prices. The diffuse character of the agreement, the fact that the agrarian sector was hardly an oligopoly, which made implementation rather improbable, and the imprecise terms of the most important promises, did not stop great emphasis from being given to this deal. Its real importance, and its symbolic meaning, was that it was part of a covenant 'concerting policies' with all sectors. In this case it was believed that 'the agrarian sector could be won over and that it would abandon its previous role, incompatible with popular aspirations' (Gelbard, on the submission of the law to Congress, 1 May 1974).

More effective than the tax law or the Agrarian Agreement were the new enlarged functions of the Meat and Grain Boards, part of the new policy of advancing the role of the State in foreign trade. These were a milder repetition of the policies of the first period, when the Government created the Instituto Argentino para la Promoción del Intercambio, which was empowered to intervene in foreign trade beyond the basic export staples. The main idea in both instances was that private oligopolies operating in the country reduced the price paid to producers, and at the same time did not maximise the export price obtained by the country; it was assumed, moreover, that the export houses through intra-company pricing policies could locate their earnings within or outside the country, according to circumstances. The argument, very common in primary producing countries, has some weight. Nevertheless, granting two State monopolies the right to buy and sell the bulk of agricultural exports, i.e. from US \$2000 to 3000 million per year, accounting for more than half of the total export trade, was indeed a drastic answer, especially as the attempt was made to reach that level practically overnight. The producers, even if they agreed at times with the essential argument, were wary of moving away from known market forces, even if they were oligopolistic, to State intervention on such a scale. In some quarters it was suggested that the boards should restrict themselves to a supervisory role, involving themselves in purchasing and selling only as an exceptional measure; these suggestions, however, went unheeded.

The jump was so extreme that serious administrative and financial problems appeared. The boards found themselves needing to use the old exporters' organisations, particularly for the sale of the produce; the curious situation arose in which the old exporters were relieved of the financing load and of most of the risks, but continued to perform some of their previous functions, acting now on behalf of the boards. When the initial decision was taken, not much consideration was given to how it was to be implemented. Taking the grand approach, one may think that small details are of little long-term significance. However, the extremely messy way in which the matter was handled compromised the whole idea. Export sales and financing were lost at the very time when the external situation was extremely delicate.

As important as these laws affecting the agricultural sector was the fixing of agricultural prices through export *ad valorem* taxes (*retenciones*) and through the exchange rate. This was equally significant in defining overall policy and in arousing the reactions of the sector. Nevertheless, for a good while relative prices of agricultural products were not as bad as might have been expected. The short-lived boom of the end of the previous government had gone beyond anything reached during the last decade, 'cattle producers having enjoyed unprecedented incomes' (*La Nación*, 22 July 1973). A reversal set in but only after the end of 1974, when the agricultural–industrial ratio went below the one prevailing in 1960, the average for the decade. While the initial reaction of the sector was coloured by the agrarian laws, as time went by pricing policies became more and more important and from 1975 to the end they were decisive in turning the sector belligerently against the government.

INDUSTRIAL AND FOREIGN INVESTMENT LAWS

The industrial laws dealt with the protection of local production (20 545/73), the promotion of new industrial projects (20 560/73), the encouragement of small and medium-sized industries (20 568/73) and, most significantly, the regulation of foreign investment (20 557/73).

The first law did not advance much on the Buy Argentine Act passed during the Levingston–Ferrer period. Nevertheless, it went well beyond the regulation of purchases of locally produced capital goods by State enterprises, and brought in quite a range of protectionist measures which could be taken to stop foreign competition. It was an extremely protectionist law with few considerations of costs and efficiency. On the other hand, it paid a lot of attention to industrial exports, which were given very high priority. This was a novelty and reflected the breaking down of the exclusively import-substitution scheme. It advanced the view, sustained by some economists who were not necessarily sympathisers of the Government (Diamand, 1973), that the higher domestic industrial prices were basically owing to some kind of 'structural disequilibria' and in no way reflected a lack of comparative advantage. Effective protection and export rebates were to be fixed for each product so as to equalise its local costs with the international ones. Some justification for such undiscriminating criteria was made on the grounds that breaking the inward-looking strategy was so important that a first stage, even if of this type, was better than none. This was a possible but dangerous argument. During the first two years the level of nominal protection was increased, although the exchange rate was gradually overvalued, which reduced net effective protection. The breakdown of the tariff structure was increased until mid-1975, when the process was partially reversed.

The industrial promotion law allowed the Government to subsidise specific projects of 'national interest'. The definition was a loose one. The basic requirements were that they should be new projects which should not compete with existing industries, and that they should be located outside developed areas. Besides the usual kind of tax concessions, the law allowed sales taxes (or later VAT) to be deferred for up to fifteen years without any kind of interest or monetary adjustment for inflation. The number and total size of the projects were not significant: in the first six months up to January 1974, 203 projects, employing a workforce of about 25,000 people, were approved, at a total investment of $215 million (US dollars).

The second significant measure dealing with the industrial sector was the creation of the Corporación para el Desarrollo de la Pequeña y Mediana Empresa to assist small and medium-sized firms. This was to be done through cheaper credit, through loosely defined measures geared to improve the level of local technology and through a whole set of services such as the supply of intermediary and capital goods, the provision of local and international market studies, and so on. Again, strong emphasis was laid on these firms' potential as exporters. What was not clear was how these industries could develop local technology, compete with foreign firms and export to world markets. The rationale was, perhaps, that economies of scale are usually exaggerated and that a local technology adapted to local conditions, is a possible and convenient objective; this position had some encouragement from academics (Katz, 1972). The role of small local firms is at the core of the fundamental discussion on how modernisation can proceed. In any case this policy – very much in line with the political base of the CGE – was implemented only to a small extent, as it was not easy to translate the general purposes of the law into practical action.

The most important of the laws affecting industries and the one that received most public attention was the one dealing with foreign investment (20 557/73). It was explicitly inspired by the well-known Resolution 24 of the Cartagena Agreement signed by the Andean Pact countries. It was a highly sophisticated law, being most concerned with the danger that excessive participation by foreign investors in the development of the country would mean

that the centre where crucial decisions [are taken] becomes located in foreign countries and in the hands of multinational corporations, that dependent countries adopt the consumption pattern of the dominant power ... that the technology which is introduced is linked with privileged groups and that the industries which are introduced are capital-intensive ... making more difficult the satis-

faction of the needs of the whole of the population.   (Considerations on the submission of the law to Congress, 7 June 1973)

The main purpose was to reverse foreign penetration of the economy,
particularly in the industrial sector. This had been increasing since
1952 and particularly since the very pro-foreign investment policies of
the Frondizi government, interrupted only during the Radical period
from 1963 to 1966. The process had reached a point where foreign
investors owned about a third of the manufacturing sector, measured
in terms of contribution to the GNP. This increase had been
dramatised by the purchase by foreign firms of some large industrial
companies and banks. A special law was passed to reverse some of
these purchases, but, in contrast with Perón's first presidency, this
was rather exceptional as no emphasis was laid on the nationalisation
of foreign firms. Initially, expropriation affected only a group of four
banks; only much later was it intended to affect the large Swiss public
utility company Compañía Italo-Argentina de Electricidad (CIAE).
This company was a very special case, to the point that its expropriation was confirmed and finalised during the succeeding pro-foreign
military government.

From a broader point of view, the increase in foreign participation
was the inevitable consequence of the autarkic policies prevailing
during the whole period. The country had switched from its pre-1945
dependence on foreign trade to a post-1958 dependence on foreign
capital. This inward-looking strategy, with its lack of emphasis on
exports, created after a while a permanent balance-of-payments
problem, which increased the crucial role of foreign financing in terms
both of credits and of direct investment (Caputo and Pizarro, 1970). It
can be argued that at such a juncture the opening up of the economy
and an increased dependence on industrial exports may reduce the
need for foreign investment. Foreign trade and foreign investment
may act in a countervailing way as far as these matters are concerned
(di Tella, 1973).

The expectations of the Government were that harsher but clearer
rules of the game would be compatible with the maintenance of a
desired flow of foreign investment. To this end, it was not too strict in
applying the law, and this lack of rigour did not go unnoticed. It was
felt that 'the government interpreted the law in a much broader spirit,
and foreign investors were able to notice it' (*La Nación*, 9 Dec 1973).
However, no significant foreign investment took place. The most
important deterrent was not so much the law in question as the
deteriorating political and economic situation.

TRADE WITH THE SOCIALIST COUNTRIES

During the late 1960s some nationalistic groups claimed that the country should not trade with the Soviet bloc. At that time the USA was applying varying degrees of discrimination to trade with those countries, although these measures were not as drastic as those advocated by the Argentines. These groups succeeded in creating a climate of suspicion around the opening up of any trade with the Soviet bloc. In 1972 President Lanusse, in an attempt to project a progressive image, championed the opposite line; however, this was then more a declaration of intent, with few practical consequences.

In 1973 the new government placed a special emphasis on the opening of trade with these countries and made it a political issue. It was quite in line with the great emphasis on foreign trade and appeared a practical way to contribute to the desired export drive. The diehard opposition from the right tried to convey the idea that the country was giving away the goods and that it was 'an absurd political machination' (*La Prensa*, 12 Jan 1974) in order to attain a dubious political goal, a suspicion which, extraordinarily enough, was shared by some of the groups of the Peronist right. However, the more general reaction after some initial hesitancy was that 'the participation of technology and capital from the socialist countries ... may be obtained on conditions ... which may be considered as extremely advantageous to the country' (*La Nación*, 7 Oct 1973).

The Minister of Economy made it a personal project and successfully carried out trade negotiations with Cuba, the Soviet Union and Poland. In the first case, the opposition of the USA to the involvement of subsidiaries of American multinationals in trade with Cuba provided the perfect opportunity for testing the determination of the Government. After some haggling and hard negotiations, the Government succeeded in forcing these companies to participate. The American automobile companies, which were those principally involved, started an active export drive. One of the incentives was the granting of extended lines of credit for up to ten years, something for which the Government was severely criticised, particularly by the business sectors. Cuba had an excellent standing in international trade, behaving quite conservatively in these matters, like most socialist countries. In the case of the Soviet Union itself, trade picked up spectacularly; in three years the USSR became one of the principal trading partners of Argentina. With Poland the deal included the organisation of joint companies, in fisheries in particular, but this was less successful, and little came out of it.

TABLE 4.2 Trade with the Soviet Bloc

(1) Exports (US $'000)

Year	East Germany	Bulgaria	Czecho-slovakia	Hungary	Poland	Romania	USSR	Cuba	Total Soviet countries	Total exports
1972	714.8	46.3	8,126.2	3,654.4	14,350.5	8,136.9	24,101.3	0.1	59,130.5	1,941,097.9
1973	3,505.0	542.3	17,256.2	2,767.5	24,705.3	3,116.8	83,091.3	12,039.1	147,023.5	3,266,002.8
1974	3,516.8	1,260.1	12,230.8	1,622.6	48,733.2	2,268.6	211,145.4	76,493.9	357,271.4	3,930,701.7
1975	1,881.5	993.2	8,533.5	2,984.6	16,188.0	418.7	288,313.8	156,540.0	475,853.3	2,961,264.3
1976	12,362.5	4,645.5	12,375.3	3,361.3	20,371.8	17,859.1	219,117.3	168,645.8	458,738.6	3,916,058.2

(2) Imports (US $'000)

Year	East Germany	Bulgaria	Czecho-slovakia	Hungary	Poland	Romania	USSR	Cuba	Total Soviet countries	Total exports
1972	178.6	298.1	2,563.9	1,020.1	12,014.3	2,805.7	2,601.5	—	21,482.2	1,904,681.8
1973	256.5	388.7	1,729.9	1,584.7	13,753.5	1,983.7	7,010.1	0.5	26,707.6	2,229,467.6
1974	410.2	303.1	5,799.3	3,327.8	16,316.7	20,637.2	10,911.5	13.1	57,718.9	3,634,917.9
1975	333.8	402.7	8,035.1	3,604.3	31,569.1	34,166.2	21,940.8	55.9	100,107.9	3,946,500.8
1976	10.3	416.2	4,982.0	2,173.4	33,627.6	28,797.2	12,784.1	9.7	82,800.5	3,033,004.4

(3) *Exports (as percentage of total exports)*

Year	East Germany	Bulgaria	Czecho-slovakia	Hungary	Poland	Romania	USSR	Cuba	Total Soviet countries	Total exports
1972	0.037	0.002	0.419	0.188	0.739	0.419	1.242	—	3.046	100.0
1973	0.107	0.017	0.528	0.085	0.756	0.095	2.544	0.369	4.502	100.0
1974	0.108	0.039	0.374	0.05	1.492	0.069	6.465	2.342	10.939	100.0
1975	0.064	0.034	0.288	0.101	0.547	0.014	9.736	5.286	16.069	100.0
1976	0.316	0.119	0.316	0.086	0.520	0.456	5.595	4.307	11.714	100.0

(4) *Imports (as percentage of total imports)*

Year	East Germany	Bulgaria	Czecho-slovakia	Hungary	Poland	Romania	USSR	Cuba	Total Soviet countries	Total imports
1972	0.01	0.016	0.135	0.054	0.631	0.147	0.137	—	1.128	100.0
1973	0.012	0.017	0.078	0.071	0.617	0.089	0.314	—	1.20	100.0
1974	0.011	0.008	0.16	0.092	0.499	0.568	0.300	—	1.588	100.0
1975	0.008	0.01	0.204	0.091	0.800	0.866	0.556	—	2.537	100.0
1976	—	0.014	0.164	0.072	1.109	0.949	0.421	—	2.73	100.0

Source: Instituto Nacional de Estadísticas y Censos (INDEC), *Boletín de Comercio Exterior* (1976).

Total exports with the socialist countries, which stood at US\$60 million in 1972, jumped to \$475 million in 1975 – that is, from 3 to nearly 12 per cent (of which Cuba represented 4 per cent) – a successful performance which, fortunately for the country, continued even after the fall of the Government. (See Table 4.2.)

THE FINANCIAL REFORM

The financial reform was more far-reaching than reforms attempted in other areas; it repeated to a great extent that of 1946 (Baliño, 1980), and was a mixture of some archaic concepts of banking and an interventionist attitude. It was hailed as a major tool in the 'liberation of the economy', and resisted on the ground that 'Its only clear [consequence] is that Government bureaucrats will have a greater capacity to distribute . . . credit between the various activities, and if its allocation does not take into consideration the basic needs of the country it will become one of the worst measures that could be imagined' (Carlos Brignone, former head of the Central Bank, *Clarín*, 12 Aug 1973).

The main purpose of the new law was to give the Central Bank more direct power in the determination of the total amount of credit and money in circulation. In the previous fractional reserve system, the credit that banks could loan was determined by the Central Bank on the basis of deposits received, i.e. the reserve requirement, and varied according to the type of deposit and the purpose, area or type of credit to be given. In order to determine the total amount of money, the Central Bank had to take two variables into consideration, one determined by the demand for money (and for its different kinds, M_1, M_2, M_3, M_4) by the public, and the other determined by the bank itself. This degree of control of the money supply seemed insufficient.

The new idea embodied in the law was to break completely the relationship between deposits made by the public in the banking system and the total amount of credit given to the community. The role of money creation, which had been shared by the banking system and the Central Bank, was now transferred completely to the latter, which was to have absolute and direct power to determine the supply of money (but naturally not the demand). The law specified that banks would receive deposits 'on behalf of the Central Bank', which in turn would grant lines of credit to each of the banks; these would grant credits at their own risk but on behalf of the Central Bank. The criteria by which the Central Bank was to make credit available to each bank depended on the amount of deposits collected by each bank *and* on the sector, area and purpose for which the credit was requested. The basic difference in the new system lay in the fact that the total amount of credit fixed by the Central Bank was now determined by a formula made up by several independent variables, i.e. independent of the amount of deposits in addition to the one dependent on deposits. The system proved to be extremely clumsy, giving rise to a whole maze of regulations and payments of compensation to the banks for their services. However, the amount of money could not be fixed as directly as was thought. In fact, banks were given maximum amounts that they could loan by type of credit, but their degree of utilisation varied, and varied differently according to the type of credit authorised. Between the total amount authorised and the amount actually granted there was a discrepancy which in a way became an equivalent to the old monetary multiplier which the new law had attempted to eliminate, although it probably varied within a narrower range.

Another consequence of the new system, although not a necessary one, was the shift of credit from private to State-owned banks (see Table 4.3). This was the consequence of the differential treatment given to the different lines of credit. In some cases, those with specifically promotional purposes were channelled exclusively through State banks. In other cases State banks were preferred but private banks also received a share. As time went by, quite a few exceptions were made; increasingly the receipt of some type of deposits gave the banks the right to grant loans automatically in certain proportions, exactly as in the previous system. At all times banks were allowed to loan their own capital within broadly defined limits. Although it was not inherent in the law, it was believed that one of its main consequences was to be a shift of credit from private to official banks, a characteristic that came to be associated with the law. In fact that shift was rather modest, 5 per cent, and could have been achieved under the old system, although it may be true that under the new one it was more easy and natural. In any case the new system was an improvement on the one tried between 1946 and 1955, as in that instance deposits in each bank at the date of the law were taken as the fixed basis for all future allocations of credit, a most arbitrary basis indeed.

The system had some formal similarities (Baliño, 1978, 1980; Gaba, 1974) with the 100 per cent reserve scheme recommended by Chicago economists in the late 1930s and early 1940s. This provided for current-account deposits to be taken away from private commercial

TABLE 4.3 Bank Loans by Type of Bank

(1) Million pesos

Year's end	Total	State-owned banks			Private banks		
		National	Provincial	Cities	Locally owned Buenos Aires	Locally owned Provinces	Foreign
1971	25,281,346	9,198,753	6,027,925	693,927	3,401,118	2,279,241	3,680,382
1972	39,120,655	15,236,856	9,209,510	897,383	4,911,917	3,711,125	5,153,864
1973	67,623,484	28,814,814	16,678,859	1,380,654	7,628,951	6,427,710	6,692,496
1974	106,621,015	50,281,953	24,111,273	1,683,291	11,161,383	9,583,683	9,799,432
1975	229,071,236	109,846,094	44,389,970	3,017,190	29,397,244	19,895,490	22,525,248
1976	1,004,511,374	411,484,124	157,002,243	5,731,791	191,474,919	101,481,176	137,337,121

(2) As a percentage of total loans

Year's end	Total	State-owned Banks			Private banks		
		National	Provincial	Cities	Locally owned Buenos Aires	Locally owned Provinces	Foreign
1931	100	35.88	23.51	2.71	13.26	8.89	14.35
1972	100	38.09	23.02	2.24	12.28	9.28	12.88
1973	100	40.34	23.35	1.93	10.68	9.00	9.37
1974	100	46.76	22.42	1.56	10.38	8.91	9.11
1975	100	47.23	19.09	1.30	12.64	8.56	9.69
1976	100	40.74	15.54	0.56	18.96	10.05	13.60

Source: BCRA monthly statistical bulletins

banks or, alternatively, for them to make a reserve deposit of the same amount. This scheme (Currie, 1934; Simons, 1948; Friedman, 1948) was also supposed to reduce the variability of the money supply, which had been so extreme in the 1930s. It had originally been designed for the opposite purpose: to reduce the degree of State intervention in the determination of the amount of money. Under the scheme, current deposits were to determine an exactly equivalent amount of loan money, while private commercial banks would operate only with time deposits, leaving the Central Bank to regulate M_2 through open-market operations.

It is strange that the differences between the two systems, technical in nature and not too substantial, should have stirred up such discussion. The reform appeared as one of the major steps taken by the new government. In the minds of important sectors of the public, it was considered a fundamental piece of anti-monetarist policy – the fact that it had formal similarities with the Chicago plan would have been considered a bad joke – and, oddly enough, as an expression of sovereignty following a line which had already been taken years ago (Cavagna Martínez, 1954; Moyano Llerena, 1949) but abandoned later on. Both the fractional reserve system and the new so-called 'nationalisation' scheme could serve the same purposes of policy. The only difference between the systems was the nature of the monetary multiplier, which in both cases was variable and not easily predicted.

THE TAX REFORM

The reform of the tax system was made up of a coherent group of laws. These embodied many of the suggestions made by professional organisations, such as the prestigious Colegio de Graduados de Ciencias Económicas (which had Radical leanings) and the Asociación Argentina de Política Fiscal. The general approach was to broaden the definition of profits subject to progressive taxation. One of the more important changes was the attempted identification of ownership of assets and of sources of income (20 643/73 and 20 627/73). Under the previous system, taxpayers could, if they so wished, avoid reporting any shareholdings or dividends, paying a fixed rate, but not the highest. Under the new law, ownership of shares had to be identified, both for tax purposes and to determine the nationality of shareholders, following practices prevalent in a number of developed countries, the USA and the UK among others. Under the previous legislation, companies paid income tax on behalf of shareholders who, if unidentified, were not obliged to pay anything more. The new law differentiated between a company's profits, making them subject to a corporation tax, and the shareholders' profits (or dividends), making them subject to a personal and progressive income tax.

Profits made by corporations but not distributed were subject to an even higher tax, an odd differentiation which tended to penalise the accumulation of capital by corporations. In the case of the capital tax (20 629/73), all kinds of ownership, including shareholdings, were to be declared and subjected to a progressive capital tax, leaving land as the only 'capital' treated differently. To compensate for this broadened definition of profits, the highest corporation tax rate was reduced from 42.9 per cent in 1972 (33 per cent plus 9.9 per cent emergency tax) to 26.4 per cent (22 per cent and an emergency tax of 4.4 per cent). The maximum personal tax rate was also reduced, but less so, from 46 to 42 per cent. Capital gains, which in the past had been taxed at a special and low rate of 10 per cent, were now treated like other kinds of profits; this implied a more than fourfold increase. This tax continued to be levied on the nominal difference between the sale and purchase price, with no adjustments allowed in the determinations of costs, as if inflation had not had any bearing on them. Foreign companies were dealt with separately, being required to pay, on top of the corporation tax, a tax equal to that paid by a local shareholder in the highest income bracket. Moreover, payments to head offices for know-how and technology were not accepted as expenses; these were treated as hidden profits and taxed accordingly.

In the case of indirect taxation, a switch was made from sales tax (*actividades lucrativas*) to value-added tax (IVA, 20 631/73) which had been suggested by most tax experts as being more rational, as it avoided 'cascading' and allowed a broader tax base. A final law (20 633/73, *coparticipación impositiva*) specified the way taxes would be shared between the State (48.5 per cent of the total), the provinces (another 48.5 per cent) and a special regional development fund (3 per cent). Something which was left out of the stabilisation programme but which was to be included late in 1975 was any consideration of the impact of inflation on the determination of profit and taxes. The only adjustment which had been previously allowed was the revaluation of fixed assets according to the wholesale price index, which in turn affected amortisation. The adjustments which were introduced in the 1975 proposals concerned the assessment of work in progress; this tried to avoid the false inflationary profits stemming from FIFO (first-in-first-out) accounting, making mandatory either LIFO (last-in-first-out) or replacement costing. Moreover, it required an adjustment for the loss of value (or gain) caused by inflation on the net amount of monetary assets (or liabilities).

A transitory but significant law (20 532/73) allowed taxpayers who had undeclared past taxes to make a special once and for all payment and avoid any further penalty. At the same time other laws empowered the tax authorities to prosecute (20 537/73) and jail (20 658/73) tax-dodgers, even for deeds committed prior to the new laws, creating a special 'tax police' (Dirección de Policía Fiscal Federal, 20 644/73).

Summarising, we can say that this was a reasonably technical reform, that it still refused to include inflation accounting for tax purposes, that it was slightly distributionist in intent, as it increased the types of profits affected by progressive taxation, and that, as with so many other aspects of this initial package, it was implemented only to a relatively small degree; this was partly owing to somewhat over-ambitious targets, but particularly to the increasing political troubles.

THE ORGANISATION OF THE STATE SECTOR

While the general policies were interventionist and advanced the role of the State, an attempt was made to improve the organisation and management of the State enterprises, an effort which lasted only for a relatively short while. Many expected demands were made on the State sector in general (and on the State companies in particular) as they provided a very important opportunity for political patronage. The initial attempt was made through the creation of a State holding company which encompassed all the State companies (Corporación Nacional de Empresas del Estado, CNEE) both in the service and in the manufacturing sectors, excluding only the military ones. Studies for this project had been already started during the Levingston–Ferrer period and were inspired by similar attempts made in European countries, particularly in Italy. The Italian Istituto per la Ricostruzione Industriale (IRI) and Ente Nazionale d'Idrocarburi (ENI) companies had been active in Argentina and were well known.

Some voices were raised – even by people who were not against the Government – pointing to the huge power that the new corporation would have, and condemning it as 'one of the most objectionable projects ... it creates a state within the State, a gigantic corporation

which, directly and indirectly, will manage a large percentage of the
national economy ... free from any political control' (Diamand, *La
Opinión* 4 July 1973). Notwithstanding, the Government was able to
bring onto the executive board some of the leading members of the
industrial establishment, some of them closely associated with the
Instituto para el Desarrollo de los Ejecutivos en Argentina (IDEA),
the highly reputed top-management association, and with the Unión
Industrial. This reflected the good relations which were being
established between the old industrial groupings and the CGE. At the
same time a group of highly qualified economists, technicians and
energy and transport experts were recruited for the staff of the new
organisation. The presence of this technocratic group, considered as
being politically somewhat to the left and suspected of being highly
interventionist, gave the CNEE a polemical image which was not
completely assuaged by the composition of the board. The formation
of the Corporation was more a declaration of intent (and an important one at that) than a real instrument of policy, as it was unconnected
with the political and social context. Nevertheless, if the
disorganisation of the State sector, which was to reach sorry levels,
was not worse, this was owing to the existence of the corporation. It
began to meet significant political resistance on the occasion of the
appointment of the heads of the State companies. The problem was
not so much with the Justicialista party as with the leaders of the
unions in the service companies, who thought it their 'natural right' to
head their respective State companies. This development was spear-
headed by the electricity workers' union (Luz y Fuerza), whose sea-
soned and able leaders were appointed to head the two largest electric
utilities (Servicios Eléctricos del Gran Buenos Aires (SEGBA) and
Agua y Energía). The unions were successful in other instances but
many of their candidates lacked the minimum qualifications. While
the whole attempt was shrouded in a workers' management philo-
sophy, it soon degenerated into a purely power-grabbing affair. A
compromise between the CNEE and the unions was sought and
found, but the initial technocratic aspirations of the corporation soon
came to nothing; it lost the support of the business community, and
this forced the resignation of their representation on the board. After
the appointment of the new Minister of Economy, Alfredo Gómez
Morales, in September 1974, the Government took a negative view of
the CNEE; it reduced its role and importance as if it also believed the
initial criticism levelled against it. The corporation enjoyed a short-lived
revival in late 1975, and this in turn created suspicions about the real

intentions of the new minister, Antonio Cafiero, and his group, who had been responsible for the new lease of life.

PRICE CONTROL POLICY

One of the most publicised cases of State intervention was the law (20 680/73) which empowered the Government to fix maximum prices, intervene in primary markets, prohibit exports and compel the production of essential products. This law was part of a long tradition going back to the 1939 law (12 591/39), passed under the influence of the World War, which had empowered the State to impose price controls. Such powers were substantially reinforced and widely used during the first Perón presidencies (laws 12 830/46 and 12 938/47) and became intimately associated with Peronist policies. They were reinstated in a milder form by the Radicals in 1964 (16 454/64) while in 1967 Krieger Vasena imposed controls on about 500 firms which were price-leaders – theoretically on a voluntary basis but in practice through direct pressure exercised by a special watchdog commission. The new laws gave the State more power than ever in these matters, including the ability to impose harsh penalties. (These had existed in 1939, but ceased in 1946.) What was more important was that the new law was used extensively, becoming one of the main tools of the initial 'social pact'. It was viewed by the rank and file as anti-establishment and as a sign of the firm determination to 'fix things' (as if things could be fixed that easily). The policy of fixing prices was used across the board, both in cases where control, even if difficult, was possible, and also where control was unlikely. Large companies, because of their limited number, were easier to control, and wholesalers' prices were easier to control than retailers'. An attempt was even made to control retailers' margins, an even more impossible proposition. One of the probable consequences of these differences in openness to control was that the wholesale price index lagged behind the retail one; this implied an increase in the retailers' mark-up, which was just the opposite of what was intended.

The price freeze lasted for the two years that the social pact was in force, during which time wages were frozen as well. The freeze was effective at the beginning, mainly because of the general scare created by political developments. The Peronist Youth created volunteer supervisory groups which checked compliance with the price freeze; this added tension to an already tense atmosphere. The price index which measures prices effectively paid in the market went down during the first month of the freeze and remained without change for the following six months. The black-market rate fell from 13 to about 10 pesos to the dollar, indicating that even the business community had changed its expectations regarding the growth of inflation.

Even critics of the Government's measures were impressed by the fact that 'the [former] yearly inflation of 70 per cent has been stopped, the stock exchange has picked up, the non-official dollar quotation has gone down, taxes have gone up and the country, surprised, can see results that nobody would have imagined . . . not even the authors of those policies' (Roberto Alemann, former Minister of Economy, *Clarín*, 12 Aug 1973). However, some doubts remained, as he went on to state that 'Some of the inflationary sources [i.e. monetary expansion] have still to be controlled . . . until then a judgement about the long-term chances of this anti-inflationary policy cannot be made.'

The Government was so surprised by the initial effectiveness of the measures that it ended up with too strong a conviction of their value: in fact, they were continued until long after they had ceased to be useful, as we shall see in the next chapter. A price freeze can be quite useful; it can create a price pause and it can change expectations, which are in themselves an inflationary factor. However, it has to be used with great care, only for a short while and over a small range of significant and controllable products, and this unfortunately was not done.

As with many of the initial measures, one gets the impression of an extremely voluntaristic approach to economic problems, as if economic laws, instead of being disagreeable facts, were the consequence of some intentional capitalistic confabulation and could be circumvented by energetic intervention.

LABOUR LEGISLATION

Labour relations merited two very different kinds of law. One was the expected Trade Union Law (Ley de Asociaciones Profesionales, 20 614/73) and the other, the Work Contract Law (Ley de Contrato de Trabajo, 20 744/74). The first had been in effect since the first Perón government; it was suspended from 1955 to 1958, but it was revived by the Frondizi government as part of the electoral deal. Initially the law had a corporativist tinge, but its use gave it a different colour. It became a crucial instrument in the preservation of trade union unity by imposing a single union on each sector, but reinforced the power and independence of the unions even *vis-à-vis* the State, something which is not precisely a corporativist aim. At the same time it gave great power to the Labour Ministry, which could recognise, cancel or change the rights of trade unions to represent their specific sector in wage and labour negotiations. Over the years the law consolidated both sides of what could be described as a duopolistic relationship between the trade unions and the government. It is precisely this ambivalent character which explains how it endured for so long and why it was upheld by both military, Radical and popular governments.

The new law was not a significant departure from the previous one, but reinforced the pro-union clauses. It made more difficult the creation of competing unions, thus tending to accentuate the tendency towards the existence of a single union per sector. At the same time it specifically allowed unions to participate in political activities and publicly to support parties and candidates for public office. It also reinforced the autonomy of the unions, reducing the cases in which the Labour Ministry could intervene in their internal affairs, and allowed union officials to stay in office longer. Significantly, special judicial rights (*fuero especial sindical*) were granted to trade-union leaders, so that they could not be subject to judicial process unless the charge was first approved by the Labour Ministry (or, rather, by the special branch, the Tribunal Nacional de Relaciones Profesionales). Trade union officials were also given special protection against being fired by their employers and given the right not to work while holding office in the unions.

The Work Contract Law was basically a compilation of most of the measures and laws already regulating labour contracts, together with a few improvements. These principally concerned a lengthening of paid leave by about 40 per cent; an increase in maternity leave, allowing a six- to twelve-month delay in the resumption of work; and a two- to six fold increase in severance pay. Absences from work were no longer to be controlled by the employer's own medical services, as had been the practice, but a private medical certificate was to be sufficient. This measure, coupled with a lax social climate, significantly increased absenteeism. Private estimates made at the time indicated that average absenteeism went up by about 10 percentage points, from 6–7 per cent to about 17–18 per cent. Its initial effect was to disrupt production; later on, it forced employers to increase their labour force by a proportion similar to the increase in absenteeism. The law was heralded as a step forward out of all proportion to its actual provisions. For its part, the business sector considered it a major factor in hindering productivity.

SOCIAL SECURITY AND HEALTH

In welfare the main measures were related to some improvements in social security and, more substantially, to changes in the National Health system. Improvements in social security (21 118/73) were not significant. The national system introduced during the first Perón presidencies had been kept up. The only important change had been connected with the financing of the system. Originally it had been launched under a capitalisation scheme, but, as the funds collected were not in fact invested (at least in any specific way), it soon evolved into a 'pay as you go' scheme. Some increases in basic retirement pay were now made; other fringe benefits were introduced, and early retirement, something which had been cancelled during the Krieger Vasena period, was again permitted. The changes were not substantial, however, and the whole subject did not create any public stir.

In the case of the health services the law (20 748/73, Sistema Nacional Integrado de Salud) was more far-reaching, attributing to the State responsibility for the provision of health services and for the funding of a single central system. The law not only covered medical assistance to patients, but also included training, research, the distribution and marketing of medical products, as well as the promotion of local industries devoted to the equipment of hospitals and the development of local technology. The law also specified that, while in the past local authorities had had the prime responsibility for the provision of health services, they were now to delegate it to the State. In the original plan, the private sector was to become an integral part of the system. The main opposition to this came from the trade unions, who resented losing control of their highly developed health services, which were an important source of power, patronage and income. They succeeded in amending the law; the private sector was to be incorporated on a voluntary basis and the unions' health organisations were specifically excluded.

The law provided as well that 'Everywhere the principles of workers' co-management would be enforced; planning would be centralised while implementation would be decentralised.' The financing of this programme was to be carried out by the State, and was to amount to at least 5.1 per cent of the Government's total expenditure. Again, one can see a voluntaristic and interventionist attitude at work, together with a lack of appreciation of the problems of implementing such an ambitious programme. Nevertheless, it has to be said that it had been the tradition of the country since the end of the nineteenth century for the State to provide free medical services through a chain of State, provincial and city hospitals.

CONCLUDING NOTE

In conclusion it may be said that reformist programmes were weak or entirely lacking for areas where pressure groups were weak or unorganised, and where what was involved was a public (free) good. A case in point is the notorious absence of any laws or programmes concerning primary and secondary education. While this kind of situation is objectionable, it can hardly be called unfamiliar.

BIBLIOGRAPHY

Baliño, T. (1978) *El sistema de reservas bancarias del ciento por ciento*, Serie de Estudios Técnicos, no. 34 (Buenos Aires: CEMYB–BCRA).

Baliño, T. (1980) *Some Aspects of the Argentine Monetary and Banking Reform of 1946–57 (a Case of 100% Reserves?)* (Buenos Aires: CIE, Instituto Torcuato di Tella).

Caputo, O. and Pizarro, R. (1970) 'Dependencia e inversión extranjera', in Caputo *et al.*, *Chile hoy* (Mexico).

Cavagna Martínez, I. (1954) *Sistema bancario argentino* (Buenos Aires) esp. chs. 1 and 2.

Currie, L. (1934) *Supply and Control of Money in the United States* (Cambridge, Mass.).

Diamand, M. (1973) *Doctrinas económicas, desarrollo e independencia: economía para las estructuras productivas desequilibradas; el caso argentino* (Buenos Aires).

Friedman, M. (1948) 'A Monetary and Fiscal Framework for Economic Stability', *American Economic Review* (June).

Gaba, E. (1974) 'La transformación del sistema monetario argentino: nacionalización de los depósitos bancarios', *Mercado de Capitales* (Washington: Organisation of American States).

Katz, J. (1972) *Importación de tecnología, actividad inventiva e industrialización dependiente* (Buenos Aires: Instituto Torcuato di Tella).

Moyano Llerena, C. (1949) 'La producción de dinero y el nuevo régimen bancario argentino', *Revista de la Facultad de Derecho* (Buenos Aires) July–Aug.

Simons, H. (1948) *Economic Policy for a Free Society* (New York).

di Tella, G. (1971) 'Teoría de la nueva planificación', *Desarrollo Económico*, no. 40 (Jan–Mar).

di Tella, G. (1973) *La estrategia del desarrollo indirecto* (Buenos Aires) ch. 6.

5 The Short-term Economic Policies

This chapter considers some of the short-term developments of the period, so as to illuminate some of the major problems analysed in Chapters 6 and 7. The basic data referred to is laid out in the Statistical Appendix.

The reformist programme was very soon overshadowed by the stabilisation scheme and by the social pact, which was an integral part of it. The control of inflation was of greater concern to most people than the more grandiose and more distant 'structural' reforms. In fact, just before the new government came in, inflation was running at more than 100 per cent per year; it gave the impression of having completely run loose and was having obvious negative political effects. Improved terms of trade, the very high demand for exports and the favourable change in the trade balance made up the positive side of the picture. On the other hand, the Government's deficit was increasing and could be expected to deteriorate even more as a consequence of the distributive aims of the new government and of the expected greater social demands. Real wages had fallen during 1972 to more than 6 per cent below their 1969 level, one of the lowest levels in the last ten years, a situation which had continued up to the last months of the previous government. It was therefore to be expected that there would be an upward pressure on wages, with an inevitable rise in costs. By election time, inflationary expectations tended to vary considerably but were on average very high.

Economic policies and conditions changed considerably during the period. For ease of exposition, it is here divided into six sub-periods, which allow us to focus on some of the more important issues.

JUNE–DECEMBER 1973: THE INITIAL ECONOMIC POLICIES

Immediately after its inauguration the Government launched a rather drastic stabilisation programme. The basic idea was to induce, or even force under State auspices, an agreement on the distribution of national income (i.e. on relative prices and taxation) between wage-earners and business as represented by their respective central organisations, the CGT and the CGE. This *política de concertación* (agreement policy), known as the 'social pact' (Ayres, 1976), had been and was absolutely essential to the Peronist tradition of inter-class co-operation. It was implemented through a very strict wage and price freeze, leaving fiscal and in particular monetary measures very much out of the picture. The price freeze included an actual reduction of prices for a selected group of 570 presumably oligopolistic firms and for a selected list of products, including beef and textiles. Prices for all other firms and products were frozen at their prevailing level, while a special watchdog group was set up at the Secretariat of Commerce. As for wages, they were to be frozen for two years, after an initial rise of 200 pesos per month. This rise came to about 20 per cent for the lower income level and somewhat less for the higher ones, in line with the attempt to reduce wage differentials. It was supposed to compensate for the fall in wages in real terms during the previous year. It was much less than the percentage demanded by union leaders, although it allowed real wages to rise above the 1969 level by 13 per cent. This increase together with the slight reduction in unemployment allowed the share of wages in GNP to rise by more than 4 percentage points, recuperating the loss that had taken place during 1972; it reached 46.9 per cent of GNP, somewhat above the level prevailing during the previous stabilisation programme.

One of the factors contributing to the initial success of the wage and price freeze was the fact that many firms had made anticipatory price increases before the new government came into office, as the policy was not completely unexpected. They were thus able to absorb the required wage increase. However, the measure tended to penalise the more labour-intensive industries, which were supposedly the base of support for the Government coalition. The impression was that a government with a strong social arbitrating power had finally arrived and that, at a price, each sector had received a not unacceptable share of the national income. While the business sector was not happy, it had been alarmed by the previous runaway inflation and even more by the political outlook and initial pre-eminence of the radical groups; this had led it to fear much more dangerous policies. Under the circumstances, therefore, the programme was viewed with a sense of relief. This situation was at the source of the very strict initial compliance with the price freeze, which helped reduce inflationary expectations quite drastically. In a way it was similar to the beginnings of the 1967–70 programme, which also had started with a drastic control of inflationary expectations, in both cases helped by the preceding political change, which gave some credibility to the new policies.

The best indication of the initial success was the downward movement in the black-market rate during the first months of the year from 12.5 to about 10 pesos to the dollar – the same as the official rate of exchange. The rate of price increases was not only reduced but the absolute level actually decreased in June by 2.8 per cent. From July to December it increased by only 4 per cent, creating the excessively optimistic expectation that inflation had come under control. This reached a point when the government began to use the expression 'zero inflation' as a political slogan. Later on this unfortunately became a straightjacket, reducing the economic alternatives and in particular forcing the continuation of rather rigid price policies well after they had ceased to be advisable.

Another factor contributing to the initial success was the very great improvement in the international situation. Argentina took advantage of the final period of international prosperity of 1972 and 1973. The terms of trade increased at the end of 1972 and continued high until the third quarter of 1973. The enormous increase in export prices of more than 60 per cent and the excellent wheat harvest partially offset a mediocre performance in the volume of exports of the other major staples. During 1973 the country had record exports of US$3266 million, exceeding by 65 per cent the value of those of previous years. Imports decreased substantially in real terms, reflecting the relatively uncertain conditions of the first half of the year and the highly devalued currency; they picked up, however, towards the end of the year, following the expansionary domestic policies and the gradual overvaluation of the exchange rate. Imports for the whole year in nominal terms increased in value by 16 per cent, reflecting the very large increase in import prices.

The terms of trade remained, during the first three quarters, at the high levels of the previous year. By the end of 1973 the country was able to accumulate a significant current account surplus of US$704 million (or about 3 per cent of GNP) compared with a deficit of US$218 million for the previous year. This began to have an effect on the expansion of the economy and the growth of GNP. In the last quarter of the year, the international oil crisis brought an abrupt reversal of the terms of trade; they fell by more than 20 per cent, a trend that was to continue until the middle of the following year. While the external situation was good, the Government allowed an overvaluation of the currency; at the same time it engaged in an expansionary policy, a dangerous combination in view of the reversal of the international situation. This expansion could be seen in the increase in the expenditure of the Central Treasury compared with its receipts, a trend that was to continue, increasing its deficit from 2.43 per cent of GNP in 1972 to 5.43 per cent in 1973. The major part of the problem was the increasing current expenditure, due partly to the increase in real wages and partly to an increase in the number of public employees.

Government income increased, partly on account of the tax reforms, but more because of the beneficial effect of the stabilisation of prices, which avoided the reduction in the real value of receipts due to the fiscal lag, i.e. to the time between the determination of taxable income and actual payment.

The money supply, which had been at the relatively high level of 23–25 per cent of GNP during 1968–70, dropped to about 16.6 per cent during 1972 and 16.1 per cent during the first two quarters of 1973. It went up to 18.6 per cent in the third quarter and to 21.3 per cent in the last, by reason of the drastic curbing of inflationary expectations and the corresponding increase in the demand for money. This was a repetition of the 1967–9 experience, when the reduction in the rate of inflation from 22.7 per cent to 7.2 per cent allowed an increase in the liquidity coefficient from 20 to 26 per cent without adverse effects.

During the second half of the year the foreign sector contributed 14.5 per cent of the monetary expansion, the Government deficit contributed 30 per cent, while credit to the private sector contributed 48 per cent. Whereas from May 1972 to May 1973 money and prices had grown roughly by 70 per cent, during the whole of 1973 money increased by 93.16 per cent while prices increased by 30.8 per cent.

Unemployment fell, but remained until the middle of 1974 at 4.5 per cent, a figure that does not seem to be lower than the national 'natural' rate, and might have been reached later on anyway.

Interest rates decreased in nominal terms, as cheap credit had been one of the slogans of the CGE, even at the time of negative rates. Paradoxically, the reduction in the rate of inflation was so drastic that the real rate, which in 1972 had been -27.4 per cent, became $+8.5$ per cent from July to December. This was a beneficial but unintended consequence of the new policies. While this increased costs, it reduced the demand for credit and improved its distribution; however, it was too short-lived to have any lasting impact on the economy. Negat've rates were prevalent once more from 1974 onwards, again contributing to the maldistribution of resources and to the flight from cash and monetary assets.

The rate of growth nearly doubled the 1972 figure, reaching 5.8 per cent in 1973. It was an export-led growth, the change in the current account making up for nearly half the total figure. This can be seen also in the sectoral breakdown of growth; the agricultural sector increased its production by an extraordinary 13.5 per cent, while industry increased by 6.4 per cent. On the other hand, construction declined by 5.1 per cent, in line with the decline in investment, which decreased in 1973 from 23.6 to 22 per cent of GNP (increasing, however, in real terms). No significant changes took place in its composition, although public investment went down from 8.8 to 7.7 per cent of GNP, while private investment was practically unchanged at 14.1 per cent of GNP, but decreased by the end of the year. The private sector had seen a reduction in the availability of credit and in its profitability. It did not yet reduce its level of investment, but this was something which was to happen in the later stages with very adverse consequences. Foreign capital was intentionally discouraged and, while local capital was officially preferred, it was not sufficient to maintain past levels of private investment.

As a transitory and rather exceptional policy, the social pact had proved its worth, at least as regards its ability to stop inflationary expectations for a short period. During the first few months inflationary expectations had been cut in a very dramatic way, more so than anybody could have expected at the beginning of the year. By the end of the year, the international reversal and local expansionary policies had begun to create some of the first clouds on the horizon. Moreover, it was not clear whether the price freeze was intended as a permanent policy or even how it would be followed up. This problem was to prove crucial, in fact the stumbling-block of the whole programme.

JANUARY–SEPTEMBER 1974: THE MOUNTING PROBLEMS

By the end of 1974 it began to be clear that the relative prices which had prevailed since the date of the freeze were far from being a rational set or, for that matter, one which could assure a smooth functioning of the economy. Those who had repriced just before the freeze had been able to make good profits, while those who had been unable to do so or had been more moderate were not doing as well. At the same time, it was increasingly clear that monetary and fiscal policies were not in line, particularly since the renewal of inflationary expectations. The absorption of the wage increase had penalised, as already mentioned, the more labour-intensive industries. Many of these were locally owned and made up precisely the political base of the CGE, the main group responsible for the policies in question. Moreover, imported prices had continued to go up, from June to December by nearly 30 per cent, while the official price policy still required that they should be absorbed by profits. In many sectors it became an impossible condition to comply with, particularly for those with a high import content for which local substitutes were not available. Some industries began to incur losses, reducing or stopping production altogether, while others began to violate price controls, selling at a premium collected in black-market money.

It therefore became clear from the very end of 1973 and even more so during 1974 that some degree of price flexibility had to be introduced. The extent and the ways in which this could be done became one of the main issues. The Government was very hesitant, since such a change could imply abandonment of the 'zero inflation' scheme and a renewal of price rises, with the danger of once more creating inflationary expectations with their dreadful self-perpetuating effects.

The first attempt was made in December 1973 and clearly exemplified this ambivalent attitude. The Government announced that the increased cost of imported products could be transferred to prices, a decision which was cancelled before being put into effect and replaced by a revaluation of the currency for a selective list of imported goods, mainly raw materials. This implied an import subsidy. The decision was taken by the President pressed by the CGT leadership. They were harassed by radical elements within their rank and file who considered the social pact a sell-out and thought that they could not withstand price increases of any kind without asking for an immediate wage increase. The excellent foreign-reserve situation and a certain disregard of the fiscal cost prompted the Government to 'buy time', postponing some disagreeable measures at the cost of making them more necessary in the future and eventually more disagreeable still.

Some 'flexibilisation', as it was called, was, however, introduced during 1974 and particularly after September, when a new Minister of

Economy took office. Prices increased during the first quarter by 3 per cent and some shortages began to appear. By March the pressures from the unions became very strong; there had been a small decrease in real wages but they were still well above those of 1972. Although the initial social pact had specified no change in wages for two years, an increase was again granted, made up of a fixed amount of 240 pesos per worker, representing about 20 per cent for unskilled workers and less for skilled ones. This wage increase, compounded by a gradual 'heating' of the economy, pushed up prices in the second quarter by a further 10.4 per cent, a trend that was to continue throughout the year. Zero inflation had become a thing of the past. During the year real wages remained on average at the same level as during the second half of 1973. However, there was greater variation, as a consequence of the by-now significant rate of inflation.

The unemployment rate, after having been reduced to about 5 per cent in the second half of 1973, decreased further to 4.2, 3.3 and 2.5 per cent during 1974, and to an all-time low of 2.3 per cent in April 1975, partly owing to the increase in State employment. It may be wondered whether it was indeed approaching a 'natural' rate of unemployment, which would have significant inflationary consequences, along the lines of the Phillips curve. It would seem, however, that at least in the short term the changes in expectations affected the inflationary process much more than the changes in the unemployment rate (Brodersohn, 1977).

One of the crucial changes, and probably the one that goes furthest towards explaining the intense strains of the end of the social pact, was the reversal of the external situation, brought about by the sharp reversal of the terms of trade, by more than a third; this was owing to the rise in import costs compounded by local expansionist policies. Export prices were maintained at their level at the end of 1973, but one of the most important problems was the ban on meat imports imposed by the EEC about July 1974 (characteristically considered by the IMF as an infant-industry protection measure and therefore not qualifying as trade-discriminatory). Import prices, on the other hand, increased by a further 35 per cent, compounded by a significant increase in the volume of imports.

The current-account surplus fell from US$704 million in 1973 to US$245 million in 1974, a figure which disguises the even greater downturn that took place during the year, from a surplus of US$395 million in the first half of the year to a deficit of US$286 million in the second.

Despite the price increases and the reversal of the external situation, the exchange rate remained unaltered. This meant a gradual over-valuation of the currency (see Table A.8.1), a significant increase in imports and a huge loss of reserves. These factors were being used to delay once more the dreadful moment when the peso had to be devalued, thus further fuelling the inflationary fire. However, it is fair to say that at the time it was unclear whether the export problems were temporary or not.

The internal ratio of imported to national prices decreased, while the agricultural terms of trade, which stood at about 130 (1960 = 100) before May 1973, moved to 110–15 in May 1974 and fell below 100 by the end of the year. The depression in meat exports accelerated the downward movement of the cattle and meat cycle, although it helped the cost-of-living index, in which meat has a weight of about 22 per cent. The situation, moreover, stirred strong unrest among producers, and this later was to have serious political repercussions over and above the purely economic ones.

The effect of the expansionary policies could be clearly seen in the increase of the Government deficit, the result of increases in both current and capital accounts. Indeed the Government acted on a most extreme cost-push interpretation of inflation, increasing the amount of money in circulation, increasing current expenditure and the number of public employees and pushing investment projects as if there were no need to consider demand.

The renewal of inflationary expectations reduced the demand for money and consequently increased the inflationary potential of even the same amount of money, let alone an increased amount. Money, which was equivalent to 20 per cent of GNP in the second half of 1973 and 24.5 per cent during 1974, decreased at the end of the year, owing to the increased inflationary expectations. The Government actually increased its role in the creation of money throughout the whole period; the foreign sector, however, after having made a sizeable con-tribution to the creation of money, began increasingly to absorb it after the middle of 1974.

The real rate of interest, having been positive, fell to a negative figure of 9.4 per cent (yearly rate) during the first half of 1974 and to 17.5 in the second. At the same time the rate of inflation moved from about an 8 per cent yearly rate in the second half of 1973 to about 40 per cent during 1974. Again the argument was put forward that higher interest rates would increase costs, thus offsetting the dampening effect that they would have on demand. This is typical of occasions when a government has to take measures that will feed the inflationary process, either from the demand side or from the supply side. The choice is usually made against the measures which would mean an increase in costs, particularly because of their more immediate impact.

Investment, which had been sluggish during the middle of 1973, accelerated from the end of the year, going from 19.4 per cent of GNP in 1973 to 20.6 per cent in 1974. This was the consequence of the increase in public investment, which compensated to a very large extent for the fall in private investment from 14.1 to 11.3 per cent.

The profits of 400-500 of the larger companies were controlled in a rather detailed fashion, and this affected them rather seriously until the policy reversal of the last quarter of 1974. The smaller companies, which were not accurately controlled, did not follow this pattern, as they charged premium prices for their goods to a much greater degree than did the controlled companies. This difference agreed with the political slant of the CGE. The reduction in profitability and in private investment may explain the view, rather common at the time, that investment was falling in absolute terms. However, the fact was that the Government was pursuing both distributionist and developmentalist policies, and both in the short term, something which could not continue.

The rate of growth of the economy was excellent; at 6.5 per cent it was slightly up on the previous year. The increase in the level of effective demand contributed to this figure. Growth in the industrial and agricultural sectors at 6.2 per cent for both was slightly below average. Overall growth was pushed up by the growth of construction, partly owing to the Government's emphasis on low-cost housing.

The price and wage freeze, which initially had been able to cut inflationary expectations, was kept up for an excessively long period. Moreover, when the external situation was reversed and imported prices increased drastically, the Government, instead of pursuing a flexible price policy and a restrained monetary policy, did the opposite. The freeze was pushed beyond what was reasonable, impairing the profitability of the business sector and the level of investment, and eventually creating shortages of all kinds. The most serious was the shortage of foreign exchange, the result of overheating the economy while maintaining a 'frozen' exchange rate.

The renewal of inflationary expectations had the opposite effect to that of the initial 'virtuous' circle. This time it was a vicious one, working through the decrease in the demand for money, which had an extremely dangerous inflationary potential.

A price freeze is a possible policy only if it is adopted at the right time so as to break expectations. This is what had happened. However, it can only be undertaken in a temporary way, as it otherwise introduces a serious degree of rigidity, which has pernicious long-term effects. It is also clear that it cannot bring under control cost-push pressures; it can only delay them for a while and runs the risk of making them worse in the future. It must be accompanied by coherent management of the demand side of the economy. The more stringent and the longer the freeze is, the more severe the restraint on demand should be. Unfortunately this was not appreciated at the time. It was a policy easier to get into than to get out of. Moreover, it can be seen in retrospect how some of the intrinsic weaknesses of the policy were compounded by the international reversal and by the particular local policies which were adopted.

SEPTEMBER 1974–MAY 1975: 'FLEXIBILISATION' AND FINANCIAL RESTRAINT

While the economic clouds were gathering, far greater ones were accumulating on the political front. The death of Perón in July 1974 meant a significant reduction in the arbitrating power of the executive, a problem particularly serious in any loose political alliance. The problem was compounded by the fact that the new president, Isabel Perón, was identified with the right wing of the party, headed by the Minister of Social Welfare, José López Rega, to an even greater degree than expected. This group tried to put across a rather straight-forward right-wing programme, an essential part of which was a drastic shift towards a rather orthodox economic line and a forceful attempt to curb the power of the unions.

While on the political front the measures were taken soon after the death of Perón, on the economic and labour fronts they were delayed. In September, a respected, middle-of-the-road Minister of Economy was named, Alfredo Gómez Morales. This was a compromise solution reached rather reluctantly, as it meant that full implementation of the right-wing programme was postponed until a later stage – in fact, until the second quarter of 1975.

As described in the preceding section, some important shifts in economic policies were in any case necessary. Two different approaches were put forward by business and political groups. One emphasised the need for a more flexible price policy and the second the need for a general 'cooling' of the economy. It could be said that there was a price approach and an income approach and that they were presented as if they were alternative policies rather than complementary ones.

The more commonly voiced opinion was in the direction of a readjustment of the prices of some goods, particularly those that at the time of the freeze had been caught at relatively low levels; those requiring a large contribution from imports; and those whose production was labour-intensive. It was quite evident that higher import prices and higher wages had reduced the profitability of the business sector, causing significant losses which had reduced or even stopped production. This situation had caused all sorts of problems on the supply side, creating shortages and imbalances in the flow of goods. At the same time the increasing violation of the price freeze and the frequency of black-market transactions had created a highly speculative quantity of untaxed and unrecorded money that was to have serious effects during 1974. These funds were more likely to be invested in financial assets that did not require the legal identification of the investor – for instance, Government dollar bonds, adjustable peso bonds (adjustable according to the wholesale price index) and black-market dollars. The stock exchange did not play any significant role.

The new economic authorities had an intermediate view regarding the liberalisation of the economy. They thought that under the circumstances a freeing of all prices might result in an enormous jump in price levels. To avoid this, they thought that the freeing of prices should be partial and should be accompanied by a policy of financial restraint, reducing expenditure of all kinds and, consequently, the Government deficit and the growth of money.

Many price adjustments were allowed, including those of some of the public services in February 1975. Prices continued to pick up, increasing by 12 per cent in the last quarter of 1974 and by 25 per cent in the first quarter of 1975, while inflationary expectations increased significantly. Wages were increased in November by 13 per cent, and were allowed to be transferred to prices as part of the policy of increasing – or at least not worsening – business profits. Wage readjustments took place again in March with an increase of about 20 per cent (actually 400 pesos per month). In both instances, the increases were granted before any significant real loss had taken place, as if inflation had made the unions overzealous in the defence of real wages. In any case, this is one of the periods when higher real wage rates prevailed, which may in part be related to the very high demand for labour and the very low level of unemployment. However, it is also true that, despite the more orthodox outlook of the new economic policy, it did not count on a reduction of real wages as one of its deflationary tools; the increase was unintentional. On the other hand, the new policy tried to maintain the 'frozen' exchange rate as a way of controlling inflation, probably counting on the dampening of demand as the main factor in bringing the foreign sector back to equilibrium. The exchange rate was maintained until March, while very significant losses of reserves took place. The black-market rate started to move above the official rate, more than doubling it by February 1975. At that time, the peso was finally devalued from 10 to 15 pesos to the dollar. This reduced but did not eliminate an overvaluation of the currency which had reached gross levels. These wide fluctuations in the real value of the exchange rate are indeed one of the more important reasons for the difficulty of developing a consistent export policy for anything other than land-intensive goods.

The fact that the official exchange rate was not lowered decreased the net level of effective protection (Corden, 1971; Berlinski, 1977), which sometimes depends much more on the level of the exchange rate than on explicit tariffs. This consequently increased the value of imports by more than 50 per cent. As devaluation was expected, however, speculative imports began to be made in significant amounts by the end of the year. The problem was compounded by the abrupt fall in export prices and by the sharp deterioration in the terms of trade, which fell by more than 20 per cent between the first and second halves of the year. All this contributed to an impressive reversal in the trade balance and in the level of reserves; these, after reaching about US$1972 million during the first half of 1974, went down to about US$1057 million by the first quarter of 1975, a trend that was to continue until the third quarter. The deterioration in the price of agricultural exports was made worse by the overvaluation of the currency and was further reduced by the policy of applying *ad valorem* export taxes. The cattle sector was further affected by the closing off of the EEC market, and by the world cattle crisis, which aggravated the downward phase of the beef cycle.

The domestic agricultural and industrial terms of trade figures were low, although only after November did they fall below the 1967–9 level, reaching an all-time low by the middle of 1975. However, the situation was still more serious, as these figures are based on industrial prices, which were also low. By the end of 1974, the problem was not so much one of relative prices as one of absolute prices – that is, of output prices compared with input prices – both for agricultural and for industrial goods.

While the various groups affected by these relative price abnormalities were pressing for what came to be called 'flexibilisation' of the economy, some less powerful groups were worried by the overheating of the economy, and asked for a more prudent financial policy. Of course, wide disagreement existed as to the areas where the cuts had to take place. Some, such as the 'developmentalist' group, even asked for an increase in Government investments, assuming rather superficially that cuts could be made to an extent that would make this strategy possible. 'Flexibilisation' and financial restraint were the alternative future avenues.

A strict programme to reduce the current expenditure of the Government was started, particularly on personnel. A reduction of some of the rather overambitious Government programmes, including cheap housing, was attempted; and, as might be expected, this created strong opposition.

While investment peaked in the last quarter of 1974 at 23.4 per cent of GNP, it had already fallen in the first quarter of 1975 to 20.8 per cent; the drastic reduction in private investment accelerated its negative trend. Public investment reached an all-time high, but could not compensate for what was going on in the private sector. At this stage money was seen, and rightly so, as having a very important impact on the inflationary situation. An attempt was made to reduce the amount of money in circulation, to some extent helped by the deficit in the foreign sector. Of the money created during this period, the Government deficit contributed 76.6 per cent of the total, credit-creation an additional 80 per cent, and the foreign sector a negative 16.3 per cent. At the same time a policy was undertaken of settling some of the conflicting cases concerning foreign capital that had arisen in the previous period and a study was started in order to liberalise the foreign-investment law. All these measures were part of a strategy to make foreign capital once more an important source of investment. This was intended to compensate for the reduction in Government investment; it was something that was desired but which in fact never took place.

The actions of the Minister of Economy were very much impaired by the ambivalent attitude of the extreme right wing of the party. It criticised some of his proposed policies, only to pursue them in a much more drastic way when it succeeded in naming its own candidate.

While quite a few of the measures undertaken were indeed necessary, they should have been started much earlier; they were, in fact, at least six months late and were milder than the situation warranted, particularly in the foreign sector. The necessary measures on prices and incomes were not taken. Probably there was too exclusive a reliance on financial restraint, which was supposed to replace the need for any direct price adjustments and in particular the need for devaluation. When the time came these measures had to be taken in a much more drastic and abrupt manner, a fact which is at the root of the final convulsion. The views which prevailed in this period on the role of the level of economic activity and the role of price movements in bringing about an equilibrium were to change quite drastically in the succeeding period.

JUNE–JULY 1975: THE DRASTIC READJUSTMENT

Many clouds had been gathering. Several groups had become quite vocal in their protests, particularly in the agricultural and the industrial sectors, but it was the most delicate situation on the foreign exchanges that forced a change. The March devaluation and wage increases had created new cost-induced inflationary pressures. These developments, coupled with rumours of imminent political change to be led by the right wing, caused destabilising speculation on the exchanges, increasing the gap between the black market and the official rates.

The change took place in June when Celestino Rodrigo – a member of the inner circle of the right wing – became the new Minister of Economy. The new group wanted to free prices, bring the exchange to a realistically devalued rate, improve agricultural prices, encourage private investment, increase prices of public services and public goods, diminish the fiscal deficit, keep down wages and, finally curb the power of the unions. Within this rather orthodox view, the role attributed to the money supply was not completely clear; a reduction in its rate of increase was implied in the reduction of the deficit, but at the same time more credit to the private sector was envisaged. The main exception to the general plan was an insistence on the continuation, and even expansion, of the low-cost housing programme. This was the main project of the Welfare Minister, who was the political leader of the right.

The Government devalued the peso from 15 to 30 to the dollar, setting the exchange rate at 300 per cent above the February figure.

Prices of public goods were increased in many cases by more than 100 per cent, reaching 200 per cent in the notorious case of petrol. Meanwhile a wage increase of less than 40 per cent was offered to the workers. Public opinion was in a state of shock. The directions of change were as expected, but their intensity was not. One may suspect that they were aimed at creating an impossible situation for the union leaders, whose replacement was indeed an avowed objective of the Government. We have to understand the increase in inflation, which moved from 74.2 per cent in the twelve months before May 1975 to 954 per cent in the following twelve, and the intense measures taken by the Government and the reactions to them as part of an all-out fight between the trade-union-based sector of the party and its political right wing. A struggle for power and political domination was fought precisely around the readjustment of relative prices, with its obvious implications for the transfer of income.

Wage discussions that had started under the previous minister were immediately broken off. What was rather odd – and was probably one of the reasons for the failure of the programme – was that the devaluation and the price increases had taken place while negotiations were still going on. Now union leaders were fighting not so much for a wage increase as for their political survival. A tentative settlement was nearly reached on the basis of a 50 per cent immediate wage increase to be followed by two 15 per cent increases (not compounded) in August and October. Finally, however, the unions rejected the agreement and mobilised their political forces. One of their main problems was that, since the economic policies had been wholeheartedly supported by the President, their opposition could bring the downfall of the Government. They were divided as to whether it was necessary to go this far or not. In the end the unions were able to get wage increases, negotiated union by union in a tumultuous fashion, ranging from 60–80 to more than 200 per cent and averaging about 160 per cent. Again, the intensity of this reaction can be understood only as an attempt to bring about the downfall of the right wing of the party. This was what actually happened, amidst military unrest. The authority of the Government was very much hurt and the possibility of its abrupt end became rather obvious, hindering the already delicate economic situation.

The immediate effect of all this was a drastic increase in the cost of living, 102 per cent in June–August or 117 per cent as judged by the wholesale price index. Import prices increased in real terms by 30 per cent compared with domestic prices, following a similar movement of the real rate of exchange. Agricultural prices decreased a further 10 per cent, the opposite of the initial objective. Real wages increased by 50 per cent, but this was very soon eroded to the pre-disturbance level. Nevertheless this meant a significant once-and-for-all transfer of about 4 per cent of the yearly wage bill. Another very important transfer of 3.7 per cent of GNP took place from creditors to debtors as a consequence of the halving of the real value of debts.

Another consequence of the price increases was that the amount of money in circulation decreased, in real terms, from 13.7 per cent of GNP in the first quarter of 1975 to 8.1 per cent in the third. This was a consequence of the flight from money coupled with the very short-term effects of an explicit policy of the Central Bank. This acted mostly on its own and avoided a worse price explosion, helping tone down the rate of inflation in the following months.

The economy moved abruptly from an overheated situation with very strong demand pressures and a very low unemployment rate in April to a situation of near crisis in July and August. Unemployment soared from 2.3 per cent to 4.8 per cent in the Greater Buenos Aires area from April 1975 to April 1976. From eminent quarters unemployment figures of more than 1 million workers were announced as an immediate possibility. Something very close to a collapse of manufacturing was feared. The external situation which had contributed so much to these events continued to be very delicate. The devaluation had been very significant, but its effect was not felt until the beginning of the following year. In the short term, the situation was helped by a massive increase of 'swaps', i.e. foreign short-term loans with Central Bank forward-exchange coverage. During the year short-term loans increased to an all-time high of US$2124 million, of which 60 per cent was in swaps. These became an essential factor in the balancing of the external situation, creating the need for a tight credit policy in the private sector in order to maintain this flow. The reliance on short-term financing for their supplies. A total credit of US$200 million was external, medium-term loans; this was attempted without success with American private banks. The Government had greater success in making a special deal with the local car manufacturers, the largest single importers of manufactured goods, allowing them to free their prices before anybody else provided they agreed to obtain medium-term financing for their supplies. A total credit of US$200 million was accordingly built up.

Despite the increase in the real price of several Government services, the fiscal situation deteriorated sharply, mainly owing to the effect of the very rapid inflation on the fiscal lag, i.e. the lag between the assessment and payment of taxes, which eroded the real value of the Government's receipts (Olivera, 1967). Taxes went down in real terms, while Treasury income moved from 6.6 per cent of GNP for the previous year to 4 and 3.8 per cent for the second and third quarters of 1975. However, the final effect of the mid-year convulsion was not felt in full until the end of the year and the beginning of the next.

Summarising the aftermath of this drastic attempt to overhaul the economy, it can be said that the devaluation of the currency and an increase in real terms of some public prices (notably petrol) were achieved, while the amount of money in circulation was drastically reduced as a consequence of the flight from cash. Contrary to intention, real wages were not reduced, and a significant difference between various labour groups appeared. The tax system was disrupted, industrial activity was seriously affected, though business firms – most of them net debtors – benefited from a reduction in the real value of their debts. Agriculture continued to decline, against the explicit wishes of the Government. Finally, the economy veered between the dangers of hyperinflation and recession, as unemployment increased to high levels.

The turmoil of this period brought about the downfall of the right-wing groups. The unions, with the support of the middle-of-the-road politicians, were able to get rid of López Rega and the Minister of Economy. The trade unions moved into the centre of the political scene and became during the following months the main backers of the regime, in a way reconstituting the alliance which had prevailed during the presidency of Juan Perón, although they now played a much larger role. A caretaker minister was named, who devalued by an additional 20 per cent. The economy was in a situation of chaos and paralysis, amidst persistent rumours of a split within the army, which opened up the possibility of a military coup.

AUGUST 1975–JANUARY 1976: THE GRADUALIST APPROACH

The previous economic fiasco had deeply hurt the authority of the President, who had obviously lost the fight against the unions. Her arbitrating power, which had always been weak, practically disappeared. The military situation was settled within the army, with the strengthening of the so-called 'professional' group and the removal of the faction that had tried to bring the army to the support of the Government's right-wing programme. The new Minister of Economy was Antonio Cafiero, one of the most respected economists of the party, who took over by the end of August. He had been closely associated with the trade unions for a long time, and did not enjoy good relations with most members of the right wing.

There were three extremely pressing problems that deserved immediate attention. The first and most critical was the redressing of the external situation, which continued to be extremely delicate despite some of the previous measures. The second alarming problem was the slide into a serious internal crisis, with increasing halts in industrial production, rising unemployment, tremendous social unrest and very strong protests from the business sectors and trade unions. The third problem, not the least important, was the need to tone down the inflationary outburst of the previous months. While it was improbable that inflation would continue at the same extraordinary rate, it was not clear whether it would be possible to return to the pre-shock levels; it seemed more probable that a new and much higher level of inflation would become the new standard. It was clear that these three problems required to a great extent contradictory solutions and that each could only be partially solved. Moreover, the new economic team was determined to achieve its objectives through rather gradual measures, i.e. through a succession of small steps. It was felt that the extraordinarily high price increases, the jump in unemployment, the collapse of the external market, the tripling of the rate of exchange, the halving of credit in real terms and the wide and abrupt transfers of income had left a deep wound and that the various sectors of the economy could not withstand further shocks.

Inflation at this stage was not viewed as a primary consequence of monetary disequilibrium. The inter- and intra-group fights had become the basic cause of inflation, which by now was as high as 10 per cent or more per month. These struggles were in turn exacerbated by inflation, by its unequal distribution among sectors and by its leads and lags. If inflations can be characterised according to different degrees of relative price oscillations, the one of 1975 was certainly one of the highly oscillatory type; this is something which we shall consider in Chapter 7. Unfortunately this type of inflation is much more resilient to orthodox treatment than the more uniform and less oscillatory ones. The variations in income consequent upon these oscillations produce intense reactions from the groups which were harmed, and these tend to perpetuate the oscillations.

The struggle for shares of the national income was significant not only when fought between wage-earners and business groups, but also when fought between different sub-groups of those categories. These considered their relative positions more significant and their improvement more attainable than the general advance of the broadly defined groups to which they belonged, whose income was to a greater extent fixed. The implication is that these sub-groups behaved in an oligopolistic manner, and that this explains to a great extent the oscillation of relative prices and the resilience of the inflationary process.

One of the worse consequences of the previous shock was that the Government had lost the strong arbitrating power it had held at the time of the social pact and had become powerless to stop this infighting. Under these conditions it was thought rather unrealistic to attempt to stop inflation altogether. It was thought that it would be sufficient to reduce it to 'somewhat below 100 per cent per year', as it was purposely and ambiguously stated, and to avoid abrupt changes in the rates of inflation, which were thought to worsen its effects even more.

Wages had emerged with gross distortions. Those unions that had been the first to sign new agreements during the explosion were the ones that fared worse, while the last got the higher increases. Those whose relative positions had deteriorated soon began to press for a reconsideration of their 'special cases', asking to go back to traditional inter-union differentials. Those which had fared better thought that any allowance made to one group should be extended to all. The Government thought that a partial redress of the situation was necessary and proposed, without any success, a typical halfway solution. Some unofficial increases began to take place. In November, when real wages had moved below the pre-shock level, the Government granted a monthly rise of about 1500 pesos per worker, which meant about 27 per cent. More important was the agreement that wages would be indexed. Every three months, starting in January, wages would be adjusted so that an average real wage of about 95 per cent of the previous year would be guaranteed. A special institute to check on the figures and police the indexing of wages was to be created with worker and business participation. Under the peculiar situation created by the explosion it was felt that keeping down wage demands to previous price increases was in itself a toning down of expectations. What was feared was that trade unions would again request the same kind of nominal increases that they had obtained in the middle of the year.

A redressing of some of the prices of important goods and services was also considered an essential part of the new policy. While this was undoubtedly necessary in the longer term, it was clear that it would have a negative impact on inflation. This was but another instance of the conflict between short-term anti-inflationary considerations and longer-term considerations of efficiency. Prices of agricultural products fixed by the Government were increased to pre-shock levels. The price of grain rose somewhat higher, while meat, despite the reduction and finally the elimination of export *ad valorem* taxes, continued at a very low level until the very end of the period, when a significant increase took place, and it reached one of the highest levels of the 1975–7 period. Two lock-outs by cattle producers took place, each suspending deliveries to the stockyards for a week. While the lock-outs were caused by the economic conditions, they were also part of a political plan to bring down the Government, particularly the second one. Internal conditions together with the closing off of the EEC market created a difficult situation which was not sufficiently appreciated by producers and would continue to worsen even after the new military government had taken office. The policy of the existing government was to maintain the real prices of agricultural products from sowing to harvest, but allow changes in real prices from year to year. Over a period of three years prices would rise to standard international levels. This was the length of time thought necessary to bring into operation a tax system based on the potential productivity of land; while this was the law, it had not yet been implemented. The prices of some public services were formally indexed, as in the case of electricity, while in other cases a readjustment was made every two to three months.

An attempt was made to index medium- and long-term loans, as well as tax debts. This was much resisted, because the new system would have brought to an end the previous implicit inflationary subsidy, and also because of the dangers of leads and lags in the prices of the specific goods produced by the debtor compared with the general wholesale industrial index used for the readjustment. These instances were part of a general indexation of the economy which was put forward as one of the few ways of diminishing the harm of continuous inflation. Some prices were indexed, but not all, as this would have assumed an initial correct relative price vector, which obviously did not exist. Moreover, it would have run the risk of making permanent a source of inefficiency which could be very harmful in the longer run.

An important consequence of the wide variation in relative prices and the leads and lags for various goods was that 'arbitrage' became at times extraordinarily profitable. A speculative climate developed, particularly noticeable on the stock exchange; this occurred not so much in shares, which were extremely weak, as in Government bonds, some of which were adjusted by the wholesale price index and some by the dollar rate. The Government policy was to permit this 'arbitrage', but to reduce its profitability by equalising the nominal cost of money with the rate of inflation. The nominal rate for deposits was increased several times but still remained below the rate of inflation. However, the part of the market where interest was fixed freely, i.e. bank acceptances, was broadened, and by October and November their rates were practically in line with inflation. After December inflation was again ahead of interest rates, allowing big margins to arbitrageurs and contributing to the speculative climate.

A tax reform was attempted, reducing some of the tax rates, which were thought under the circumstances to be unrealistically high and running the risk of increasing the already high level of evasion. Firms were to be required to depart from traditional accounting practices for the determination of taxes, which ignored the inflationary process, and report on a 'real' basis, i.e. to take into account the effect of price variations, particularly on debts and credits, on inventories and on amortisation allowances. This tax package was sent to Congress but was never approved, as it became involved in the intense political bickering which was already going on even within the Government party.

The external situation was really desperate, although some of the basic measures necessary had been taken by the previous administration – for example, the severe devaluation of the peso. The immediate problem was tackled by departing from the traditional anti-IMF attitude of the Peronist party. Negotiations were started with the Fund in order to obtain the 'fall in exports' financing, which was automatic, and the 'oil facilities', which required the presentation of a coherent plan, but a less stringent one than a 'tranche I' agreement. The Fund did not like the programme, as it did not contemplate any drastic reduction of wages and had a full-employment target while only aiming at a reduction of the deficit to about 6 per cent of GNP. After hectic negotiations in which crucial US State Department co-operation was sought, an agreement was reached. This opened up the possibility of obtaining short-term financing from other public and private institutions. US$250 million was obtained from the Fund. The group of local private banks, who were members of the Asociación de

Bancos Argentinos (ADEBA) group, had initially quite a positive response. After two months, however, the increasing political difficulties and the lukewarm support of the Fund induced some of the lending groups to pull out.

This short-term 'breathing space' was accompanied by the firm decision to maintain the devalued exchange rate reached after the end of the previous shock. This was achieved through small and frequent devaluations at intervals of ten to twenty days at most, each time by 3–5 per cent. At the same time, other indirect devices were used to increase the cost of imports. The small and indirect devaluations were supposed to diminish the unfavourable expectations and the immediate repricing that had followed the more spectacular ones.

One of the indirect and less obvious ways of devaluing was through significant increases in the cost of the forward-exchange insurance given to importers in return for cash deposits of equal value to imports. Even at very high nominal charges, forward-exchange insurance implied a subsidy to imports. On the other hand, the total amount of money tied up in the prepayment of the insurance was very substantial, exceeding the equivalent of US$1000 million or about 2 per cent of GNP. A complete elimination of this practice would have meant the release of money with dangerous inflationary potential, while retaining advance payments without exchange coverage would have been considered a restraint of trade by the IMF. The typical solution was to halve the deposit requirements by the end of the year, so reducing the forward coverage accordingly. The cost of forward coverage for financial loans was moderately increased, as the policy was to maintain and increase the implicit subsidy on these transactions in view of the still delicate external situation. At the same time, a scheme of several exchange rates was maintained as a transitional set-up, as it allowed the pace of devaluations to accelerate in a less obvious way through the movement of goods from the lower to the higher exchange rates, something which had been done rather successfully in 1972. The idea was to end with just one exchange rate, officially fixed and frequently adjusted, for most goods, and a freely fluctuating exchange rate for a proportion of exports and imports and for financial transactions. By November the lower exchange rate was eliminated, and by January a free exchange was opened where foreign currency could be bought for tourism, freight and some minor remittances and where a proportion of exports, initially 3 per cent, could be sold. The real weighted rate of exchange for this mixture was maintained at the very devalued level reached after the mid-year explosion, in fact about 50 per cent below the real rate prevailing during the previous six months. The policy was to maintain a relatively devalued currency as a basis for an external balance and also as a better way of protecting industry. In the case of the export exchange, the spread between the 'best' and the 'worst' exchange, which in some cases was more than 3:1 (for instance, the exchange rate for automobile products compared with the exchange rate for wheat), was reduced. It was thought that some differentials were justifiable but that they were excessive and should be toned down. At the same time the differential between the average export exchange (minus export taxes) and the average import exchange (plus tariffs) was reduced, as it was considered an anti-export bias. These policies did not bear fruit immediately, although they helped to maintain a precarious balance. Nevertheless, in the first quarter of 1976 a surplus appeared in the current account for the first time in five quarters.

The other fundamental problem which the economy was going through was the abrupt reduction in the level of activity and the imminence of what seemed an industrial breakdown amidst price increases which were still extremely high.

The amount of money in real terms remained at practically the same level, 11.8 per cent of GNP. It is not easy to appraise the changes in expectations; in the early stages of the outburst they were lower than the rate which actually ensued, while later on they were well above it. Prices had changed so abruptly that both businessmen and consumers were utterly confused as to what to expect next. A policy of increasing the rate of interest was attempted, the avowed target being to move towards positive rates either through higher nominal rates or through indexation. Inflation, however, was too high and indexation could not be implemented, so that the rates continued to be negative. Money creation was basically owing to the Government's deficit and to the increased credit given to the private sector. By the last quarter of 1975, the Treasury had reached a deficit of 16.4 per cent of GNP; this was caused by a combination of a high level of expenditure and a further reduction of income owing to the fiscal lag. The foreign sector, which had been absorbing money, became neutral by the end of the year.

Industrial production continued to slide, from -5.6 per cent in the third quarter to -8.9 per cent in the last. GNP, which had gone down by 3.2 per cent in the third quarter of the year, went down by 6.3 per cent in the last quarter. All these figures, including those for construction and investment (-26.3 and -20.2 per cent respectively), reached extremely low levels in the last quarter. The first signs of a reduction in the intensity of the crisis began to show rather modestly in the first quarter of 1976, when most of these figures moved upwards, though they were still below the levels of the previous year. The policies avoided a major disaster in the level of activity, but by January an increase in inflationary pressures could be detected, compounded by the very serious destabilising effects of the political crisis which began the year.

As mentioned in Chapter 3, the political situation had begun to deteriorate again since the beginning of November, when the President staged a partial comeback. Isabel Perón had been on leave for a month and a half while the Government was run by an interim president, Italo Luder, but by then she was able to reject a second period of leave and make some changes in the Cabinet. However, she could not touch the leaders of the middle-of-the-road coalition, who were in charge of the Ministries of the Interior and of Economy. A stalemate between this group and the right wing emerged, creating a difficult political situation and a complete loss of authority for the Government. The trade unions then jockeyed to improve their positions in a rather anarchic way, making life for the Government very difficult. The two lock-outs carried out by the cattle sector, the several producers' strikes, the creation of a new business organisation, the APEGE, with the avowed purpose of creating a pre-revolutionary climate contributed to a feeling of social chaos and had a destabilising economic impact.

In January the President attempted a complete comeback, trying to control the situation on her own terms. This opens the last act of our story.

JANUARY–MARCH 1976: THE END

The right-wing comeback was this time attempted in a moderate way. The President dismissed all the middle-of-the-road ministers and made new appointments further to the right, including Emilio Mondelli (who up to that moment had been head of the Central Bank) as Minister of Economy. The trade unions were shocked by the abrupt political change which had taken place without their prior knowledge. Initially they reacted violently and for a while were undecided whether to opt for an open confrontation as in mid-1975 or for some kind of accommodation. This time the latter attitude prevailed; the end of the regime was in sight no matter what was done and an open fight did not seem worthwhile. The military had reached the point where its strategy was to let the situation deteriorate until the need for a coup became evident to everybody. Until this happened, the stalemate between the main factions within the Government coalition, the increased and unchecked power of the unions and the by-now blatant opposition of the business sectors created a very anarchic situation, making normal management of the economy impossible.

By the beginning of 1976 it was becoming clear that the dangers of a deep recession had been overcome. Nevertheless the upturn was not completely clear at the time, owing to the coexistence of recessive conditions and strong inflationary pressures coupled with expectations of destabilisation influenced by the political climate. A new restrictive set of policies was in fact necessary, as no improvements could be counted upon on the political side. The existence of an 'expected' coup contributed very much to the price explosion, which again more than doubled prices from February to April. Wholesale prices increased more than consumer prices, implying a reduction of the retailer's margin. This relative movement was a repetition of what had happened during the previous explosion, suggesting that in both cases the cost-push factor was more influential than the demand-pull. All groups were frantically jockeying for an improvement in their relative positions in view of the imminent change of government. Although the tremendous increase in prices apparently repeated the experience of the middle of the previous year, the causes were different, as this time the disintegration of the Government and the pre-coup atmosphere were the crucial factors.

Wages were increased at the beginning of March by 20 per cent but the promise of any further automatic readjustment was withdrawn. The Minister did not hide the fact that real wages were expected to decrease by something around 20 per cent. He argued that this sacrifice was necessary to reduce inflation.

The real prices of agricultural products, which had been moving upwards, reached a high level by February, falling thereafter as they did not keep pace with the general price increases of March.

The frequent devaluations were soon stopped, but a new exchange rate was introduced for a list of products which maintained the highly devalued real rate inherited from the previous administration. The freely fluctuating rate moved sharply upwards, pushed by very strong destabilising speculation, well beyond what any purchasing-power estimate might indicate. International reserves continued to be extremely precarious, owing particularly to the policy of the private foreign banks of making less credit available, a policy which was continued up to the day of the military coup but reversed directly after. A new and more open policy with the IMF was pursued; an attempt was made to qualify for 'tranche I', which required a more comprehensive programme, but it found the Fund reluctant to the point of not even wanting to receive the proposal, conscious as it was of the imminent military coup.

The attitude regarding wages, the exchange rate and the readjustments of medium- and long-term loans (which were abandoned) indicated a change of attitude regarding indexation in general. It would seem that indexation was considered partly responsible for the increase in inflationary pressures. The strategy was probably to make once-and-for-all adjustments, but the period was too short to appraise this point properly.

The external situation, despite the improvement in the current account, which produced a small surplus in the first quarter, continued to be extremely delicate.

The amount of money in circulation fell from 11.8 per cent of GNP in the last quarter of 1975 to 8.4 per cent in the first quarter of 1976. This was partly caused by the drastic price increases, which, as in mid-1975, produced a new intensification of the flight from cash. The Treasury deficit, which stood at 12.9 per cent of GNP, was again affected by the price jump and the erosion of receipts caused by the fiscal lag.

The level of activity continued low, −4.4 per cent compared with the same quarter of the previous year, but not as bad as in the preceding quarter. Manufacturing activity showed a small improvement (from −8.9 per cent to −6.7 per cent), while construction and investment continued at extremely low levels (−26.3 per cent and −20.2 per cent on the previous year).

Although the economic measures were basically right of centre, they repeated in a more moderate way some of the mid-1975 policies. Despite this, the Government's loss of authority, the anarchic behaviour of the members of the coalition and the very high level of price increases created a sense of chaos and doom. The opposition, both economic and political (excluding the UCR), counted on the support of the army. This created the necessary political climate for the military coup, which finally took place at the end of March.

BIBLIOGRAPHY

Arnaudo, A. (1979) 'El programa anti-inflacionario de 1973', *Desarrollo Económico*, no. 73 (Apr–June).

Arnaudo, A. (1980) *La base monetaria en cuatro economías inflacionarias: Argentina, Brasil, Chile y Uruguay*, Estudios IEERAL (Buenos Aires) Jan–Mar.

Arnaudo, A. and Bartolomei, J. (1977) *El doble mercado cambiario argentino, 1971–76*, Ensayos económicos, BCRA (Buenos Aires) Dec.

Arnaudo, A. and Domenech, R. (1979) *El déficit fiscal de los años 70*, Estudios IEERAL (Buenos Aires) Jan–Feb.

Ayres, R. (1976) 'The Social Pact as Anti-inflationary Policy: the Argentine Experience since 1973', *World Politics* (July).

Bajraj, R. (1976) 'La inflación argentina en los años 70', paper presented to the Seminario sobre la Inflación Reciente en América Latina (Caracas) Nov.

Baliño, T. (1977) *Algunos resultados sobre la demanda de dinero en la Argentina*, Ensayos económicos, BCRA, Jan–Mar.

Berlinski, J. (1977) 'La protección efectiva de actividades seleccionadas de la industria manufacturera argentina' (Buenos Aires, mimeo).

Brodersohn, M. (1977) *Conflictos entre los objetivos de la política económica de corto plazo*, Documento de Trabajo no. 77 (Buenos Aires: CIE, Instituto Torcuato di Tella).

Canavese, A. J. and Montuschi, L. (1975) 'Efectos redistributivos del pacto social', paper presented to the Xth Annual Meeting of the Asociación Argentina de Economía Política (Mar del Plata) Nov.

Canitrot, A. (1975) 'La experiencia populista de redistribución de ingresos', *Desarrollo Económico*, no. 59 (Oct–Dec)

Canitrot, A. (1979) *La viabilidad económica de la democracia: un análisis de la experiencia peronista, 1973–1976*, Documento CEDES no. 11 (Buenos Aires).

Corden, W.M. (1971) *The Theory of Protection* (Oxford).

de Pablo, J. C. (1974) 'Relative Prices, Income Distribution, and Stabilization Plans: the Argentine Experience, 1967–1970', *Journal of Development Economics*, vol. I, pp. 167–89.

de Pablo, J. C. (1977) 'Estimadores de la inflación reprimida: Argentina 1973–1976', *Economía*, no. 92 (Buenos Aires: IDEA).

de Pablo, J. C. (1978) *Cuatro ensayos sobre la economía Argentina* (Buenos Aires).

de Pablo, J. C. (1980) *La economía que yo hice*, El Cronista Comercial (Buenos Aires).

de Pablo, J. C. (1980) *Economía política del peronismo* (Buenos Aires).

Díaz Alejandro, C. (1980) 'Exchange Rates and the Terms of Trade in the Argentine Republic 1913–1976', paper presented to the International Symposium on Latin America (Bar Ilan University, Israel).

Feldman, E. (1976) 'Comportamiento de la demanda de bienes durables en un período de alta inflación: Argentina 1974–1975', paper presented to the XIIIth Meeting of Central Bank Economists (Ottawa).

Ferrer, A. (1977) *Crisis y alternativas en la política económica argentina* (Buenos Aires).

Guisarri, A. (1980) *Tamaño del sector público* (Buenos Aires: Fundación Idea y Acción).

Martirena-Mantel, A. M. (1980) *Minidevaluaciones y estabilidad macro-económica: el caso Argentino 1971–1978* (Buenos Aires).

Nuñez Miniana, H. and Porto, A. (1976) 'Análisis de la evolución de precios de empresas públicas en la Argentina', *Desarrollo Económico*, no. 63 (Oct–Dec).

Olivera, J. (1967) 'Money Prices and Fiscal Lags: a Note on the Dynamics of Inflation', *Banca Nazionale del Lavoro Quarterly Review* (Sep).

Parino, G. and Cartas, J. (1979) *Evolución del precio real de las divisas entre 1967 y 1978*, Estudios IEERAL, no. 17.

Sommer, J. (1977) 'La deuda externa argentina, entre 1972 y 1976', paper presented to the XIVth Meeting of Central Bank Economists (Bariloche, Argentina).

Tanzi, V., (1978) 'Lags in Tax Collection and the Case for Inflationary Finance: Theory with an Application to Argentina', Department Memoranda Series (Washington, DC: IMF).

van Rijckeghem, V. (1972) 'La velocidad del dinero y el diseño de la política económica', *Revista argentina de finanzas* (Buenos Aires) no. 1, pp. 97–116.

6 Some of the Major Economic Issues: Investment, Profits and Trade

After having presented some of the more significant facts, it is time to examine some of the major questions posed by the experience of these years. Quite a few of them were thrown up by the extraordinary intensity of the economic and political processes, which brought to the surface what in more moderate times tends to remain concealed. In some of the discussions that are beginning to take place the implication is too often made that the alternative strategies of the various governments differed completely and were opposed to each other in each and every aspect. Fortunately for the country, this has not been so, and one can see how many policies begin and end independently of the political changes.

Any analysis should allow for shades within strategies and for continuities between them. The all-too-common practice of labelling some periods as 'liberal', 'populist', 'monopoly capitalist' or 'bureaucratic authoritarian' gives the false impression of clear-cut homogenous periods. Many of the schematic statements that have been made about various periods are based on their initial stages and ignore their endings as being unrepresentative. This has reached the point where several authors dismiss the last three years of the first Peronist experience and the last year and a half of the recent one altogether, although this comprises nearly 40 per cent of the total stay in government. A better approach would be one that takes into account the fact that Peronism encompasses the whole period, even if that may disturb some of the grand generalisations.

An analysis of the major economic questions must also consider the degree of internal coherence in the sets of economic policies. One should bear in mind that policies based on some kind of consensus

139

which has to appeal to wide sectors of society tend to be less coherent than those pursued by more authoritarian governments, of the right as well as of the left. These are able to pursue policies which are more coherent though distasteful to a wider spectrum of public opinion; this is a 'luxury' in which more broadly based regimes cannot indulge.

We cannot hope to analyse all the major issues posed by this period. All we can do is to tackle a few which have impressed us as being more relevant and on which we have been better able to reach some kind of conclusion.

In this chapter we analyse the pattern of investment, an issue intimately connected with the alleged conflict between distribution and accumulation, which has given rise to a much heated controversy.

There follows an analysis of the evolution of profits in the agricultural, industrial and construction sectors, compared with the evolution of wages; this gives an indication of the distribution of income.

We conclude with an analysis of the evolution of Argentina's foreign trade, and attempt to discover the variables which are most relevant to its behaviour.

PATTERNS OF INVESTMENT

One of the major questions posed by this period relates to the behaviour of investment under various governments, a question full of political implications, even if the various governments' policies cannot be held totally responsible for what went on. This question has given rise to a most heated controversy in Argentine journals (*Desarrollo Económico*, 1978).

Some (de Pablo, 1978) take the view that periods when popular governments have been in charge have tended to show low or declining rates of investment. Others (Lavagna, 1978) have tended to think that, on the contrary, these governments have as good a record in investment as the more 'liberal' ones have, despite their alleged better distribution of income, as if upper-income groups have a very feeble or even a negative propensity to save and to invest. There are several problems in trying to tackle this question.

One of the first, although not one of the more fundamental ones, is the identification of the so-called 'popular' governments, as it is further implied that in both Peronist experiences, 1946–55 and 1973–6, there were initial 'popular' periods (until 1951 and 1974, respectively), followed by second stages which 'departed from the historic tradition of Peronism' (Ferrer, 1977) and should be dismissed. It would probably be nearer the truth to say that Peronism has been strong enough (or weak enough) to change its course, and that both strategies (lasting eight and nearly five years, respectively) are an integral part of the historical tradition of Peronism, whichever one may prefer. As there is a similar problem in identifying the 'liberal' periods, we prefer to make a comparison between the years of the Peronist governments and all other regimes. As we shall see, this study throws more light on certain peculiarities of the pattern of investment than on any differences in the behaviour of various governments.

A good part of the discussion is concerned with the puzzling fact that investment has apparently increased independently of the types of government. If a comparison is made of any period with a previous one, a growth in the level of investment will be observable. As such is the case, it is therefore necessary first to determine the trend of growth and then to determine the deviations from that trend.

ANALYSIS OF THE TRENDS

We have analysed two periods, one covering the years since 1950 on a yearly basis (Table 6.1), and the other one the years since 1968, when quarterly information becomes available (Table 6.2). The latter effort is justified in view of the significant variations in the course of some of the years, particularly since 1973.

To begin with, we have taken gross fixed-investment figures because they are related to the saving and investment effort made by the community. Besides, they are the only reliable figures (or, rather, the least unreliable) as the net figures take amortisation at historical values(!). Moreover, we take fixed investment as it is related to the longer-term perspectives of the economy, while investment in stocks has a transitory character and can behave in quite an unintended way.

We have broken down the total fixed-investment series into investment in construction and investment in durable equipment. Another different but most interesting breakdown of total investment is the one between public and private investment. The behaviour of each of the component series differs significantly. Private investment seems much more sensitive to the general investment climate and to the policies of the governments than public investment does.

All series are measured in constant 1960 prices. The extraordinarily wide relative price variations, particularly of the last years of the

TABLE 6.1   Total and Sectoral Investment, 1950–78 (yearly data, in absolute terms and as a percentage of GDP)

Year	Total	Construction	Durable equipment	Total	Construction	Durable equipment	Public	Private
	(millions of 1960 pesos)			(as a percentage of GDP)				
1950	1133.5	746.8	386.7	13.4	8.8	4.6	4.2	9.2
1951	1395.5	799.4	596.0	15.7	9.0	6.7	4.5	11.2
1952	1241.6	721.9	519.7	15.1	8.8	6.3	4.2	10.9
1953	1227.1	735.2	492.0	14.5	8.7	5.8	4.6	9.9
1954	1178.4	710.6	467.7	13.1	7.9	5.2	3.9	9.2
1955	1367.0	738.1	628.9	14.0	7.6	6.4	3.1	10.9
1956	1454.7	749.8	704.9	14.7	7.6	7.1	2.5	12.2
1957	1595.0	824.7	770.4	15.2	7.9	7.3	2.6	12.6
1958	1738.5	949.5	789.0	15.7	8.6	7.1	4.0	11.7
1959	1375.5	722.3	653.3	13.3	7.0	6.3	3.3	10.0
1960	2079.1	873.1	1206.0	18.4	7.7	10.7	4.5	13.9
1961	2423.7	912.7	1511.0	19.9	7.5	12.4	4.9	15.0
1962	2207.2	822.0	1385.2	18.4	6.9	11.6	3.6	14.8
1963	1870.3	768.7	1101.5	16.4	6.7	9.7	4.8	11.6
1964	2075.4	825.4	1250.0	16.4	6.5	9.9	4.7	11.7
1965	2167.5	853.9	1313.6	15.8	6.2	9.6	4.1	11.7
1966	2238.1	903.0	1335.1	16.3	6.6	9.7	4.0	12.3
1967	2349.5	979.7	1369.8	16.7	7.0	9.7	4.8	11.9
1968	2641.3	1140.9	1500.4	18.0	7.8	10.2	5.5	12.5
1969	3169.2	1379.9	1789.3	19.6	8.5	11.1	6.4	13.2
1970	3334.0	1470.0	1864.1	19.7	8.7	11.0	7.0	12.7
1971	3648.9	1459.8	2189.2	20.5	8.2	12.3	7.0	13.5
1972	3838.2	1550.4	2337.8	21.3	8.5	12.8	8.2	13.1
1973	3850.7	1435.8	2414.9	20.0	7.5	12.5	7.3	12.7
1974	4001.0	1427.4	2381.0	19.4	7.8	11.6	9.1	10.3
1975	3670.0	1443.0	2227.0	18.1	7.3	10.8	10.4	7.7
1976	3514.0	1297.2	2217.0	18.0	6.6	11.4	10.9	7.1
1977	4230.5	1424.0	2806.5	20.6	6.9	13.7	—	—
1978	3886.2	1553.2	2333.0	21.3	8.5	12.8	—	—

Source: BCRA.

period, takes quite a bit of reliability from the series. Other series, derived from different base years with widely different relative prices, could show rather different results, a problem which is well known but has no satisfactory solution. The series are expressed both in absolute terms and as percentages of gross domestic product.

A trend for each of these series has been fitted. Three different alternatives were tried for each one: a decreasing rate of growth, a constant rate of growth, and an increasing *or* decreasing rate of growth.

$$y_t = a_1 + b_1 t \tag{1}$$

$$y_t = a_2 (t)^{b_2} \tag{2}$$

$$y_t = a_3 (b_3)^t \tag{3}$$

The last two cases were used in their linear versions

$$\ln y_t = \ln a_2 + b_2 \ln t \tag{4}$$

$$\ln y_t = \ln a_3 + \ln b_3 t \tag{5}$$

Of all these we have used the one with the best fit, measured by the adjusted multiple correlation coefficient R^2.

They all showed significant non-zero correlation coefficients with the exception of investment in construction expressed as a percentage of GDP. Self-correlation was, however, observable in all cases, but was removed by assuming it to be of the first order (and applying the Cochrane–Orcutt method). The results can be seen in Table 6.3 and show significant non-zero trends in all cases (again with the same exception) and no self-correlation.

TABLE 6.2   Investment Series, 1968–78 (quarterly data in millions of 1960 pesos)

Period		Total	Construction	Durable equipment	Period		Total	Construction	Durable equipment
1968	I	578.0	259.0	319.0	1973	III	909.7	337.0	572.1
	II	641.0	276.0	365.0		IV	1019.2	387.8	631.4
	III	676.0	293.0	383.0	1974	I	889.9	398.8	491.1
	IV	746.0	312.0	434.0		II	1001.5	381.6	619.9
1969	I	676.0	297.0	379.0		III	987.8	389.8	598.0
	II	776.0	305.0	471.0		IV	1122.1	447.5	672.4
	III	814.0	327.0	487.0	1975	I	938.9	427.3	511.6
	IV	795.0	327.0	468.0		II	1001.2	364.7	636.6
1970	I	732.0	312.0	419.0		III	887.3	350.2	537.1
	II	827.0	335.0	491.0		IV	886.4	344.3	542.1
	III	864.0	367.0	495.0	1976	I	794.1	323.3	470.8
	IV	863.0	373.0	489.0		II	867.3	313.9	553.4
1971	I	795.0	340.0	455.0		III	931.1	318.0	613.8
	II	909.0	356.0	553.0		IV	974.9	341.0	633.9
	III	896.0	361.0	535.0	1977	I	958.1	339.7	619.0
	IV	920.0	371.0	563.0		II	1128.1	344.0	784.1
1972	I	867.0	369.0	501.0		III	1195.0	374.0	821.1
	II	929.0	372.0	557.0		IV	1068.1	389.0	679.0
	III	946.0	359.0	587.0	1978	I	833.3	368.6	464.6
	IV	962.0	354.0	608.0		II	1015.7	369.5	646.2
1973	I	936.9	368.4	568.5		III	1010.5	397.2	613.3
	II	985.0	342.0	643.0		IV	1026.7	417.9	608.9

Source: BCRA.

TABLE 6.3　Estimated Variables (corrected from self-correlation)

Variable	Constant	t	ln t	R^2	F	SE	DW	ρ	N
(a) ln total investment (1960 pesos)	6.9738364 (96.5)	0.0490212 (12.2)		0.93	147.3	0.111	1.76	0.36	28
(b) ln construction (1960 pesos)	6.3698101 (50.2)	0.0342715 (5.2)		0.90	27.1	0.092	2.01	0.67	28
(c) ln durable equipment (1960 pesos)	6.154757 (58.7)	0.0629427 (10.8)		0.92	116.8	0.155	1.60	0.38	28
(d) ln total investment (% of GDP)	2.629427 (46.1)	0.0139682 (4.4)		0.69	19.6	0.081	1.64	0.40	28
(e) ln construction (% of GDP)	1.9796308 (6.4)		0.0171317 (0.2)	0.45		0.079	1.74	0.70	28
(f) ln durable equipment (% of GDP)	1.2481202 (5.3)		0.3841052 (4.5)	0.81	19.9	0.126	1.62	0.52	28
(g) ln public investment (% of GDP)	0.7755793 (3.155)	0.0546089 (4.055)		0.83	16.26	0.164	2.18	0.68	26
(h) ln private investment (% of GDP)	2.9895854 (8.243)	−0.0310309 (1.744)		0.50	3.06	0.125	1.54	0.82	26

Trend (t), R^2 adjusted, F test; SE = standard error of the regression; DW = Durbin–Watson; ρ = estimated value of rho; N = number of observations
Source: Derived from Tables 6.1 and 6.2.

The first of the series, gross total fixed investment, shows a significant non-zero trend. It actually grows at a compound rate of 4.9 per cent per annum. Therefore, any inter-period comparison will prove, more than anything else, the existence of this trend. From the point of view of growth, this trend is quite an encouraging fact. It seems as if there has been an increasing desire to make the current sacrifices required by investment in exchange for the expected future goods and services. We would readily accept that, instead of revealing preferences, the trend might be revealing the ability to enforce those sacrifices. However, it is interesting to note that in the Argentine context even the popular parties are, at least in their rhetoric, very much investment-oriented. Elsewhere such a pro-investment policy would usually be associated with an austere attitude more typical of the right or of the Stalinist left ('Stalinist' at least in these matters) rather than with a popular left-wing line.

Another equally significant fact has been the evolution of the components of the investment series, i.e. construction and durable equipment. The latter has in fact grown at the highest rate, 6.29 per cent per year. Durable investment has therefore increased its participation in total investment at the expense of construction. While during the period it averaged 51.4 per cent, by 1978 it had increased to 60 per cent. This conclusion is reinforced by an analysis of the investment series expressed as a percentage of GDP. In this we can see that the growth of total investment relative to GDP is wholly due to the growth in durable equipment. In fact investment in construction in relation to GDP is the one series which shows no significant trend.

This change in the composition of investment is, in a way, an indication of the increasing technological complexity of the Argentine economy. At earlier stages of development construction looms larger. Construction is, initially, one of the more needed and more easily tackled kinds of investment. Durable equipment, on the other hand, contains a more diversified and complex assortment of goods, which require a more sophisticated knowledge for their use. Moreover, technological progress is embodied in durable equipment rather than in construction. The evolution of the three series is a healthy sign in terms of growth, both because of the general growth of gross fixed investment and because of its increasingly sophisticated composition.

The other significant way of breaking down investment, i.e. between public and private, is equally illuminating. In fact it shows the greater relative importance of public investment. Public investment has also shown a steadier performance and has been less sensitive to political changes, having fewer significant deviations than the private-investment series.

DEVIATIONS FROM TRENDS

As important as the analysis of trends is the analysis of the deviations from those trends: this can be seen in Tables 6.4 and 6.5, expressed in standard deviations. This is a quick way to detect the periods when the behaviour of investment has been significantly different from what might be expected given the existence of the trends.

If we start with the 1950s, we can see that the earliest years were

TABLE 6.4   Deviations of Investment from Estimated Trend Values, 1951–78, yearly data (measured in standard deviations of each regression, corrected from self-correlation)

Year	Total	Construction	Durable equipment	Total	Construction	Durable equipment	Public	Private
	(from series in absolute values)			(from series expressed as a percentage of GDP)				
1951	1	1	0	0	0	1	0	0
1952	0	0	0	0	0	0	1	0
1953	0	0	−1	0	0	0	1	−1
1954	−1	0	−1	−1	0	−1	0	−1
1955	0	0	0	0	0	0	0	0
1956	0	0	0	0	0	0	0	0
1957	0	0	0	0	0	0	0	0
1958	0	1	0	0	1	0	1	0
1959	−2	−2	−1	−2	−2	−1	−1	−1
1960	1	1	2	2	0	2	1	2
1961	1	0	2	1	0	1	0	0
1962	0	−1	0	0	−1	0	−1	0
1963	−1	−1	0	0	0	0	0	−1
1964	0	0	0	0	0	0	0	0
1965	0	0	0	0	−1	0	0	0
1966	0	0	0	0	0	0	0	0
1967	0	0	0	0	0	0	0	0
1968	0	0	0	0	1	0	0	0
1969	1	1	0	0	1	0	0	0
1970	0	0	0	0	0	0	0	0
1971	1	0	0	0	0	0	0	1
1972	0	0	0	0	0	0	0	0
1973	0	0	0	0	−1	0	0	0
1974	0	0	0	0	0	0	0	−1
1975	0	0	0	−1	0	0	0	−2
1976	−1	−1	0	0	−1	0	0	0
1977	0	0	0	0	0		1	
1978	−1	0	−1	0	2	0		

either in phase with the trend or, as in 1951, better if judged by total investment, and that there was a significant emphasis on construction as compared with durable equipment. This is in line with the idea that in the middle years of Peronism there was a lot of investment in construction projects. The year 1954 was, however, bad for total investment, durable equipment and private investment. This was partly the consequence of the austerity policies imposed at the end of Peronism.

The performance of the military government was neutral until 1958, the year when the new civil administration came in; construction and public investment then picked up, without, however, affecting the total figures. These and all other series were to suffer in 1959. The initial effects of the 'developmentalist' policies of the Frondizi government were very bad for investment, the opposite of what it was claiming as its main objective. This was partly owing to the monetarist

TABLE 6.5 Deviations of Investment from Estimated Trend Values, 1968–78, quarterly data (measured in standard deviations of each regression, corrected from self-correlation)

Period	Total	Construction	Durable equipment	Period	Total	Construction	Durable equipment
1968 IV	0	1	0	1974 I	−1	0	−1
1969 I	0	0	0	II	1	0	1
II	0	0	1	III	0	0	0
III	0	0	0	IV	0	2	0
IV	−1	0	−1	1975 I	−1	0	0
1970 I	0	0	0	II	0	−1	0
II	0	1	0	III	−1	−1	−1
III	0	1	0	IV	−1	−1	0
IV	0	0	0	1976 I	0	−1	0
1971 I	0	0	0	II	0	0	0
II	0	0	0	III	2	0	2
III	0	0	0	IV	0	1	0
IV	0	0	0	1977 I	0	0	0
1972 I	0	0	0	II	1	0	1
II	0	0	0	III	0	1	0
III	0	0	0	IV	−1	0	−1
IV	0	0	0	1978 I	−3	0	−3
1973 I	0	0	0	II	1	0	1
II	0	−1	0	III	0	0	0
III	−1	0	−1	IV	1	0	1
IV	1	1	0				

Source: Derived from Table 6.2.

policies imposed at the end of 1958 – certainly not among the better ones, even of their kind – and also to the inflationary outburst of more than 100 per cent, which had its effect in 1959. This is one of the few years when a clearer statement can be made about the behaviour of investment. However, during the following two years a relatively significant reversal took place, vindicating to a great extent some of the policies of the Government. This was either the consequence of the 'price paid during the previous year' (as the Government put it) or, more probably, because of the maturing of its investment policies, which indeed required time. The improvement was noticeable not only in the increase in total investment but also in the increase in durable equipment, which was even greater; this shows the effects of the modernisation process with which the Government was pushing ahead, particularly through the promotion of foreign investment. The recession of 1962 affected first construction and public investment and, in the following year, total and private investment as well. The latter was quite sensitive to the price explosion of the previous year and to the unsettling effects of the confused political situation.

The Radicals did not perform as badly from the point of view of investment as was believed at the time; in fact their years show no deviation from the trend. On the other hand, Krieger Vasena's policies, presumably investment-oriented, had no significant effect for the first two years. Then in 1969 and again in 1971, beyond his period but still under the influence of his policies, a positive deviation appears – in 1971, very much helped by investment in construction. Whether the country was deepening its technology cannot be detected in these series, but then they are not supposed to illuminate those matters.

The initial reaction to the new policies of the Peronist government in the third quarter of 1973 was negative, but at the end of the year and the beginning of the next this was overcome, helped first by investment in construction and then by investment in durable equipment.

The balance in 1974 was not bad. Actually the second quarter shows a positive deviation in total investment and, equally important, in durable equipment, while the last quarter shows a positive deviation in construction. In 1975 there were already some faltering signs in the first half of the year, prior to the outburst of inflation but nothing too serious: there was a negative deviation in total investment in the first quarter and in the second a negative deviation in construction, with total investment at the trend value.

The problem, however, came in the third quarter, for which all values of the series depart negatively from the trend, a situation which is basically repeated in the last. This was, of course, the consequence of the mid-year price explosion, which more than doubled prices in three months, and of the terrible political situation, which affected private investment in particular. What is strange is that deviations were not greater.

Although this book generally refrains from going beyond 1976, it is tempting to see whether what happened to investment after that date can give a better perspective on the intensity of the deviations of 1975. In fact, investment in the first half of 1976 was, surprisingly enough, just on the trend. It increased thereafter in the third quarter of 1976 and the second of 1977, dipping again by the end of 1977 and dramatically by the first quarter of 1978 (minus three standard deviations), possibly as a consequence of the restrictive monetary policy of the period. Thereafter it recovered somewhat (this time helped by the increase in durable equipment), but 1978 was still a poor year for investment.

ANALYTICAL CONCLUSIONS

Unfortunately (or fortunately) this analysis does not support many of the easy generalisations made about the behaviour of investment. In fact it limits drastically what can really be said, and supported by data with statistical significance.

The most striking fact is not so much the different behaviour of investment under different kinds of government as the very clear long-term growth in investment (as a percentage of GDP) of 1.4 per cent per year. This astonishing trend requires more explanations than those given here. It is indeed an indication of an increasing bias towards investment in Argentine society. This fact, coupled with an equally firm growth in durable equipment (compared with construction), is an indication of an increasing sophistication and technological complexity and speaks well for the future.

So far as differences in performance are concerned, it has to be said that Peronism fares a bit better than might have been expected, at least by its critics. Its performance in the 1950–5 period is if anything better than the trend, although somewhat biased towards construction. On the other hand, its performance in 1973–6 was basically neutral during the first two years – just on the trend. It was, however, already bad for private investment in 1974, and very bad in 1975 (two standard deviations) reflecting an equally bad business climate. This left its mark, so that it is not easy for many people to reconcile what they remember with the fact that only after the middle of 1975 did investment fall below the trend. Then total investment behaved badly, but within certain limits (one standard deviation). All in all it was a basically neutral performance with a bad end.

As for the performance of investment under other kinds of government, it is difficult to pin down any particular year or period. Probably the exceptions are the 'developmentalist' policies of President Frondizi, which, after a very clear negative initial reaction, had a beneficial effect, both in the total amount and in the composition of investment. On the other hand, the pro-investment policies of Krieger Vasena only had a positive effect in 1969, a year in which most statistics – GDP, investment, prices, wages and distribution – showed very positive signs. Oddly enough, this was the year of very serious political upheavals.

Of the twenty-seven years for which deviations have been computed, total investment departs from the trend ten times. Nine of the twenty-seven years correspond to Peronist governments. Out of these nine years, one (1954) shows a positive deviation and two a negative one. During the other eighteen years, when very different policies were pursued, there were positive deviations in four years and negative ones in three (one by two standard deviations). This is slightly better than the record of the Peronist years, but not significantly so. The conclusion is unchanged if lags of one year are assumed between policies and results. Public investment, on the other hand, has behaved slightly differently. It was more variable before 1965 and less variable afterwards. In fifteen years up to 1965, public investment deviated in ten, in half of them positively and in half negatively. After 1966, however, public investment has shown no deviation from the trend, even in recent years.

It is, therefore, the persistence of the growth in total investment and its persistence and steadiness in the case of public investment that is significant and not the difference between periods. What is interesting is not so much what can be claimed, which is indeed little, as what cannot – a conclusion by omission.

SECTORAL PROFITS

One of the bitter discussions of the 1973–6 period was about the profitability of the agricultural, industrial and construction sectors, particularly when compared with the evolution of wages, a matter which had a direct bearing on the distribution of income. To this end three series have been compiled, to reflect the evolution of the profitability of the three sectors; we can then compare this with the evolution of wages. The profitability of each sector is derived from the evolution of its prices compared with that of its input costs. In the case of agricultural profits we are actually interested in rent-*cum*-profits and not in profits alone, the separation being neither possible nor necessary for our purposes. Our estimate of the costs is based on the structure of the demand for inputs, sector by sector, as determined by the input–output matrix of 1963. Knowing the price of the product and the composition and prices of the inputs, the profitability of sector i ($PROF_i$) can be easily derived from the following formula:

$$PROF_i = \frac{P_{it}}{\sum_{j:1}^{n} W_{ij} P_{jt}}$$

where

P_{it} is the price index of sector i at time t;
W_{ij} is the demand coefficient from sector i to sector j;
P_{jt} is the price index of sector j at time t.

The numerator is linked to the price of the product, while the denominator is linked to the costs, i.e. the quotient should be a good indicator of the evolution of the profitability of the sector.

There are several important limitations to this kind of analysis. The first is that it assumes no price substitution, a problem which haunts not only these series, but also some much more fundamental ones, such as the GDP series. The wider the price variations, the greater the problem, and there is unfortunately no good statistical solution. The only possible one – which is not precisely statistical – is to avoid price variations; these, although they are fundamentally dependent on the intensity of the inflationary process, may be affected by specific policies, as analysed in the following chapter. Another problem in the method used is that it assumes full use of all factors without allowing for variations in output. A larger profit ratio may still mean a smaller total profit if total production is reduced. The way in which we use the input–output table implies a strong rigidity, i.e. it implies the price and volume structure existing in the Argentine economy in 1963.

Having mentioned some of the serious limitations of the method used, we can go ahead with the analysis of the profit series as shown in Table 6.6, to which are also added the series of real wages. The agricultural sector fared better than at the time of Krieger Vasena (1967–9), a period which can be considered in some ways 'normal' and used as a fair reference, even if the agricultural sector, particularly the cattle sector, was not too happy in those years.

The agricultural sector tended to compare its situation with the peak year of 1972, which had resulted from a combination of a very devalued currency and very good international prices. The trend was very bad, but average profitability was somewhat better than in Krieger Vasena's period, 1975 standing out as a particularly bad year, when prices were worse than the average by more than 10 per cent. The industrial sector was somewhat worse off than in the 1967–70 period by about 5 per cent. This, however, hid significant differences within the sector, caused by, among other factors, the system of price controls, and maximum mark-ups, which were not equally imposed and

Argentina under Perón

TABLE 6.6   Evolution of Profits (1970 = 100)

Year	Agri-culture (a)	Indus-try (i)	Construc-tion (c)	Wages (w)		Jan	Apr	July	Oct
1966	99.3	103.3	98.1	103.3					
1967	95.2	99.7	97.8	96.6					
1968	97.0	100.8	99.5	96.1					
1969	98.4	99.6	100.9	100.0					
1970	100.0	100.0	100.0	100.0					
1971	108.8	101.1	98.2	106.8					
1972	128.6				(a)	119.7	123.3	132.6	137.0
		99.9			(i)	97.7	101.2	100.5	98.0
			98.8		(c)	98.9	98.7	101.2	98.3
				93.5	(w)	95.1	94.5	92.5	92.0
1973	115.6				(a)	125.2	128.4	108.0	111.4
		97.8			(i)	95.4	100.5	97.2	96.4
			102.7		(c)	102.3	103.6	103.5	103.5
				96.4	(w)	101.9	83.2	105.3	102.9
1974	100.8				(a)	109.6	102.4	101.4	101.6
		96.4			(i)	96.9	93.7	95.6	99.5
			106.0		(c)	104.1	105.5	106.6	110.9
				105.3	(w)	100.1	115.9	106.1	95.0
1975	85.6				(a)	105.3	92.7	71.9	97.0
		98.8			(i)	99.5	100.9	98.3	100.4
			112.4		(c)	112.6	112.2	122.2	115.0
				106.3	(w)	114.3	98.1	120.1	94.7
1976	112.4				(a)	98.7	108.6	120.2	131.9
		105.5			(i)	98.0	106.9	106.1	105.4
			114.5		(c)	116.7	121.7	113.0	107.0
				62.4	(w)	104.0	58.7	55.5	49.3

Source: Input–output matrix 1963, BCRA; wholesale prices, INDEC; public-ultility rates and wages, Ministerio de Economía.

monitored. It is quite certain that the larger firms were controlled to a much larger degree than the smaller ones, which, profit-wise, fared much worse than the average. The medium-sized and small firms, which were the political base of the CGE and of the first Minister of Economy, escaped the regulations on prices and mark-ups. Another of the serious problems is that even in such a year as 1975, when the industrial sector did not do so badly, the tremendous price oscillations and the unexpected changes in the rate of inflation created an equally tremendous uncertainty. These anxieties carried more weight than the profit figures as they actually emerged, a clear confirmation of the fact that businessmen put a high value on certainty and will trade off larger profits for lower but more certain ones. The evolution of profits in the construction sector is even more puzzling; it was better throughout than in the 1967–9 period, and had a significantly positive trend, which peaked at the end of 1975 and beginning of 1976. Although it is not easy to explain this behaviour, one can point out that, to the extent that the construction sector built for the public sector, they were protected by very strong indexation clauses. The construction sector was one of the first to pay attention to indexation and was able to participate with the corresponding state agency in the determination of the price index for construction, which exceeded the wholesale index throughout.

Previous views about the profitability of the agricultural and industrial sectors are dimmed still further if they are compared with the evolution of wages, another commonly used criterion. If profits are expressed in terms of wages in something like wage units, the conclusions do not change, but agricultural and industrial profits so expressed justify to a greater extent the outcry of those years. Even so, the outcry was the result not so much of the economic performance, which was not so bad in terms of profits, as of the general uncertainty and the serious intra-group struggles; last but not least, it was owing to the non-economic causes, which became ever more pressing, particularly as viewed by the business and propertied sectors.

DETERMINANTS OF THE TRADE BALANCE

During the 1973–6 period, the foreign sector played a most significant role. Although the situation had been critical around the third quarter of the year, the 1972 increase of nearly 40 per cent in the dollar value of exports, compared with an increase of less than 10 per cent in that of imports, improved the outlook rather drastically. However, this situation was reversed as a consequence of the deterioration in the terms of trade which preceded the oil crisis. When the crisis came, they worsened even more; by the end of 1974 they were half what they were at the end of 1972. This had a drastic effect on the trade balance, where a surplus of nearly US$200 million in 1973–4 was transformed into a deficit of $850 million by 1974–5. The international recession affected Argentina's main markets, and the reduction in the demand for its exports was compounded by the ban on meat imports imposed by the EEC in July 1974. These foreign factors were aggravated by the policy of overvaluing the currency, a consequence of the maintenance, during the first twenty months of the new government, of a fixed rate of exchange in face of domestic inflation of more than 50 per cent. The external crisis, culminating in mid-1975, was redressed to a great extent by a drastic devaluation. Despite its being counterbalanced by a huge domestic inflation, the net result was a real devaluation of about 40 per cent from February to July 1975. This devalued rate was maintained during the last months of 1975 through a series of so-called 'mini-devaluations'; this kept up the pressure on the level of prices but helped the trade balance, which in the first quarter of 1976 achieved its first positive level in six quarters. It must be stressed that the emphasis of our account is on the terms of trade, the international oil crisis and its effects in terms of income on Argentina's main trading partners, and on the real exchange rate. Our account leaves out, among other variables, the behaviour of money, which is assumed to have played a passive role during most of this period and to have had more significance for the non-trade items of the balance of payments. We also leave out the role of the quota system for imports, as it was bypassed by most importers.

We have been largely repeating what has already been said in Chapter 5. The intention now is to subject these statements to a statistical test. To this end three variables have been chosen: the terms of trade, T; the real exchange rate, R; and the foreign demand for Argentina's exportables, D. The terms-of-trade series are not excessively reliable; instead of the Central Bank's figures, those of the Fundación de Investigaciones Económicas Latinoamericanas (FIEL), with some minor adjustments made by CEMA, are used, since, owing to their more recent base, these seem more reliable. The two sets differ widely in 1973–4: FIEL's figures show a sharp downturn one year earlier than those of the Central Bank and this tallies better with what happened in the economy. In dealing with the real exchange rate, two different series have been used, one for exports (R_x) and another for imports (R_m). Each one takes into account the weighted rates of exchange and tariffs for imports, and the weighted rates of exchange and drawbacks for exports. The figures are the ones produced by the IEERAL, based on Argentina's purchasing power relative to a selection of its principal trading partners. These seem to produce better statistical results in the several cases in which they have been tested than alternative figures produced by CEMA, which are better for other purposes; but this is still an open question. Our third variable (*D*) attempts to reflect the situation of Argentina's principal markets. The idea is that the demand for Argentina's exportables is intimately connected with the level of economic activity of its principal trading partners. For this use has been made of a composite index of the evolution of GDP of a group of seven countries which receive about 60 per cent of Argentina's exports, the USA, the UK, Italy, France, Japan, the German Federal Republic and Holland – weighted by their respective trading importance. The first stage was to correlate the first two variables, i.e. the terms of trade (*T*) and the real exchange rate (*R*), with the value of imports, and all three variables – including the international demand for Argentina's goods (*D*) — with the value of exports. The second, serving as a check on the first two correlations, was to correlate the three variables with the difference between exports and imports, i.e. with the balance of trade (see Table 6.7).

Imports

It is fair to assume that the terms of trade (*T*) and the real exchange rate for imports (R_m) will have a lagged effect on the value of imports. It was further assumed that these lags can best be taken into account by choosing a function in which the independent variables take a polynomial representation (Almon, 1965). (This avoids multi-collinearity.) We shall assume, moreover, that the lagged effect and thus also the coefficients of the variables diminish geometrically with time: this suggests the choice of a polynomial of the first degree. The following is the functional relationship between imports at time *t* (M_t), the terms of trade (*T*) and the real import exchange rate (R_m), the *B* terms of the variables representing the polynomial. We use quarterly data, from the beginning of 1972 until the end of 1976.

$$ln M_t = -0.36 \ln T_A + 0.09 \ln T_B - 0.38 R_{mA} + 0.11 \ln R_{mB} + 13.99$$
$$(-3.91) \qquad (1.94) \qquad (-4.27) \qquad (2.74) \qquad (16.47)$$

The distributed lag coefficients are

variable	coefficient	t	variable	coefficient	t
$\ln T_t$	−0.36	−3.91	$\ln R_t$	−0.38	−4.27
$\ln T_{t-1}$	−0.27	−5.61	$\ln R_{t-1}$	−0.27	−4.96
$\ln T_{t-2}$	−0.18	−7.68	$\ln R_{t-2}$	−0.15	−4.20
$\ln T_{t-3}$	−0.09	−1.53	$\ln R_{t-3}$	−0.037	−0.66
$\ln T_{t-4}$	−0.004	0.04	$\ln R_{t-4}$	0.08	0.83

TABLE 6.7   International Trade, 1970–6

Period		Foreign demand (1970 I = 100)	Exports X_t	Imports M_t	Real export rate R_x	Real import rate R_m	Terms of trade T
			(US $ million)			(1970 I = 100)	
1970	I	100.0	422	379	100.0	100.0	98.68
	II	101.5	539	425	103.6	104.2	96.30
	III	102.9	453	438	108.9	109.4	101.32
	IV	104.2	358	451	108.7	108.5	105.00
1971	I	104.5	368	433	100.0	99.8	106.38
	II	105.3	806	503	94.4	94.6	106.64
	III	106.7	421	522	98.7	99.4	105.11
	IV	107.6	443	407	107.4	110.5	106.27
1972	I	108.8	430	448	114.3	126.2	113.242
	II	110.4	482	469	121.2	128.1	121.49
	III	111.2	466	494	120.4	120.8	127.46
	IV	114.9	561	492	112.8	113.8	138.77
1973	I	116.6	732	444	104.3	101.6	134.97
	II	118.14	753	476	93.0	90.0	125.20
	III	120.0	916	533	92.5	86.7	124.54
	IV	121.6	863	775	95.5	85.4	115.67
1974	I	121.3	889	634	93.3	84.8	87.81
	II	121.6	1066	855	91.2	83.6	68.58
	III	122.5	849	902	86.0	78.5	71.92
	IV	120.1	1125	1243	77.8	70.6	72.30
1975	I	117.5	633	1043	81.2	66.6	67.55
	II	117.3	807	1060	108.5	92.5	71.36
	III	117.7	759	942	120.2	117.0	74.102
	IV	121.6	761	900	111.7	110.7	70.63
1976	I	123.3	713	645	132.7	125.7	69.06
	II	125.3	1008	660	145.4	133.8	69.15
	III	126.3	1076	883	131.5	115.5	67.53
	IV	127.7	1120	843	121.6	110.0	61.57

Sources: BCRA, CEMA, IEERAL, International Financial Statistics (IFS) and FIEL. Quarterly figures are averages for the whole quarter.

SC (sum of coefficients)	$= -0.89$	SC	$= -0.76$
SE_{sc} (standard error of SC)	$= 0.116$	SE_{SC}	$= 0.18$
t_{sc}	$= -7.67$	t_{sc}	$= -4.22$
ML (mean lag)	$= 0.975$	ML	$= 0.492$

When corrected for problems of self-correlation, the characteristics of the correlation are

$$R^2_{(tv)} = 0.9134 \quad DW = 2.33 \quad SE = 0.126 \quad F = 48.44 \quad \rho = -0.25$$

As can be seen, the match is very good, as the R^2 of the transformed variable (tv) exceeds 0.9 and the statistic F is very indicative. Moreover, the statistics t of the B terms are also significant at the 5 per cent level, which indicates that the variables behave in the way suggested by the polynomial. In the case of the terms of trade and the real exchange rate, the coefficients of the lags are quite significant, and the real exchange rate and effects of the terms of trade diminish as time goes on, as can be seen by the reduction in the values of the coefficients, very much as one would expect. The effects of a change in the terms of trade and the real rate can be detected in the value of imports during a period of up to nine months; taken together they explain more than 90 per cent of the evolution of imports. This is a most significant conclusion, particularly as all other possible factors account for less than 10 per cent of the phenomenon.

Exports

As in the previous section, we make a correlation between exports and the three chosen independent variables, the terms of trade (T), the real exchange rate for exports (R_x), and export demand as measured by the level of activity of Argentina's trading partners (D). We also consider the lagged effects of these variables; their decreasing intensities are represented by a polynomial of the first degree. Self-correlation is eliminated by the Cochrane–Orcutt method. The results are

$$\ln X_t = -0.046 \quad \ln T_A + 0.14 \quad \ln T_B + 0.175 R_{xB} + 0.05$$
$$(-0.42) \qquad\quad (1.92) \qquad\quad (1.97) \qquad\quad (0.99)$$
$$\ln R_{xB} + 0.804 \quad \ln D_A + 0.643 \quad \ln D_B - 34.15$$
$$(0.68) \qquad\quad (0.82) \qquad\quad (-0.955)$$

lag	variable	coefficient	t	variable	coefficient	t	variable	coefficient	t
t				$\ln R_x$	0.175	1.97			
t_{-1}	$\ln T$	−0.046	−0.42	$\ln R_x$	0.227	4.31			
t_{-2}	$\ln T$	0.094	2.03	$\ln R_x$	0.280	4.90	$\ln D$	0.804	0.68
t_{-3}	$\ln T$	0.234	4.40	$\ln R_x$	0.330	3.44	$\ln D$	1.450	3.47
t_{-4}	$\ln T$	0.374	3.14	$\ln R_x$	0.385	2.66	$\ln D$	2.090	4.98
t_{-5}							$\ln D$	2.733	2.31

SC	= 0.657	SC	= 1.400	SC	= 7.08
SE_{sc}	= 0.136	SE_{sc}	= 0.286	SE_{sc}	= 0.60
t_{sc}	= 4.831	t_{sc}	= 4.895	t_{sc}	= 11.80
ML	= 2.57	ML	= 2.38	ML	= 1.95

When corrected for problems of self-correlation, the characteristics of the correlation are

$$R^2_{(tv)} = 0.9526 \quad DW = 2.35 \quad SE = 0.092 \quad F = 61.24 \quad \rho = -0.68$$

In this case, more than 90 per cent of exports are explained by the three chosen variables T, R, D. However, the B terms are significant at 5 per cent in the case of the T, but in the cases of R and D only at a 20 and 30 per cent limit respectively. This means that the polynomial which has been chosen is not very good. However, the values of the lagged coefficients are highly significant, either from the first lag onwards, as in the case of R or from the third lag, as in the case of D.

Trade balance

As a check on the previous results, the trade balance as a percentage of total trade was correlated with the three variables, using as the real exchange rate the average of the export and import real rates. It was decided to use the value of the dependent variables in the previous period as an indication of the effect of previous lags, because it gives better results than the Almond method. Self-correlation has also been eliminated; logarithms have not been used, because of the negative values in the trade balance in some years. The results are

$$\left(\frac{X-M}{X+M_t}\right) = \underset{(2.07)}{0.396} \left(\frac{X-M}{X+M}\right)_{t-1} + \underset{(3.15)}{0.00346}\, T_t + \underset{(1.95)}{0.00179}\, R_t + \underset{(2.78)}{0.0047}$$

$$\underset{(-3.11)}{D_t - 2.65}$$

Once self-correlation is eliminated, the characteristics of the correlation are

$$R^2_{(tv)} = 0.8047 \quad DW = -1.31 \quad SE = 0.079 \quad F = 19.54 \quad \rho = 0.37$$

All the variables have the expected signs and are significant at the 5 per cent level. More than 80 per cent of the trade balance can be explained by the three variables, confirming the conclusions arrived at from independent consideration of exports and imports.

Exports, imports and the trade balance

After these analyses, we can conclude that the three variables chosen do explain from 80 to 90 per cent of the behaviour of the trade balance and of imports and exports. We can also add the following conclusions:

(a) The terms of trade are very significant in explaining the increase in the value of imports. In the case of exports they are also significant, but less so, pointing to a certain price inelasticity for exports.

(b) The real exchange rate is significant for both imports and exports. Again, it is less significant in the case of exports but with less difference. This reinforces the previous conclusion.

(c) Exports are very dependent on the level of income of Argentina's trading partners. The inclusion of this variable was crucial in the improvement of the correlations. Without it, the correlations for exports and for the trade balance were rather poor.

(d) The three previous conclusions are somewhat surprisingly in line with some of the views of the old structuralist school, i.e. a certain price inelasticity for exports, in both international and national prices, and a certain foreign-income elasticity for Argentina's exports. The first two conclusions show that devaluations have to be rather severe to produce effects on the export side, but need not be as severe to produce effects on the import side. This emphasises the importance of foreign disturbances such as the oil crisis.

(e) Of the three variables, the first (the terms of trade) and the third (foreign demand) were beyond the control of Argentina's policy-makers. The internal terms of trade was the only one which could to some extent be determined locally. Given the fact that the balance of trade had turned so strongly against the country, one of the few measures that could be taken was a significant devaluation. In nominal terms its severity was unquestionably exaggerated, but in real terms what was done was probably in line with the avowed objective, which was attained less than nine months later.

BIBLIOGRAPHY

Almon, S. (1965) 'The Distributed Lag between Capital Appropriation and Expenditures', *Econometrica* (Jan).

de Pablo, J. C. (1977) 'Aldo Ferrer y la política económica en la Argentina de postguerra', *Desarrollo Económico*, no. 67 (Oct–Dec).

de Pablo, J. C. (1978) 'Inversión, liberalismo y populismo', *Desarrollo Económico*, no. 68 (Jan–Mar).

Ferrer, A. (1977) *Crisis y alternativas de la política económica argentina* (Buenos Aires: Fondo de Cultura Económica).

Ferrer, A. (1978) 'Crisis y alternativas de la política económica argentina, una respuesta', *Desarrollo Económico*, no. 68 (Jan–Mar).

Lavagna, R. (1978) 'Aldo Ferrer y la política económica en la Argentina de postguerra (II)', *Desarrollo Económico*, no. 68 (Jan–Mar.)

Lavagna, R. (1978) 'Inversión, liberalismo y populismo', *Desarrollo Económico*, no. 69 (Apr–June).

Machinea, J. and Rotemberg, J. (1977) *Estimación de la función de importaciones de mercancías*, Serie de Estudios Técnicos, no. 21 (Buenos Aires: CEMYB, BCRA).

7 Yet Another Major Issue: Inflation

The extraordinary inflation of these years gives rise to a whole set of topics. The first of these has to do with the role of oligopolies and of the conflicts between and within groups in the inflationary process. This subject leads rather naturally into the study of the oscillation of relative prices and of the possibility of correlating it with inflation, to the point of suggesting that inflations can be characterised according to their oscillatory character. Another connected problem is the cyclical character of the inflationary process, a problem distinct from the stop–go character of the economy, which has to do with movements in income rather than movements in inflation rates. The last issue we tackle is the role of indexation and its connection with the effeciency of the economy and with the rekindling of the inflationary process.

This selection of topics leaves out a host of other equally interesting issues: for instance, the role of money, of capital movements and of expectations. Some of these are touched on indirectly in what is said, but they all deserve special studies; some of these, fortunately, are in the process of appearing.

SECTORAL CONFLICTS, OLIGOPOLIES AND INFLATION

Inflation is a complex phenomenon that cannot be explained simply in terms of one or a few economic variables (Hirsch and Goldthorpe, 1978). In this section the aim is to bring clearly into the picture yet another factor, the oligopolistic behaviour of increasingly large sections of the economy. Not only does this kind of behaviour start inflation, but it also perpetuates it by creating a vicious circle. Oligopolistic behaviour was much more pervasive than has been generally acknowledged; however, it can be clearly distinguished if one looks attentively.

During this period, many groups priced their products or services far beyond their equilibrium level, giving rise to non-competitive reactions. If their behaviour had been based purely on competitive considerations, other producers would have adapted to the new situation, reducing their consumption and production in accordance with the higher prices requested by the deviant producer. He, in turn, would have found his turnover and presumably his profits reduced; and if, for whatever reason, he had persisted in his pricing strategy, he would have suffered losses. In fact, this was not what happened. On the contrary, price increases triggered a chain reaction: each group tried to recoup its lost position, increasing its prices in turn.

This kind of oligopolistic behaviour became much more widespread than ever before. Groups which normally behaved in a competitive manner, such as agricultural producers or small businessmen, were able to organise quite effective lobbying groups. This was quite clearly the case with landowning groups such as the Sociedad Rural and CARBAP and business groups such as the CGE and, later, the APEGE. These were quite able to manipulate public opinion, influence Government policies and organise several lock-outs and producers' strikes.

These oligopolistic struggles were one of the major reasons why the inflation was so intense. This could be clearly seen during the 1975 price explosion; inflation was then set at a new and much higher level and it continued to rise for more than four years at monthly rates of about 5 per cent before showing any downward trend, despite relatively orthodox monetary policies. When a relative price movement took place, it had the dubious virtue of showing that the share of the national income of a certain group could be altered. The group which benefited from it resisted all attempts to redress the situation. When the affected groups raised their prices in an attempt to adjust to the disturbance, the first group raised its prices yet again, disequilibrating the relative prices set and thereby perpetuating the price spiral. If the rise in question had been the first disturbance after a long period of price stability it might not have triggered further disturbances – at least, to such an extent; stability is the consequence of the acceptance of a certain distribution of income among the various participants, and it in turn contributes to such an acceptance if for no other reason than the force of habit. On the other hand, a long and fluctuating inflation such as Argentina's teaches all groups the absolute necessity of fighting for their share of the national income. The mere idea of an equilibrium set of prices and incomes is poorly understood by or even unknown to the contending groups. A considerable degree of anxiety develops and the struggle for relative shares becomes very acute and a permanent feature of the whole inflationary society. However, from the point of view of the oligopolistic groups, it still makes sense to push for individual gains even at the cost of a reduction in the general level of welfare.

Another and even more serious problem was that the broad groups to which we have been referring – workers, landowners, capitalists, and so on – did not behave at all in a homogenous way. They were in turn composed of quite distinct sub-groups, which also behaved in an oligopolistic manner, and this gave rise to serious internal group conflicts. In fact, it appears that these internal conflicts come nearer to explaining the inflation than do the struggles between different groups. More could be gained in this way, and gains could be maintained for a longer period. Many examples can be found. Each trade union, instead of focusing its attention on a general rise in wages, tended to concentrate its efforts on improving its own position in relation to the general level. Trade unions competed among themselves for workers of similar industries, as in the case of the metallurgical and mechanical workers' unions. The difference between a specific and a general rise in wages was considered the real net gain. Past experience pointed to the fact that the general rise was associated with rises in prices, so that the value of the wage rise was cancelled out. The general rise was viewed as self-defeating, while the fight for a specific wage rise was considered to be particularly fruitful. At times this forced a reduction in the actual volume produced by the industry, but it none the less brought very important real benefits for the workers. It is possible that the reduction of profits and the increases in the prices of some specific industries went too far, reaching a point where they became self-defeating for the trade unions and the workers involved. On rational grounds, however, to put up a good fight was a sensible thing to do.

Wage increases were not uniform. In industries, such as the car industry, which were more profitable and had stronger trade unions, wages increased above the national average; in other cases they tended to lag. These situations strained the traditional wage structure, but the wages and prices explosion of mid-1975 created real havoc. Some unions got increases of less than 80 per cent, while others got up to 250 per cent, completely breaking traditional wage differentials. The struggle between the different groups of workers to maintain their new relative positions, and the successive rises in prices which these caused were fundamental causes of inflation in this period, in particular during late 1975.

This kind of infighting was repeated in the business sector. Instead of pushing for a general increase in the return on capital, industries strived to improve their own positions. They tried to increase the prices of their products by pushing for higher specific tariffs while insisting on very low ones for their imported inputs.

Struggles between and within groups were brought under control for a short while during the Krieger Vasena period but afterwards increased, reaching dangerous proportions just before the new government came in. The 'social pact' was an attempt to impose a solution under the aegis of the State upon explicitly recognised oligopolistic antagonists. However, there was less awareness of the importance of struggles within groups, as these were a rather new development. Even more explicitly than in the late 1960s, an attempt was made to impose a long-term distribution of national income which took into account not only the traditional balance but also the new and changed distribution of oligopolistic power among groups. However, it was not easy to organise a long-term solution when each group was not particularly disciplined, and struggles within groups soon took precedence, compounding the difficulty and precariousness of the solution.

RELATIVE PRICE OSCILLATION AND INFLATION

It might be worthwhile to examine one of the significant characteristics of the inflationary process, at least as experienced by Argentina: i.e. the wide variations in relative prices (di Tella, 1980). That there should be variations may seem somewhat obvious, as it is difficult to imagine cases where all prices move to the same extent. A certain disparity is bound to exist between the overall rate of inflation and the price changes of particular products. We have to separate out (relative) price variations which are the result of long-term structural changes from those which are caused by the inflationary process.

Inflation, also, produces permanent and transitory variations in real prices. The more lasting changes may reflect a permanent inability – or engrained ineptitude – adequately to replace a particular good, factory, service, or rate of interest. However, inflation also changes relative prices in a transitory fashion as a result of the oligopolistic struggles mentioned earlier, in which victories are seldom of a lasting character. Leads and lags in prices occur more rapidly as the intensity of inflation teaches more and more groups how to defend themselves. This means that prices lag only for a while before bouncing back to their previous position and even taking the lead. This alternation of leads and lags causes rapid price oscillation and an equally intense but short-lived transfer of income from one group to another.

Rather than a permanent change in relative prices, it is this transitory process which has characterised inflation, at least in Argentina. In the past these oscillations may not have been so central, but in the 1972–6 period they were at the root of the way in which inflation was transmitted and maintained. Price oscillations have nowadays become a more pervasive problem, and this is true for other Latin American countries as well. In the Argentine case, one finds that more intensely inflationary periods were associated with more intense oscillations in (relative) prices compared with the rates of inflation.

This is quite an interesting conclusion. Although it is to be expected that at higher rates of inflation prices will oscillate more, it is not so obvious that they will do so out of proportion to the rate of inflation. An important inference is that it may be possible to differentiate equally intense inflationary processes by their oscillatory character. This may be important, as the more oscillatory inflations are probably the ones which are more intractable to standard anti-inflationary medicine.

The degree of price oscillation is differently affected by cost-pushed or demand-pulled inflationary processes. The increase in a particular cost may be brought about by an exogenous factor, such as the so-called 'imported' inflation of 1973–4, or by an intentional policy, such as the devaluations of 1975, but in all cases the price vector is distorted more directly and probably to a greater degree than in the initial stages of demand-induced inflations. However, if the demand pull is the consequence of a deliberate shift in the distribution of income from some income brackets to others, the demand for different products will alter; this was quite noticeable during the end of 1973 and the whole of 1974. The increase in consumption relative to investment was connected with this shift; it caused an increase in the prices of consumer goods relative to the prices of investment goods and of landed property.

We tried to test these hypotheses statistically. Inflation was defined as the rate of change of the wholesale price index, slightly more reliable in the Argentine case than the cost-of-living index, and free from seasonal effects. In both cases, the indexes are measured on the basis of prices paid at actual market transactions, disregarding official prices theoretically in force. Inflation then becomes

$$\frac{\bar{p}_t}{\bar{p}_{t-1}} = a_1 \frac{p_{1t}}{\bar{p}_{t-1}} + a_2 \frac{p_{2t}}{\bar{p}_{t-1}} + \ldots + a_n \frac{p_{nt}}{\bar{p}_{t-1}}$$

where $\bar{p}_t$ and $\bar{p}_{t-1}$ are the wholesale price indexes at times t and $t-1$ respectively, and p_{it} is the price of the ith component at time t. a_i and p_{it} are the weight and the price of the components of the index also at time t.

Alternatively, and more usefully, we can express the overall rate of inflation in terms of the rates of price change of its components, so that

$$\frac{\bar{p}_t}{\bar{p}_{t-1}} = b_1 \frac{p_{1t}}{p_{1t-1}} + b_2 \frac{p_{1t}}{p_{2t-1}} + \ldots + b_n \frac{p_{nt}}{p_{nt-1}}$$

But in this case new weights b_i have to be introduced, different from the a_i and varying from period to period:

$$b_{it} = a_i \cdot \frac{p_{it-1}}{p_{t-1}}$$

Relative price oscillation can be defined in several different meaningful ways. For our particular purpose the one that has proved most useful is the ratio between the standard deviation of the rates of change of the components of the wholesale price index and the rate of change of the index itself over a specific period. This can be expressed

$$Y_t = \frac{\sigma_t}{\bar{p}_t/\bar{p}_{t-1}} = \frac{\sum\limits_{i=1}^{n} \frac{p_{it}}{p_{it-1}} - \frac{\bar{p}_t}{\bar{p}_{t-1}} \left(a_i \frac{p_{it-1}}{p_{t-1}} \right)}{\bar{p}_t/\bar{p}_{t-1}}$$

where

Y_t is the relative price oscillation between time t and time $t-1$;
σ_t is the standard deviation of the rates of change of the prices of the components of the wholesale price index;
p_{it} is the price of the ith component of the wholesale price index at time t;
$\bar{p}_t$ is the wholesale price index at time t;
a_i is the weight of the ith component of the wholesale price index.

TABLE 7.1   Weights of the Components of the Wholesale Price Index
(1960 base)

(1)	LOCALLY PRODUCED	*0.954*
(a)	*Agricultural and animal*	*0.295*
	Agriculture	*0.151*
	Cereals and linseed	0.074
	Industrial crops	0.034
	Fruit	0.015
	Vegetables	0.028
	Animal origin	*0.143*
	Cattle	0.106
	Wool	0.009
	Dairy	0.028
	Fisheries	*0.010*
	Fish	0.010
(b)	*Non-agricultural*	*0.695*
	Food and beverages	0.235
	Tobacco	0.013
	Textiles	0.076
	Garment	0.059
	Wood	0.022
	Paper	0.011
	Chemical products	0.040
	Petroleum	0.023
	Rubber	0.008
	Leather	0.023
	Glass, ceramics	0.025
	Metal, excluding machinery	0.054
	Non-electrical machinery	0.046
	Electrical	0.016
	Extractive industries	0.009
(2)	IMPORTED	*0.046*
	Food and beverages	0.008
	Wood	0.006
	Paper	0.001
	Chemical products	0.008
	Rubber	0.002
	Metals	0.018
	Extractive industries	0.009

Source: INDEC.

TABLE 7.2   Relative Price Oscillation (Y_t), Residuals (Z_t) and Inflation (X_t), 1972–6 (on a monthly basis)

Year	Month	Y_t	Z_t	X_t	Year	Month	Y_t	Z_t	X_t
1972	Jan	5.68		1.138	1975	Jan	6.75	−0.742	1.063
	Feb	5.88	−1.852	1.062		Feb	7.67	−0.449	1.126
	Mar	4.09	−1.125	1.038		Mar	5.86	0.045	1.059
	Apr	5.09	−1.312	1.052		Apr	7.26	1.345	1.038
	May	3.53	−1.307	1.035		May	8.69	0.947	1.052
	June	5.31	−1.080	1.065		June	23.77	0.865	1.436
	July	5.31	−0.762	1.040		July	17.73	3.279	1.321
	Aug	3.77	−0.753	1.023		Aug	17.46	4.127	1.153
	Sep	4.67	−0.948	1.047		Sep	13.55	3.181	1.130
	Oct	4.27	0.547	1.033		Oct	7.49	4.491	1.090
	Nov	4.83	0.362	1.018		Nov	20.01	3.491	1.099
	Dec	7.15	1.003	1.033		Dec	9.28	3.614	1.094
1973	Jan	6.67	−0.095	1.049	1976	Jan	11.04	−0.058	1.195
	Feb	3.96	−0.844	1.069		Feb	15.12	−2.439	1.286
	Mar	6.12	−0.778	1.065		Mar	21.01	−2.231	1.541
	Apr	6.28	0.338	1.040		Apr	14.00	−3.180	1.263
	May	6.62	2.425	1.056		May	5.50	0.096	1.048
	June	9.19	1.202	0.985		June	8.38	1.195	1.047
	July	2.55	0.455	0.992		July	10.21	−4.304	1.111
	Aug	2.82	−0.726	1.012		Aug	0.24	−4.877	1.080
	Sep	4.36	−1.091	1.004		Sep	8.46	−4.329	1.088
	Oct	2.01	−0.268	1.001		Oct	6.34	1.176	1.044
	Nov	4.50	0.245	0.989		Nov	8.59	1.410	1.069
	Dec	7.30	1.535	1.013		Dec	8.12		1.065
1974	Jan	4.72	1.457	1.003					
	Feb	4.82	−0.608	1.004	Mean		7.41		1.078
	Mar	1.59	0.407	1.004					
	Apr	9.67	−0.202	1.025	Variance		22.62		0.010
	May	6.12	1.590	1.044					
	June	5.32	0.490	1.035	Standard				
	July	5.70	−0.422	0.027	deviation		4.76		0.101
	Aug	3.16	1.042	1.029					
	Sep	3.45	−1.467	1.035					
	Oct	4.50	−0.565	1.036					
	Nov	7.00	−0.162	1.044					
	Dec	4.19	0.203	1.029					

Source: Derived from INDEC.

The different kinds and degrees of disaggregation of the wholesale index which can be chosen may produce different results, as some of the more significant oscillations may disappear if the sector is aggregated. Moreover, some crucial prices, such as rates of exchange, rates of interest and wages, are left out of our definition. A different definition would be necessary in order to include them.

The breakdown and the actual weights of the wholesale price index can be seen in Table 7.1, while the monthly and quarterly relative price oscillations, residuals and rates of inflation are given in Table 7.2.

On the basis of these series it has been attempted to correlate the monthly relative price oscillation, Y_t, to the monthly rate of inflation, X_t, as expressed by the change in the wholesale price index. The results from January 1972 until December 1976 are as follows:

$$Y_t = 38.4248 \ X_t - 34.0047 \qquad R_2 = 0.66808 \qquad DW = 1.697$$
$$ (10.8119) \quad (-8.84)$$

The correlation coefficient is practically the same, even slightly better, when the data is analysed on a quarterly basis:

$$Y_t = 40.9639 \ X_t - 37.1765 \qquad R_2 = 0.7174 \qquad DW = 1.949$$
$$ (5.76) \quad (-5.68)$$

On the other hand, these results clearly worsen when the relative price oscillation is correlated with the inflationary rate of the previous month:

$$Y_t = 26.8367 \ X_{t-1} - 21.4907 \qquad R_2 = 0.3266 \qquad DW = 1.7570$$
$$ (5.26) \quad (-3.89)$$

or of the following month:

$$X_t = 0.0125 \ Y_{t-1} + 0.9844 \qquad R_2 = 0.3470 \qquad DW = 1.589$$
$$ (5.50) \quad (428.0)$$

When three-month moving averages are taken into consideration, the high correlation is maintained:

$$Y_t = 41.6756 \ X_t^{111} - 37.924 \qquad R_2 = 0.7663 \qquad DW = 0.643$$
$$ (13.55) \quad (-11.43)$$

A most interesting result appears if we analyse two clearly divided periods, i.e. before and after the price explosion of June 1975. During the period beginning June 1973, just after the inauguration of the Peronist government, until April 1974, the monthly rates of inflation averaged 0.6 per cent (with a high of 2.5 and a low of -1.4), while the relative price oscillation was

$$Y_t = 25.1336\ X_t\ -\ 20.5467 \qquad R_2 = 0.1258 \qquad DW = 2.015$$
$$\quad\ (1.74) \qquad\quad (-1.38)$$

During the succeeding period, which covers the twenty months from May 1975 until December 1976, the monthly rate of inflation averaged 15.76 per cent (ranging from a high of 54.1 to a low of 4.4 per cent), while the relative price oscillation was

$$Y_t = 32.9393\ X_t\ -\ 26.4798 \qquad R_2 = 0.6009 \qquad DW = 1.884$$
$$\quad\ (5.21)$$

Between these two periods one can see a significant increase in the correlation coefficient from 0.1258 to 0.6009; this points to an equally significant increase in the possibility of explaining the oscillatory character of the economy as a consequence of the degree of price changes.

This is by no means to imply that inflation can be wholly or even mainly explained by the degree of relative price oscillation. One should be suspicious of any explanation of such a complex phenomenon in terms of just one variable, be it a monetary or a structural one. All that has been done here is to present a special correlation between relative price oscillation and inflation which is particularly impressive for the 1972–6 period in Argentina. It is probably a concept which will have to be included, among others, in any further explanation of the process of inflation. Moreover, the significant jump in price oscillation which took place after the 1975 price explosion differentiates the preceding and subsequent periods over and above alternations in the rate of inflation. It also throws some light on why inflation became so much more difficult to bring under control, even more than would have been expected from its higher rate.

INFLATIONARY CYCLES

The 1973–6 experience, if observed against a longer-term background, may point to the existence of a kind of cyclical behaviour in inflation rates. This is the consequence of a complex underlying situation the explanation of which is the purpose of this section. Moreover, it is claimed that these inflation cycles are distinctively different from the income cycles which are the basis of the 'stop–go' character of the Argentine economy (Díaz Alejandro, 1970; Brodersohn, 1977; Heyman, 1980). There is a certain relationship between them, but it is neither simple nor straightforward. That the alleged inverse correlation between price and income variations is in fact weak is demonstrated in the following sub-section.

TABLE 7.3   Logarithmic Changes of Prices and GDP, 1947–76

Year	Consumer prices	Wholesale prices	GDP
1947	12.70	3.30	12.86
1948	12.31	14.45	1.19
1949	27.07	20.78	−4.70
1950	22.75	18.42	1.50
1951	31.42	39.87	3.81
1952	32.75	27.18	−5.16
1953	3.90	10.97	5.16
1954	3.70	3.06	4.05
1955	11.61	8.55	6.82
1956	12.61	23.13	2.74
1957	22.09	21.57	5.05
1958	27.44	27.10	5.92
1959	75.93	84.74	−6.68
1960	24.13	14.61	7.58
1961	12.68	7.97	6.86
1962	24.73	26.46	−1.60
1963	21.56	25.29	−2.40
1964	20.00	23.22	9.80
1965	25.15	21.44	8.77
1966	27.67	18.23	0.64
1967	25.64	22.78	2.61
1968	15.02	9.19	4.21
1969	7.31	5.88	8.19
1970	12.75	13.18	5.24
1971	29.79	33.28	5.73
1972	46.03	57.11	3.74
1973	47.19	40.58	4.60
1974	21.68	18.25	3.93
1975	103.96	107.33	−0.87
1976	169.38	179.02	−1.72

Source: Derived from INDEC.

Inflation and income cycles

An analysis was made using yearly data over the relatively long span from 1947 to 1976. This covers most of the post-war period and includes the six inflation cycles described later on. The consumer price, the wholesale price and the GDP series were used, the first approach being based on yearly data. Inflation was measured as the logarithmic change either in consumer or in wholesale prices and the rate of growth was measured as the logarithmic change in GDP (Table 7.3). For the regressions the ordinary-least-squares method was used, self-correlation being corrected by the Cochrane–Orcutt method; accordingly, the R^2 corresponds to the transferred variable.

For consumer prices, the main results were as follows:

(1) $P_t = 6.5397 - 2.15\ Y_t$
   $\quad\quad\quad (-1.0)\,(-3.36)$
   $R^2_{(tv)} = 0.2692$
   $F \quad\quad = 11.32$
   $DW \quad = 1.31$
   $SE \quad = 0.2185$
   $\rho \quad\quad = 1.0$

If wholesale prices are taken instead, we get:

(2) $P_t = 1.3706 - 2.44\ Y_t$
   $\quad\quad\quad (1.37)\ \ (-3.2)$
   $R^2_{(tv)} = 0.2479$
   $F \quad\quad = 10.23$
   $DW \quad = 1.47$
   $SE \quad = 0.2539$
   $\rho \quad\quad = 0.96$

The inverse correlation between price and income changes is partially confirmed, as only about 25 per cent of the change in prices – whether consumer or wholesale – can be explained by changes in income. A similar analysis was then made taking into consideration leads and lags and, as a second step, taking quarterly data. In the first case, results worsened; in the second, not only did they worsen but the correlation disappeared altogether. It would seem that, whatever inverse connection there is between price and income changes, they are more adequately detected within the year.

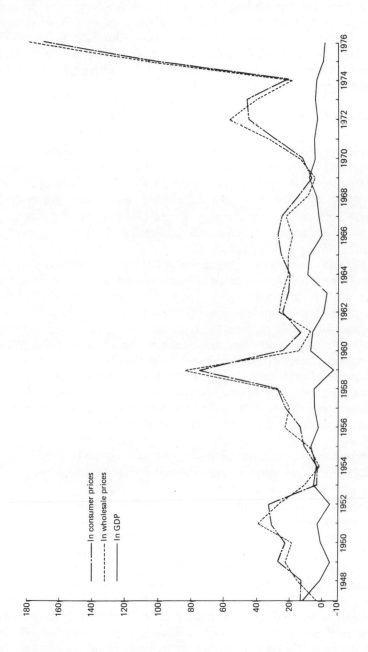

FIGURE 7.1 Consumer and Wholesale Prices and GDP (logarithmic changes)

The basic conclusion that emerges is that the factors or policies which affect the level of income affect only to a minor extent the rates of price change. A large proportion of these – up to 75 per cent – is accounted for by other, unexplained variables. This gives grounds for an initial assumption of two fundamentally different processes: the inflation cycle and the growth cycle.

The cyclical pattern

An analysis of the evolution of prices, consumer or wholesale, from 1947 to 1976, as depicted in Figure 7.1, shows a quite distinct cyclical pattern. During the period we can detect six cycles: these peaked in 1951, 1959, 1962, 1965–6, 1972 and 1975–6 respectively. An analysis of these cycles is made in the appendix to this chapter, and may give an idea of the kind of experience which has given rise to the specific interpretations presented here.

Argentina's inflationary pattern is very much the consequence of policies which had little chance of being sustained for long. One can detect an alternation between stages when inflation was tackled through the 'repression' of some particular set of prices and stages when the previously repressed prices were 'loosened up', redressing some of the imbalances but unleashing the upward spiral of prices once again. The first stage usually succeeded in restraining inflation at the expense of some serious imbalances, and these eventually forced a reversal of policy. The second succeeded in redressing the imbalances at the price of rekindling the inflationary process. This in turn created strong pressures to 'do something', opening the way for a new 'repression' stage. At times, it was thought that the various governments could be associated with one or the other of these stages. In fact these stages sometimes overlapped political boundaries, or the same government, after starting upon one strategy, would veer towards the other. This happened during the first ten years of Peronist government; during the Frondizi and Krieger Vasena periods; and, most notoriously, during the later Peronist governments. The Radical period was one of the few without such a change in policy.

Moreover, as we can see by reading the histories told in the appendix, some of the better successes and some of the worse failures among the various governments depended to a great extent on the particular moment of the inflationary cycle in which they made their appearance. Moreover, one of the longest periods, that from 1963 to 1970, depended for its success on a particularly felicitous blend of the

Radical policies pursued up to 1967 with Krieger Vasena's policies pursued thereafter; these had a continuity in some relevant aspects which has been disguised by the very different rhetoric used by the two groups.

On the occasions when inflation began to increase, rising prices of various kinds have been considered the main culprits: wages, business profits, agricultural profits and the exchange rate have been deemed the most responsible for inflationary pressures. They have been frozen, fixed or kept within boundaries by various means. Wages have been kept under control either by fixing the mark-up (1955, 1975, bargaining (1959, 1976) or fixing them directly by law. Profits have been kept under control either by fixing the mark-up (1967, 1975, 1977) or by freezing the prices of the goods produced in the face of mounting costs (1953, 1973). Agricultural prices sensitive to the export market have been controlled through the overvaluation of the exchange rate and/or by the imposition of *ad valorem* taxes on exports. The control of import prices has played a smaller role, but it was tried in 1967–70, mainly through a reduction in import tariffs. The overvaluation of the exchange rate has had a similar role, although its alleged main justification was usually to cheapen the price of exportables, i.e. to cheapen food and improve distribution, and only incidentally to cheapen imports.

Not all of these policies were adopted simultaneously and at times they were not completely coherent. There were also times when they seemed aimed at cancelling out other policies already in existence, i.e. overvaluing the exchange rate while import tariffs were being increased (1954, 1974). These strategies for reducing inflationary pressures were in general initiated after a previous period of relatively high and unrepressed inflation. The repressing of a specific price (or prices) produced in general quite an effective downward pressure and succeeded for a while in reducing inflation. The repression of the price of a strategic variable was generally carried out in disregard of the possible equilibrium price. It has to be admitted, however, that such a concept was difficult to determine in situations of rapid price changes and wide variations in relative prices.

What was characteristic of these stages was the simultaneous reduction in the inflationary rate *and* the increase in a situation of disequilibrium. In other words, while economic inefficiency as measured by price distortion increased, inflation in the short run diminished. It is not that we get minimum inflation at the moment of maximum distortion. Minimum inflations preceded maximum distortions by about one year or so. This was normally owing to the fact that the repression of prices was particularly effective in the initial stages. As soon as inflation began to fall and the danger stemming from the imbalances seemed to be over, concessions on other fronts were demanded. Some of these pressures were yielded to, and this began to push prices up. These were probably the worst moments; it can be seen, with hindsight, that in 1961, 1970 and 1974 distortion was at its highest and some of its negative effects on the economy had already begun to be evident and worrying. While low agricultural prices, low expectations, low profits or low wages were at different times characteristic of the distortion stage, at a certain point the external situation always came into the picture. Prior to this, the pressures for a change in policies could come from any of the repressed areas, but it was the situation in the foreign sector which left no other option, not only because of negative trade balances but also because of the destabilising capital movements typical of the times when clouds begin to gather.

Nevertheless, these situations were not normally resolved quickly but dragged on for a while. The disagreeable option was to redress the distorted set of relative prices and start the inflationary process all over again, losing at a stroke what had apparently been gained in the anti-inflationary fight. One can well understand the hesitancy and the wish to delay the hard decision until the last possible moment, at the price of making the reversal even more sharp. The more it was delayed, the greater the adjustment that would have to be made to relative prices.

The essence of the reversals and of the unloosening of prices is that they had to move in different proportions, so as to change the relative price set. A non-proportional price jump was therefore a necessary part of this adjustment, and a reason for the oscillating character of inflation at such times. The repressed prices had to move much more than the others, so as to attain a new equilibrium set. Usually a short-term equilibrium set was aimed at rather than a long-term one, in view of the immediate pressures and needs. This short-term equilibrium set normally meant that prices overshot their long-term values. The devaluations are a good example of this, as on many occasions they exceeded what proved necessary in the longer run, as in 1975.

In some unfortunate circumstances the reversal was aggravated by quite independently created political disturbances, as in 1961–2. In other instances, the tensions built up during the 'repression' stage prompted political disturbances, although seldom really creating them. In yet other instances, the reaction to the reversal was what created the political problems, as in mid-1975.

The subsequent stages were in many ways the opposite. While the repressed stages were associated with price distortions and a loss of economic efficiency, the freeing of prices, by contrast, increased economic efficiency. These more efficient economic conditions gave rise to some of the economic improvements so badly needed. Again we can detect here the odd inverse relationship between inflation and efficiency. After the balancing of the 'real' situation it became tempting – and possible – to try once more for a reduction in the rate of inflation. The whole set of measures mentioned earlier was reintroduced. This started periods of lower inflation and increased price distortion, repeating the cycle all over again.

Of course, there is nothing inherently obligatory in this story. One could imagine a different scenario in which prices would be set at the optimum long-term equilibrium values and the various groups would accept the implicit income distribution, thus making efficiency and low inflation compatible. But, as we have seen, the essence of the alternation of policies lies in the difficulty of setting an exact course, of hitting the correct long-term equilibrium relative price set. Moreover, it has to be accepted that the control of inflation cannot be achieved on any permanent basis through the manipulation of relative prices, even if this means the abandonment of some tempting but treacherously short-lived solutions.

This is not an easy proposition. When a society persistently strays far from its optimal path, it is not easy to get back to it. It is even more difficult to agree to stop the bickering between groups that has been going for so long and that has been continuously exacerbated by the oscillation of relative prices, which is so much a part of the story. One can easily see how, under these conditions, inflation becomes resilient to any kind of measures, orthodox or unorthodox.

Destabilising effects of monetary behaviour and capital flows

The behaviour of money has so far been mentioned only in a marginal way, despite the fact that there are at least two monetary phenomena which, given the setting described, contribute to the intensity of the inflationary cycle.

The first of these paradoxes – as they have been called – relates to the extreme variability of the velocity term in the monetary equation.

The variation of this presumed long-term constant is one of the more crucial variables of the whole inflationary process: it can make cycles even more intense and reversals more sharp.

When inflation falls one is bound to expect a reduction in expectations and a tendency to move back into monetary assets (Salama, 1978; Baliño, 1977; Fernández, 1980). In the case of non-interest-yielding money M_1, the cost of holding will go down with a corresponding increase in demand. In the case of interest-yielding money $(M_4 - M_1)$, it depends on the behaviour of the real rate of interest. It has not been uncommon to see an increase in the real rate in these downward inflationary stages (1953–4, 1960, 1968–9 and 1973–4). The ceilings which were responsible for the negative real rates in the upswing are more than enough to allow for a positive real rate and an increase in the demand for money during the downswing.

In these stages, it is possible to have a reduction in inflationary pressures and an increase in credit and the amount of money in circulation. These are the periods of 'easy credit' which have usually been heavily criticised by the more orthodox groups. However, the set of policies is perfectly coherent, even if money is issued to finance the government's deficit. The possibilities afforded by this monetary issue are clearly restricted, but it is a most useful 'cushion' in such stabilisation schemes. However, if the process is continued beyond the bounds imposed by the greater, but not unlimited, demand for money, or if for any other of the reasons mentioned before prices begin to pick up, the monetary situation may become very dangerous. As cash-holders see the disequilibrium or notice the price increases, they try to move away from monetary assets. If yields are increased to catch up with the increased price expectations, something which it has not been found easy to do, it is taken as a signal that the government is envisaging a most serious inflationary threat, and this helps to increase inflationary expectations even more. It has been increasingly typical that, at this juncture, inflationary expectations increase more than inflation, partly because of the community's similar experiences of disaster in the past. People move away from money in all its forms. Even if the amount of money in existence is not increased, its inflationary potential rises and is soon fully felt. The pressure on prices becomes even more intense and the stage is set for a big inflationary jump. Through this jump in prices a reduction in the real amount of money takes place. It is one of the few factors checking the jump; however, it is one that has usually been very small. If the government then tries to restrict the issue of money, this reduces the price jump which is necessary to reduce money holdings to the desired levels; however, this restrictive policy is normally beyond its means at this juncture.

The reduction of the amount of money in circulation in relation to GNP is not necessarily a reflection of a restrictive monetary policy, but could be a reflection of the flight from money. In fact in some instances the only restriction has come through the increase in the nominal value of the denominator, i.e. through an increase in prices. This behaviour of money in relation to expectations, so helpful during the initial stabilisation stage, makes things much worse at this stage and accentuates the cyclical behaviour.

International capital flows have also, in turn, behaved in an unsettling way immediately after the reversal and at the beginning of the price-distortion stage. This has commonly happened when the rate of exchange has either been fixed or devalued at a lower rate than inflation. The difference between these two rates, plus the fact that interest rates have become positive, makes it highly convenient to bring in money from outside the country and loan it internally. This has not always been possible, as there have sometimes been restrictions. However, as foreign loans are now badly needed to correct the previous external imbalance, they have usually been welcomed, even during such nationalistic periods as 1965 and 1971. This inflow of foreign currency improves the balance of payments and increases the possibility and attraction of devaluing even less. It also contributes to the supply of money. Counterbalancing measures are possible, but have usually been delayed so as not to hinder the inflow. While inflation continues to decline, the process is self-reinforcing and stops only if inflation goes down to the rate of devaluation. However, as we are speaking of instances when a slow or zero rate of devaluation has been used to pull down the rate of inflation, a positive difference between the rate of inflation and the rate of devaluation is rather essential to the strategy. As mentioned before, the successful stage of this strategy reinforces the possibility of devaluing even less as, owing to the capital inflows, the balance of payments may show positive results and allow the price-distortion stage to last longer. However, when clouds begin to appear, either because of a persistent deterioration in the trade balance or for any other reason, the continuation of the strategy is put in question. Capital flows, uneasy about a sharp devaluation, not only stop but are reversed. The balance of payments becomes critical. Not only is the trade balance negative but so also is the capital account. While the inflow allowed an excessively small devaluation, the outflow forces an excessively large one. In general terms, long-term equilibrium does not actually include any kind of capital flow, as does short-term equilibrium. The only contribution that the capital outflow makes to stability is in reducing the quantity of money. This helps to lower the rate of inflation but at the same time may contribute to a reduction in the level of economic activity.

The so-called paradoxes of money and of capital flow help to make good times even better, at the expense of making bad times even worse. They accentuate the sharpness of the reversal and by so doing accentuate the intensity of cycle. They are not long-term disequilibrating forces, but they make the movements around equilibrium rather sharp.

The conclusion, if any, is that it might be better to go about controlling inflation more quietly and slowly, trying to avoid excessive price distortions. This will take longer, but it may in fact prove much more effective to approach equilibrium in a less oscillatory way. The quicker and more distorting approach may be much more successful in the short term but it is bound to produce periodical outbursts, and create the cyclical inflationary pattern that has haunted Argentina during the last few decades.

INDEXATION, EFFICIENCY AND INFLATION

Some of the problems mentioned in the last two sections have prompted the development of ways to reduce the harm done by persistent inflations. Indexation, i.e. the more or less automatic readjustment of economic variables, has been one of these ways. This definition is purposely ambiguous so as to encompass the various approaches that have been thought up and put into practice in Argentina.

One of the criticisms raised when indexation was first suggested was that it implied 'a clear admission of the expectation of defeat by the one agency in the economy which has the power and responsibility for combating inflation' (Nevin, 1972). Although it is true that, if the authorities expected to bring down inflation in a relatively short while, they would not bother to tackle all the complexities and cost of indexation, it is debatable whether governments ever really have such a power. It seems that most governments have either lost it – if they ever had it – or are faced with a problem which goes far beyond the single issue of inflation. Governments and the monetary authorities come into the picture, but only as part of a much wider scenario.

The spread of inflation all over the world, particularly since the 1973 oil crisis, and, in Argentina, its extraordinary resilience against all kinds of policies, would suggest that a more realistic approach should start by recognising that inflation will not be brought under control in the short term and that some way of reducing its harmful effects might be desirable. Although the emphasis on the necessity of fighting inflation should not be diminished in any way, it is nevertheless true that the will to do so may be impaired by the knowledge that it might be made less harmful. This is one of the inevitable dilemmas so often found in economics.

It is here contended that, under the circumstances, a partial indexation has made and can make, particularly if it is consistently carried out, a big improvement in the management of the economy. It is, however, a poor substitute for a stable economy, although probably more easily attainable. We shall try to analyse the two fundamental aspects of indexation, i.e. its contribution to the general efficiency of the economy and its contribution to the reduction – or rekindling – of inflationary pressures.

These problems are in turn closely connected with three basic disturbances caused by inflation. The first is purely monetary, and is due to the fact that the cost of the non-interest-yielding money necessary for transaction purposes is increased by inflation. The second is due to the fact that inflations are quite variable and therefore very difficult to predict, while the third results from the fact that inflation proceeds at different rates in different sectors, altering relative prices for reasons not associated with structural changes. As we shall see, the three problems are made worse by increases in the rate of inflation and are differently affected by indexation.

Indexation and money

The effect of inflation on cash balances is equivalent to a tax. As a consequence there is a reduction in the amount of non-interest yielding money demanded by the public and an allegedly negative effect on production. Although it is difficult to follow some of the estimates that put the loss at around 1 per cent of GDP (Fernández and Hanson, 1976), there is no doubt that there is a social cost inherent in this flight from money. A more measurable effect is the implicit tax, which is basically equal to the erosion of the value of money holdings due to inflation. From 1973 to 1976, the tax on non-interest yielding money was equal to 4.1, 2.4, 3.6, 7 and 4.9 per cent of GNP; that it was not larger was owing to the reduction of M_1 from about 14 per cent in 1974 to about 6 per cent of GNP in 1976. These figures slightly overestimate the transfers, as interest on demand deposits (which are part of M_1) began to be made, even if in a minor way, during this period.

Inflation also affected interest-yielding money during the periods when real interest rates were negative. The implicit tax in those years was 2.4, 1.6, 2.2, 3.7 and 1.6 per cent of GNP. Indexed bonds were not affected by this problem and increased accordingly from nil in 1972 to 23 per cent of M_4 in 1976.

In the strained months after the 1975 outburst, adjustable national bonds – Valores Nacionales Ajustables (VNAs) – began to be used as a means of payment, and in Government circles some consideration was given to whether this trend should be encouraged. This was the nearest approach to indexed money; this will probably never come into being, as it is hardly a practical alternative.

On the other hand, indexation is particularly necessary in the case of the longer-term financial instruments (Bathia, 1974), as a lack of predictability makes long-term fixed interest rates rather meaningless. The alternative to indexation is a variable rate, i.e. a rate that changes during the life of the financial instrument. The problem remains that, if the nominal rate is fully paid throughout its lifetime, an unduly steep depreciation in value takes place; this is because nominal rates include both an element of compensation for inflation and a real rate. The solution which has been adopted in Argentina is that the proportion of the nominal rate equivalent to the expected inflationary rate is added to the capital value while the real interest part is paid out.

Indexation based on a general price index (and this, as we shall see, is not a necessary procedure) is very similar to a policy of variable nominal interest rates, particularly if partially capitalisable. Nevertheless, the erratic behaviour of real interest rates, which have ranged from -72 per cent in 1975 to $+36$ per cent in the fourth quarter of 1977, leaves a strong element of uncertainty when interest is variable. Indexation on a selective sectoral basis is, on the other hand, a very different matter, as we shall see when analysing relative price movements.

Indexation and the variability of the inflation rate

If the rate of inflation is relatively constant over long periods, inflation may become a predictable event, allowing a better adjustment of economic agents. Unfortunately, the higher the inflation, the more variable and less predictable will its rate become. This has been found in, among others, a study of eighteen Latin American countries from 1950 to 1969 (Fernández and Hanson, 1976). In that study it can be seen that the standard deviation of the rate of inflation increases almost proportionally to the rate of inflation, as indicated by the following functional relationship:

$$SD = 0.95 + 0.87P$$

where *SD* is the standard deviation of the rate of inflation and *P* is the average rate of inflation over the period 1950–69. (The value of the statistic *t* of the inflation coefficient is 8.0 while the coefficient is not significantly different from 1.) These conclusions are very similar to those reached by Logue and Willet (1975) for a group of forty-nine countries for the period 1948–70, as well as for the twelve Latin American countries included in the study. The higher inflations are, therefore, more harmful because their more intense variability (Fernández, 1980) means greater unpredictability, more difficult and less accurate economic decisions and a worse economic prformance.

Some of the ways in which predictable inflations can be tackled become impossible in these variable conditions. In the case of financial instruments, the variable-interest clause performs less well; it is necessary to shorten the intervals for readjusting the rate, as in the case of Argentina, down to six months, three months or even one month. Worse still, the risk that the rate may end by being highly positive increases, even if this is compensated for by the possibility of negative rates. The other strategy used in predictable inflations is to predetermine rates of increase at specified times. This has been done in the case of the prices of public services, of goods bought or sold and for wages, but it is impossible when inflation varies erratically. The problem is also particularly bad in the case of investment projects, which have long gestation periods and long delivery dates. In such conditions it soon becomes impossible to avoid readjusting according to some kind of index. We can safely say that indexation is more necessary the more variable and unpredictable inflations are. The problem then is to relate each particular case to the index used. This is a new subject which we discuss in the following sub-section.

While indexation performs a very useful role in improving the general level of efficiency of the economy, it does not make any signi-

ficant direct contribution to reducing the variability of the inflation
rate.

Indexation and relative prices

We now come to one of the most central problems of inflation:
namely, its disturbing effect on relative prices. The basic problem is
that relative price movements are the consequence of two distinct
phenomena. On the one hand we have a trend associated with deep-
rooted changes in the structure which should not be hindered; on the
other, we have the price oscillations which characterise high
inflations. As we have seen, the latter are by definition transitory
changes that rekindle the inflationary process. This is the area where
indexation can make its most important contribution, but equally do
the greatest harm, if it ends up creating a rigid economy which does
not allow short- and long-term economic adjustments.

One of the significant problems with which indexation is faced,
when adopted, is the choice of an initial relative price set which will be
in line with the long-term equilibrium set. This will rarely be achieved,
but in highly inflationary situations, characterised by intense oscillations, its achievement is even less likely. Indexation – if it is all-
encompassing – freezes relative prices; and, if they are set at non-
equilibrium values, these disequilibriums will be made permanent and
worse. Even if we initially have the adequate relative price set, it
should be allowed to change, as economic conditions also change, in a
structural way, i.e. with changes in technology, changes in supply and
demand conditions and even with long-term structural changes in the
relative power of the various oligopolistic groups. All these changes
have to be reflected in the price mechanism if the economy is to
maintain its ability to change and grow.

Even in the short term a fully indexed economy will have its
problems, as it will lose some of its equilibrating qualities. The fixity
of relative prices will not allow substitution effects, one of the
essential mechanisms for the absorption of economic disturbances. In
the case of the indexation of money (which even if unlikely throws
light on the general problem), indexed-cash holders will not suffer any
loss of income from the rise in prices, and will not – in the Pigou
fashion – reduce their demand for goods. In this case, and in most
others as well, the protection of a particular group contributes in the
short term to the resilience of inflation. However, this will be partly
(or even wholly) compensated for by the benefits of larger cash
holdings and of reduced pressures to move into other assets.

The reduction in the self-equilibrating qualities of the economy is at the root of Patinkin's (1965) and Baumol's (1966) arguments about the indeterminacy of the price level, although it has been pointed out that this depends on the specific ways in which the indexation of money is made (Auernheimer, 1979). The indeterminacy argument, however, is strengthened if full indexation is extended to the whole of the non-monetary sector. In such an extreme case a disturbance in one sector, if maintained, would have indefinite repercussions on the economy and create an indefinite rise in prices.

Bearing these problems in mind, it would seem sensible to think that indexation should aim at a reduction of relative price movements but should stop short of their complete elimination. This can be achieved by simply indexing those sectors of the economy which are more prone to react belligerently to price changes. Better still, it can be achieved by the use of mixed indexes which combine a general price index, such as for wholesale prices, with a sectoral one. If only the latter is used, the sector would be basically insulated from price variations whatever their source. The halfway solution tones down price oscillation while still allowing some relative price movements; it is to be hoped that at the same time it tones down the reactions of the sectors which have suffered. The view taken here is that partial sectoral indexation is an attractive policy (Gray, 1976) despite the fact that it has never been tried and there has been little demand for it. On the other hand, the demand for exclusively sectoral indexation has been rising in Argentina. The authorities' resistance to it has been based on its alleged complexity, on the possibility of 'arbitrage' and, in the case of bank loans, on the argument that banks should not get involved in problems of 'production'. These are not really damaging arguments but the excessive rigidity of the ensuing system is. The fact has been missed that one of the essential and unique opportunities opened up by indexation is the possibility of partial sectoral indexation. This special kind of indexation can not only contribute to the efficiency of the system but also reduce the self-perpetuating action of price oscillation on the inflationary process.

The experience of indexation

Although there had earlier been isolated cases of indexation, indexation as a policy was first announced in the middle of 1975, just after the price explosion, and was made the central strategy from August 1975 until January 1976, when it was partially abandoned. The most important area that was indexed, but in a non-automatic way – which may prompt some people to question whether it was indexation at all – was the rate of exchange. Previously, devaluations had taken place in discrete and substantial jumps (from 50 to 100 per cent in March and June 1975); after August, it proceeded in fortnightly intervals at from 3 to 5 per cent each time.

The basic idea was to maintain the real rate; this was deemed essential to balance the critical external situation. It was quite clear that this objective ran counter to the anti-inflationary strategy, which would have benefited (as in the past) from an increasingly overvalued rate of exchange – again a case of conflict between efficiency and short-term stabilisation. That it was not automatic was the consequence of an attempt to retain some degree of flexibility in case the real rate had to be changed in the future. The discretionary element maintained some uncertainty, which was considered rather desirable in order to discourage arbitrage. At the price of maintaining strong cost pressures, this exchange policy was instrumental in reversing the critical external trade situation by the first quarter of 1976.

The other important area which was indexed was wage determination. From October 1975, wages were to be readjusted every three months, and a special institute was to be set up to administer this policy. The idea was that, as the previous wage rise had been on average about 160 per cent, exceptions had been created, if not necessarily of similar increases, at least of increases of an extraordinary nature. It was assumed that a guaranteed real wage would mean lower nominal increases than those expected. Moreover, while the wage 'fight' had been responsible for the price explosion, it was felt that the real wage that had prevailed before and after the jump was not a fundamental cause of inflation. In fact real wages were less than 10 per cent above the 1968–9 level, a rather reasonable increase, particularly if rises in productivity were taken into account.

Indexation of wages faced two major hurdles. One was their increased variability. While the average rise was about 160 per cent, there were groups who had achieved less than 60 per cent and others whose wages had more than tripled. For many unions the central aim was not so much to have a general indexation of wages, something about which they had become rather sceptical, as to improve their own particular positions. An attempt to halve the differentials between gains made during the June outburst was strongly opposed by those who had done best. Some of the losers, such as the Luz y Fuerza union, succeeded in obtaining specific rises; this began a new round of pressures and of wage rises. This situation lasted until the new military government reduced the general wage level by a third and set relative wages back to the pre-June situation – an unfortunate example of the difficulties of achieving a consensus solution as opposed to one imposed from the outside.

It was much easier to agree on the basic level at which wages were to be indexed. The unions asked for the real wage level reached just after the June increases, but just before the price jump. The Government argued for a certain average, to which the unions surprisingly agreed. Although indexation was applied only twice, it can probably be said that it helped to tone down some of the wild expectations that had been created since the middle of the year. On the other hand, it did not help to tackle the inter-union differentials, which at the time were the most burning issue.

Prices of public services were also indexed, but in this case by a predetermined monthly (or bimonthly) percentage. This was a halfway solution; it did not preclude discrete changes over and above the automatic ones. In the case of Government purchases, indexation was more complete and more specific. It had previously been the practice of State companies to fix their suppliers' prices according to special formulae based on the suppliers' costs. The price of the exchange rate, of some significant raw materials and of wages were the usual variables. This was made even more complete by taking into consideration delays in payments.

In the case of agricultural products, prices in real terms were guaranteed up to harvest. Nothing was promised about prices for the following season, and this left a certain leeway for discretionary long-term real changes. This solution was reached after much heated internal controversy about the different degrees of rigidity and certainty of the various alternatives.

Indexation of taxes was not actually implemented, although a set of laws to that effect was sent to Congress by the end of 1975. These laws established that, for tax purposes, companies were to follow inflation-accounting practices; these were duly defined in line with what the local professional board had suggested on a voluntary basis (Mar del Plata convention of 1963). It made three basic corrections to traditional accounting, i.e. work in process was to be valued at replacement cost instead of by the previous LIFO system, amortisation was to take into account the increase in nominal values of the original investment, and the net debtor or creditor position was to be corrected by the effect of inflation on its real value. The first two corrections reduced profits and accordingly reduced taxes on profits, while the third, in the quite common case of companies having a net indebtedness, increased profits and taxes at times by very considerable amounts. The corrections were in line with the stock approach, and left aside the more sophisticated flow approach, which requires a notional idea of profitability under normal conditions (Scott, 1976).

Another important innovation included in the tax laws was that delays in the payment of taxes were to be indexed, eliminating a very important source of implicit subsidy. The indexation of financial contracts, already referred to, was the one case where there was more agreement as to the advisability of indexation; this was accordingly continued by the new military government. The most used indexed financial instrument was the adjustable national bond (VNA), adjusted to the industrial wholesale price index, with a yield of about 2 per cent per year in real terms. In 1973–4 the Government had a hesitant attitude, as VNAs were the subject of strong speculative movements; arbitrage operations had at times been quite profitable. After the middle of 1975 VNAs became an important part of monetary policy, as their issue was one of the few ways to mop up the purchasing power of the public. They eventually reached 24 per cent of the total money supply, giving rise to the M_4 concept. The policy of indexing bank loans and bank deposits was attempted, but never implemented (with the exceptions of very small deposits in the National Mortgage Bank). The idea was that a certain growing proportion of bank loans – even short-term loans – should be indexed, starting in February 1976. The real rates of interest were to be only marginally superior to that of VNAs. However, after the change of ministers in February this attempt was cancelled. The new military government went ahead with indexation, but at much higher rates. Deposits in State banks have yielded up to 6 per cent and those in private banks up to 15 per cent; the real rate for loans has been up to 50 per cent higher.

Indexation and the economic performance

At this stage it must be abundantly clear that the view advanced here is that the main role of indexation lies in its contribution to the maintenance of a minimum level of economic efficiency and not in its contribution to the toning down of inflation. The compatibility of these two objectives is much greater in the longer than in the shorter term. Indexation can work through the reduction of the effects of relative price changes, through the protection of some sectors and through the reduction of uncertainty.

As far as relative prices are concerned, the main effect of indexation if made on a sectoral basis is to diminish the pernicious consequences of relative price changes. The maintenance of a minimum level of efficiency requires that the set of relative prices should be maintained within a certain range, avoiding transitory price movements and costly transfers of resources which are unnecessary from a long-term 'structural' point of view. But the attempt to reduce the range and effects of certain long-term movements should not go too far, in order to avoid an excessive degree of economic rigidity. There is an optimum degree of ease of price variation, which is indeed not easy to attain. To the extent that indexation does give a certain protection to various groups, it may make it quite clear that struggles between groups are not worthwhile and diminish the belligerent attitude of those who in a non-indexed world have to fight for their survival.

At the same time indexation will hinder those stabilisation plans which are based on drastic reductions of the price of some good or factor. These stabilisation plans are, under immediate pressures from specific lobbies, quite tempting; unfortunately, they have proved transitory and have given rise to serious imbalances which have caused the reversal of the cycle. During their successful stage they are indeed hindered by indexation; but, on the other hand, an indexed economy is probably less prone to the inflationary cycles which have typified the Argentine experience.

The effect of indexation on expectations is ambiguous and will depend on previous expectations. As mentioned earlier, expectations may be of something much worse than actually occurs as a result of indexation. After so many years of rapid inflation and so many dangerous situations for the contending groups, the speed at which producers and consumers react ('velocity of readjustment' we have called it) has become astonishing. Readjustments are made, or fought for, immediately and strongly, in a mood near to despair; this in turn feeds back into the inflationary process. Under these conditions indexation may not worsen an already bad situation. If, on the other hand, inflation is recent or moderate and reactions are still slow, indexation may speed up the readjustment process and increase inflation; this is the main argument of those opposing indexation in the low-inflation countries (Radcliffe Committee, 1959).

To reiterate, our basic conclusion is that the case for indexation is stronger in the long term than in the short, and that it is better at maintaining a minimum level of efficiency than at toning down the inflationary process.

APPENDIX: ARGENTINA'S INFLATIONARY CYCLES, 1946-76

In this chapter the more general statements and interpretations concerning the inflationary cycles have been based on the behaviour of prices over a thirty-year period, from 1946 to 1976. It may be worth undertaking a brief review of the six particular price cycles which can be identified, and sharing with the reader some of the experiences which have given rise to our more general interpretations. It is better to identify these cycles simply by their peak years, as these are a bit clearer and less arbitrary than any starting or finishing dates. Cycles are continuous processes and any particularisation or splitting is artificial and can only be justified as a descriptive convenience. The peak years were 1951, 1959, 1962, 1965-6, 1972 and 1975-6.

An attempt will be made to analyse the continuities and the changes in policies which took place, sometimes independently of the changes in governments. As we shall see, policies are begun by one government and continued by the next, despite the usual disclaimers about 'absolutely new courses'. At the same time we shall see how drastic reversals sometimes took place within the same government, at times disguised as if nothing new had taken place. Our review will not be excessively detailed and will only try to highlight those aspects more relevant to our specific problem.

The 1951 cycle

The inflation caused by the Second World War had already subsided by 1947, when the impact of the policies of the first Peronist government began to be felt. These were strongly distributionist, transferring more than 10 per cent of GNP to labour, and strongly expansionist, producing a short-lived boom which culminated in an inflationary peak in 1951 of about 50 per cent. Despite a brief improvement in the terms of trade, typical of the post-war period, a deficit in the current account developed. Reserves were reduced from $1686 million in 1946 to $173 million in 1952, despite rather early devaluations in 1949-51. Before 1951 there was no significant attempt to reduce inflation. The significantly low relative prices were the agricultural ones, low because of the distributionist policies. In 1951 that was the only restraining element, but it was soon joined by the exchange rate, which remained basically fixed. After 1952 an explicit anti-inflationary policy was instituted, based on the one hand on fixed multiple exchanges and on the other on an elaborate but rather efficient system of price controls. Many shortages appeared, although these were less intense than might have been expected.

The reduction in imports as a result of the internal recession and a new improvement in the terms of trade allowed an improvement in the external situation. The rate of inflation declined for three successive years, building up a good degree of repressed inflation. This could be seen by the shortages and by the fact that the unofficial exchange rate was triple the official rate. However, this might exaggerate the importance of price repression, as in 1954–5 the political troubles which culminated in the overthrow of the Government began to appear, giving rise to speculative movements against the peso.

The 1959 cycle

When the new military government came in, in 1955, it vehemently denounced the inherited economic situation. As a matter of fact it was not really too bad; the worst aspect was the strongly repressed inflation, repressed but at a rather low level. The new set of policies loosened most of the repressed and distorted prices, wiping out price controls, reducing exchange controls and devaluing in real terms. The internal prices of agricultural goods improved relative to industrial prices. Accordingly prices picked up in the following three years at increasing rates.

The terms of trade continued to deteriorate and trade deficits began to pile up. The new civilian government of 1958 drastically increased the liberalisation policy. This was not a departure from the previous policy, as it was represented at the time, but an intensification of the same line. Actually, both policies had the support of the IMF (informally or formally). Devaluation, which had already been substantial, was increased. In 1959 the exchange rate was doubled in two steps. Internal prices also doubled, cancelling most but not all of the intended effects. Agricultural prices remained unchanged in real terms, while devaluation in real terms was after a while not more than 5 per cent. Wages, however, ended up lower by 27 per cent in real terms, partly as a consequence of the changed relative oligopolistic situations. This was clearly a 'loosening up' stage, i.e. a stage when prices were left free to settle at new and presumably equilibrium levels.

The upheaval of the year affected the level of economic activity and an important, but short-lived, recession took place (−6.5 per cent). In this instance there was a negative relationship between the inflation and the income cycle. Some of the benefits of the rebalancing of relative prices were noticeable in the following three years. Again, the previous outburst had probably involved a certain overpricing, and this helped the next stage, when a fixed exchange rate was in operation. After the previous doubling of prices, in 1960 they were practically constant. A buoyant situation developed; income and investment went up. Prices started to rise as well, pulled by demand. This gave rise to a certain (but not substantial) overvaluation, compounded by a deterioration in the terms of trade (particularly in 1961), contributing to an increasingly negative trade balance. Stability seemed in doubt and a run on the exchanges took place, contributing to a substantial loss in reserves. Although the fixity of the exchanges in the face of increasing inflation and the bad terms of trade were beginning to create an unsustainable situation, it is clear that the political events of 1962 accelerated and magnified the economic problems and shortened the end of this cycle.

The 1962 cycle

The new government of 1962 found itself in the midst of destabilising speculation in the exchanges, with the probability of having to face an even greater run as a consequence of a military coup and the ensuing open internal disagreements. Its first act was an important devaluation, moving the exchange rate from 80 to 120 pesos to the dollar. It was greater than expected and took the business community by surprise. Prices jumped, but not quite to the same extent, allowing for a devaluation in the real rate of about 20 per cent. A negative rate of growth followed, both in 1962 and in 1963. The price increases subsided somewhat, less so than in the previous period, as this time there had not been any previous overpricing. Nevertheless, the increases in prices again eroded the real rate of exchange. Fortunately the terms of trade improved, owing to a short decline in the price of imports. This is one of the few instances when an improvement in the terms of trade gave rise to deflationary pressures. (This is just the opposite of what happens when export prices increase or, even worse, when both export and import prices increase, as in 1972.) The trade balance improved substantially, a situation that was to last for more than five years and become the basis of one of the more prolonged 'good times' in recent Argentina. In the downward stage of this inflationary cycle there were less intense price distortions than in previous cycles, not to mention later ones. It merged quite well with the policies of the new government elected in 1963, despite the apparent and proclaimed differences. In fact in 1964 inflation was still lower, while the terms of trade, the trade balance and the growth rate improved – certainly an auspicious beginning.

The 1965–6 cycle

This was a quite exceptionally smooth cycle compared with the others. From 1964 to 1970 the country evolved in a relatively less troublesome way, to the point of creating expectations that the Argentine economy had overcome its stop–go character. Inflation went up during the following year but in a moderate way (28 per cent). It came down during each of the three following years, only to go up, but not by very much, during the next (7 per cent in 1969). It really picked up again in 1970.

The period was characterised by two apparently opposed policies. That of the Radicals was, apparently, more distributionist, more nationalist, less fiscally oriented and less inclined to monetarism. What is undisputed is that they had more restrictions on the foreign exchanges, and started a timid crawling peg. The other policy, launched by the military government in 1967, was supposedly the opposite. In fact, from many significant points of view, there was no substantial dividing line between the two. One could even say that Krieger Vasena's success was to a great extent owing to the previous policies and to the not too distorted set of relative prices he inherited. It was also owing to his intelligent way of taking advantage of and continuing some of the previous policies, despite appearing to act very differently. This is not conventional opinion, but it is probably more in line with what really happened. One of the essential threads connecting both governments, curiously enough, was the exchange-rate policy. The Radicals pursued for the first time in Argentine history a kind of limited crawling peg, which allowed a certain over-valuation of the currency but of no more than 10 per cent. This policy was continued by Krieger Vasena. His devaluation of about 30 per cent was accompanied by an *ad valorem* tax on exports which left only a very small (2 per cent) net advantage to exporters. Thereafter this tax was reduced, bit by bit, which in fact meant for exporters a continuation of the previous crawl. A similar development took place with imports, where the impact of devaluation was partially compensated for by a reduction in tariffs; there were for a while excessive tariffs, but these were not fully used.

Of course, there were many and important differences between the two administrations. The biggest novelty was probably the ability to reduce the drastically inflationary expectations which – according to the new authorities – were the basic source of the inflationary process. This manipulation of expectations was probably overdone and was only possible because of the impact created by the emergence of the new military government, apparently strong and with a good chance of staying in power for a long while. The new policies were helped by several years of good (though diminishing) terms of trade, and harmed by an overvaluation of the exchange rate and by the downward movement of the characteristic cattle cycle. This created a disproportionate opposition from the cattle producers, and they were joined by the rest of the agricultural sector, which was not faring too well either. If we take the period as a whole, from 1963–4 up to 1969–70, one would say that the two principal distortions were cattle prices and expectations of future prices, and that these were probably less severe than in previous and later programmes. What really broke the programme were the political problems and the conflicts among the military, which had an adverse effect on expectations.

The 1972 cycle

While inflationary expectations had previously played a positive role, from 1971 onwards this was reversed. Before they had helped to increase the demand for monetary assets; now they contributed to the flight from money. Prices picked up. Devaluations were tried again and, in view of the deterioration of the trade balance, at an ever-increasing pace, very much forced by the IMF. Destabilising speculation appeared on the exchanges. Export prices began to increase and this helped agricultural prices, particularly for cattle. While 1971 was admittedly a bad year, measures taken in 1972 were a bit excessive. Of course, this is easily said after the event.

By the end of 1972 it was clear that the external situation had suddenly become favourable. Prices of exports were good, contributing to an improvement in the trade balance and in inflationary pressures. However, the price jump was made worse owing to the wild expectations that began to develop as soon as it was realised that a new Peronist government was about to be elected. There were a number of precautionary price increases, and these involved overpricing. The new government found itself in an ideal situation to impose some kind of ceiling. The price freeze served this purpose well, helped by the initial strong image of the new government. Expectations were cut, evidenced by among other things, the fall in the black-market rate. But, while this policy was justified for a short while, it continued for an abnormally long time in a very rigid fashion and with contradictory income and monetary policies. All this has already been fully analysed. Suffice it to say that from June 1973 until the end of the year the economy moved into a 'repressed' stage, this time through price controls and a fixed exchange rate. The exchange rate remained fixed despite an extraordinary jump in the terms of trade through both high import and even higher export prices. The pretence of a zero inflation rate in the midst of the international oil crisis was a bit unrealistic.

The 1975–6 cycle

In 1974 the terms of trade moved against the country by nearly a third through the particularly unfortunate combination of increased export and import prices. This was unfortunate because on the one hand it intensified important inflationary pressures, and on the other it created a huge trade deficit in the second half of 1974. Price distortion became quite serious, although the degree of overvaluation (about 20 per cent) seems today, when viewed in perspective, a bit less severe than it seemed at the time to its critics (and to the author as well).

In this instance the 'price rebalancing' stage was more abrupt than ever. It took the form of two devaluations during the first half of 1975. The second in particular, coupled with a particularly strained situation within the ruling coalition, produced the biggest price explosion ever known in Argentina. There is no need to describe again what has been one of the special subjects of this book. It is enough to say that the big reversal in the external situation can be traced to the policies of mid-1975. As had happened in the past, the extremely critical situation forced in the short run a rather exaggerated devaluation, which was maintained by a crawling peg until the end of the year. These policies caused a current-account surplus as early as the first quarter of 1976. This was thus another price-loosening stage. Although we do not venture beyond 1976 in most of this work, it is worth looking a little further. Initially the greatest change was a drastic reduction in wages, approximately by a third. What had been a timid liberalisation policy now became clear-cut and aggressive. However, the continuation of inflation at rates of about 150 per cent per year induced the Government once more to rely on a persistent policy of overvaluing the exchange rate, which started another price-repression stage. This time there was an explicit attempt to make the price distortion stick – that is, to move the economy to a different set of relative prices. Whether this will be a new equilibrium or a new distorted set will depend on whether a structural change takes place or not.

BIBLIOGRAPHY

Arriazu, R. (1979) *Movimientos internacionales de capitales,* Cuadernos de la CEPAL (Santiago de Chile).
Arriazu, R. (1980) 'Elección de un sistema cambiario en inflación: ventajas y desventajas de la indexación' (Buenos Aires: BCRA, mimeo).
Auernheimer, L. (1979) 'The Indexation of Money' (University of Texas at Austin, mimeo).
Baliño, T. (1977) *La demanda de dinero y sus componentes en la Argentina. Estimaciones anuales 1935–69,* Serie de Estudios Técnicos (Buenos Aires: CEMYB, BCRA).
Bathia, K. (1974) *Index Linking of Financial Contracts: A Survey of the State of the Arts,* Bank Staff Working Paper no. 192 (Washington, DC: IBRD).
Baumol, W. J. (1966) 'The Escalated Economy and the Stimulating Effects of Inflation', *Revista internazionale di scienze economiche e commerciale* (Feb).
Blejer, M. and Leiderman, L. (1979) *Inflation and Relative Price Variability in the Open Economy,* Documento de Trabajo (Buenos Aires: CIE, Instituto Torcuato di Tella); and forthcoming in *Review of Economics and Statistics.*
Brodersohn, M. (1977) *Conflictos entre los objetivos de la política económica de corto plazo,* Documento de Trabajo no. 77 (Buenos Aires: CIE, Instituto Torcuato di Tella).
Canavese, A. (1977) 'Sobre inflación estructural, dinero pasivo e indexación: reflexiones y precisiones sobre un trabajo de de Pablo', *Desarrollo Económico,* no. 67 (Sep–Dec).
Díaz Alejandro, C. (1970) *Essays on the Economic History of the Argentine Republic* (Cambridge, Mass.).
Fernández, R. (1980) *Inflation and Relative Price Uncertainty* (Buenos Aires: CEMA).
Fernández, R. and Hanson, J. (1976) 'El rol de la indexación en los procesos inflacionarios de América Latina', *Desarrollo Económico,* no. 63 (Oct–Dec).
Friedman, M. (1973) 'Monetary Correction', in Giersch, H. (ed.), *Essays on Inflation and Indexation.*
Gaba, E. (1977) 'Indexación y sistema financiero', *Revista argentina de finanzas* (June).

Giersch, H. (ed.) (1973) *Essays on Inflation and Indexation* (Washington, DC: American Enterprise Institute).

Gray, J. (1976) 'Wage Indexation: a Macro-economic Approach', *Journal of Monetary Economics* (Jan).

Grinblat, L. (1978) 'Inflación y precios relativos' (University of Tucumán, mimeo).

Guisarri, A. (1980) *Producto, empleo y precios en Argentina 1961–78* (Buenos Aires: CIE, Instituto Torcuato di Tella).

Heyman, D. (1980) *Las fluctuaciones de la industria manufacturera argentina 1950–78*, Cuadernos de la CEPAL (Santiago de Chile).

Hirsch, F. and Goldthorpe, J. H. (1978) *Political Economy of Inflation* (London).

Liesner, T. and King, M. (eds) (1975) *Indexation for Inflation* (London).

Logue, D. and Willet, T. (1975) 'A Note on the Variability of Inflation, its Measurement and Cause', Office of the Assistant Secretary for International Affairs, Research Discussion Paper (Washington, DC: US Treasury).

Nevin, E. (1972) *Public Debt and Economic Development* (Dublin: Economic Research Institute).

Olivera, J. (1964) *On Structural Inflation and Latin American Structuralism*, Oxford Economic Papers (Nov).

Olivera, J. (1967) 'Money Prices and Fiscal Lags: a Note on the Dynamics of Inflation', *Banca Nazionale del Lavoro Quarterly Review* (Sep).

Parks, R. W. (1978) 'Inflation and Relative Price Variability', *Journal of Political Economy* (Feb).

Patinkin, D. (1965) *Money, Interest and Prices* (New York).

Pou, P. (1979) *Variabilidad de la tasa de inflación, riesgo y la demanda por dinero*, Ensayos Económicos, BCRA (Buenos Aires).

Radcliffe Committee (1959) *Memoranda of Evidence*, vol. 3, and Minutes and Report (London).

Salama, E. (1978) *Demanda de dinero y formación de expectativas: Algunos resultados empíricos*, Serie de Estudios Técnicos, no. 32 (Buenos Aires: CEMYB, BCRA).

Scott, M. (1976) 'Some Economic Principles of Accounting: a Constructive View of the Sandilands Report' (Oxford, mimeo).

di Tella, G. (1979) 'Price Oscillation, Oligopolistic Behaviour and Inflation: the Argentine Case', *World Development*, vol. 7, no. 11–12.

8 Political Epilogue

This story is now coming to an end. It has been a hectic and a sorry one. Some of its characteristics are indeed unique, in particular the intensity of its conflicts; others are not so unusual, particularly if viewed against the background of the economic and political instability which has haunted Argentina over a period of more than fifty years. One should not forget that since the Second World War the country has experienced four civilian governments and five military interventions and has had, in all, ten appointed and seven elected presidents, of whom only one finished his constitutional term.

It would seem that hectic and sorry times have not been the privilege of any one period.

Argentina is one of the few countries in Latin America which has attempted a mass democracy with full participation, a fact that may be – paradoxically – at the root of the conflict-ridden political and economic history of the last fifty years. At times one wonders whether this troubled evolution is not the more likely one, and that the real exceptions are the USA and the Western European countries (and very few others) who have been able to establish democratic electoral regimes in conditions of political stability, developing 'well behaved' left-of-centre parties and a whole set of accepted and legitimate formal and informal bounds which have allowed consensual and moderate results. After all, it should not come as a surprise that such an extraordinary idea as democratic representation should produce a collision with established interests. The economic power structure is inevitably in tension with the political power structure if the latter is democratic. How this tension can be resolved without pronounced political instability is particularly problematic. The optimism of the 1960s on the prospects of development bringing about democracy has diminished (O'Donnell, 1973). Old questions about the 'governability of democracy' and about the threats to it 'from the internal dynamics of democracy itself' are coming back again (Crozier et al., 1975). A conflict between democracy and stability, between consensus and growth, unfortunately seems less strange now than it used to be.

The developed countries have, in the past, had their share of turmoil, but seldom has it been of the kind that topples governments. This may have been partly owing to the early beginnings and the slow pace of their democratisation.

Argentina, a late developer, adopted full democratic procedures rather suddenly in 1916, reaching overnight one of the highest levels of electoral participation known at that time. It has been struggling ever since to make the system work. The political stability which the country had enjoyed from the end of the last century was lost in the 1930s, while the economic stability, which proved to be more resilient, was lost some time during the 1940s and 1950s. This instability should not hide Argentina's achievements. It has attained an intermediate level of per capita income of US$2700, while its rate of economic growth has not been negligible, averaging 3.8 per cent per year since 1950, and slightly over 2 per cent on a per capita basis. The puzzle is not why the economy has not grown at the higher rate of, say, Brazil, but rather how it is that it has done so well under extraordinarily unstable political circumstances.

Despite the instability, a 'system' of sorts has been developed, which should not be disguised by the continuous formal interruptions of the political process. The system has worked in such a way as to allow Argentina to see all its major groups take their turn in power, to the point where one of the tacit political beliefs is that no government has the chance of lasting for long. This has not, however, prevented the political climate from becoming very intolerant at times. The ruling group has usually exercised power in a rather immoderate way to the exclusion of opposing groups, although it is fair to say that the middle-of-the-road Radical governments have been less prone to this behaviour. The essence of the underlying 'system' is that changes of government, though brought about in a hectic way, rather than power-sharing, have been used to handle diversity and to accommodate the various social groups. Argentina has even developed something like a three-party system, each one attaining power by different means. Since the war the labour-based party has won all the relatively free elections, in 1946, 1952 and 1973 (March and September), while the parties with middle-class support were successful in the two restricted elections of 1958 and 1963, when the labour-based party was banned. The conservative groups have in their turn taken power three times, in 1955, 1966 and 1976, always through military interventions.

Elections have been tried over and over again, as if Argentines were great believers in the electoral process, but the results have then been deemed unacceptable by a substantial part of the power structure. In theory, democratic values have not been questioned, and alternative political systems have been flatly rejected. *De facto* violations of democratic procedure have been accepted on the assumption that they are unfortunate necessities, presumably temporary in nature. Since 1955, the peculiar political dilemma has been that the Peronist alliance has been the sure winner of any electoral contest, but it was not considered capable of behaving in a democratic and tolerant way while in power. This was the situation which placed Argentina 'in a blind alley' (Halperín, 1964); democracy was defined in such a way that it required the exclusion of the majority. No wonder that Peronists were not really convinced of the democratic ideals of their opponents.

While the Peronists' own performance in 1946–55 might have justified apprehensions about them, the behaviour of the allegedly democratic groups from 1955 to 1976 in permanently interfering in the electoral process gave rise to even worse apprehensions about their democratic ideals, at least among the Peronist militants. Oddly enough, the anti-Peronist alliance ostensibly favoured principles which meant its electoral doom, while Peronism was much more hesitant in its devotion to democracy, despite the fact that its principles and their practice were the basis of its legitimacy. The reason for the allegiance of the established sectors to liberal democratic ideals may be connected with the fact that they make up a set of familiar values upon which alliances can be based. A departure from them has a dangerous ring, suggesting unpredictable and unknown consequences. Over and above their objective content, these democratic values have a symbolic function and serve as a rallying cry. Opposition to these values, on the other hand, seems to have an anti-establishment ring, and in its turn serves as a rallying cry for those who want 'change'.

However, certain modifications took place. Anti-Peronist attitudes became more openly critical of democratic values and procedures, as in the Onganía episode. On the other hand, it is clear that the Peronist regime from 1973 to 1976 was more tolerant, particularly with the opposition, and that a 'conciliatory and pluralistic attitude (could) be seen in the general conduct of the government' (*La Nación*, 29 July 1973), an attitude that did not, however, extend to 'cultural matters' or to the resolution of internal feuds.

The intense chaos that was so characteristic of this period warrants much consideration. To an extent it was the consequence of a combination of some new factors, such as armed subversion and policy reversals, and some old, such as the too-broad Government alliance, the high degree of mobilisation and the established sectors' stubborn opposition to change.

Subversion undermined civilian rule. Each new act of violence performed by the guerrillas strengthened the hardliners – first among the Government, giving rise to the temporary ascendancy of the López Rega faction, and later helping to convince the military that the nation's problems could be properly tackled only if they took full command of the situation. Subversion may succeed if it takes advantage of the initial surprise and unpreparedness of a society which has not previously known such a threat. If it does not succeed in the very short term, it will give rise to repression, the normal reaction of any society subject to a threat of this seriousness. Repression may be more or less humane, more or less legal, but repressive it will be. At this juncture – at least, this is how it happened in Argentina – demands to tackle the deeper-rooted reasons for subversion, even assuming that they are known, lose relevance. For this would require long-term efforts, while public tranquillity is a short-term objective. The protests of the guerrilla groups about the mounting of a campaign of repression seem therefore rather hollow; it is precisely the reaction that could be expected.

The Montoneros' strategy was even more puzzling, as their assumption was that their acts would make them more popular with the masses and would intimidate the Government, which, confused and afraid, would yield power in the midst of a popular uprising. The Marxist-oriented ERP had a more likely scenario, at least in the initial stages. It purported to want to topple the democratically elected government and to induce the military to come to the forefront, thus forcing a harsh repression which would enhance the 'contradictions of the system' and expose its 'true face'; the end would be a popular uprising and a precipitation of the revolutionary process. But this strange and messianic reasoning had more the flavour of a dogmatic creed than of any reasonable estimate of a possible social evolution. The first part of the scenario indeed took place in Argentina, Uruguay and Chile; however, the 'socialist' horizon does not seem any nearer, to say the least.

Since its appearance in the late 1960s and up to 1976, all the various governments, military and civilian, have failed to solve the guerrilla problem. In the case of Argentina, the civilian parliamentary system was put under a terrible strain. To face such a threat in a determined, but legal and sober way is an absolute must, but it is certainly not easy. As one of the theoreticians of counter-insurgency has put it, 'terrorism is such a virulent poison [because] the cure can damage society as much as the disease can' (Clutterbuck, 1975). The acts of violence, purposely spectacular, produced a degree of fear and excitement greater than their real danger. In such a psychological climate, parliamentary and legal procedures were deemed to be a serious hindrance to wiping out the guerrillas. Expediency became the overwhelming criterion and a 'different' government and a different political system were looked upon as a solution as if the system, as such, had been responsible for the problem.

The role of subversion changed during the Peronist period. Before 1973, the fact that the Government was illegitimate gave the impression that subversion would lose its *raison d'être* if a democratic government could be elected. It is clear that, in this first stage, the subversives contributed to the return of a democratically elected government. It was to be expected that after the elections either they would lay down their arms or an open confrontation would take place. What was surprising was their apparent disappointment at the policies of the Peronist government. From then on, the situation worsened. It has to be said that no government, of the right or the left, unless it was in the process of dissolution, could have tolerated organisations partly legal, partly illegal, such as the Montonero youth groups and the PPA. In this second stage, then, subversion was instrumental in the ascent of the López Rega faction, in the hardening of the opposition to the Government, which was accused of being too lenient, and finally in the military takeover.

Subversion alone was not the only significant element in bringing democracy to an end. The alliance on which the Government was based was indeed too wide and loose. This is an intrinsic characteristic of populist groupings, aggravated in this case by the wide appeal attained by a charismatic leader during his long exile.

The three significant changes in policies which broke up the internal relations within the original group created an abnormal degree of disorganisation. The initial left-wing stage shocked the established groups and quite a few of the not so established. For the first time in the history of the country, it seemed that a radicalisation of policies was possible. Although this was drastically corrected by Perón, he was also deemed responsible for the experiment's having taken place at all. This swing, even after it was corrected, was very costly. It undermined confidence in the whole movement and left many blemishes behind. The only more or less 'normal' period was when the

Government was headed by Perón himself – 'normal' in the sense that the Government had authority and that the alliances on which it was based and the opposition which it aroused were the ones that could be expected. The criticism directed against the incoherencies of this stage certainly have some basis. Peronism was as usual trying to appeal to too wide an audience. But to say that the Government was in an unsustainable situation in mid-1974 is to go too far. Some rebalancing was necessary. The segregation of the youth groups simplified the Government's strategy, and a certain change in economic policies was bound to come in any case. One has only to remember the changes that took place in the middle of Perón's first period of government to realise that something similar was quite probable. This was not, however, what happened. The movement towards the right attempted by Isabel and López Rega was even more shattering than the initial left turn, as it split the Peronist alliance right down the middle. The line was drawn between the union-based majority and the President, creating a profound crisis both within the leadership and among the rank and file. It was successfully resisted, but this resistance created the chaotic finale. There was a contest for authority, in which a stalemate created a vacuum of power.

It has to be pointed out that the way the majority of the alliance was able to reject the left-wing assault, and later on the right-wing assault as well, is evidence of its clear-cut boundaries and its strong tendency towards the middle of the road. These boundaries were to a great extent the consequence of the trade-union basis of the alliance; this is what gave it a certain anchorage in the middle of the political spectrum. The impression that some people got that Peronism was 'capable of anything' was not really true; on the contrary, these reactions showed the wide but limited range of what it was able to do. The fact that the alliance was prone to these opportunistic swings was in itself a serious structural weakness. The way it reacted, on the other hand, showed its strength. Unfortunately, this strength was not accompanied by an ability to put out a disciplined effort, and this gave rise to an unnecessarily violent opposition which finally endangered its success.

The death of Perón was certainly an important factor in the ensuing problems, as it meant a reduction in the arbitrating capacity of the presidency, but initially the result was less noticeable than expected. What reduced the authority of the President to its lowest level was the head-on confrontation with the unions brought about by the surprising swing to the right and the attempt to impose policies which were quite contradictory to the social and political base of the Government coalition. The chaotic end was not the consequence of a government running adrift under an incompetent leadership – though this may have also been the case – but the consequence of the attempt to impose a very clear-cut right-wing programme with Francoist overtones on a mildly left-of-centre coalition based on the trade unions. This confrontation is what lies behind the extraordinary price explosion of 1975, and is at the root of the chaotic climate of the end.

When the defeat of the President's policies pushed the unions to the forefront, their unrestrained behaviour added fuel to an anarchic situation, undermining the attempt of the middle-of-the-road groups to return to a middle course. Reform, even though it may be intrinsically moderate, requires a great degree of firmness from a government, not only in dealing with opposition groups, but also in dealing with its own base of support. This strength is not easy to muster when, as in this case, the reformist group is a rather loose and undisciplined alliance. Part of this lack of discipline was inherent in the popular coalition, but a good part was owing to the shattering consequences of the assaults from the left and right wings referred to earlier.

Another of the unsettling factors of this period, and one that frightened the establishment, was the high degree of popular mobilisation. This developed at the very end of the Lanusse period and picked up during the electoral campaign, when it soon reached one of its highest levels. It continued to be very high until the return of Perón, abating thereafter, only to revive again on a quite different basis in 1975, when the workers mobilised against the Government during the mid-year upheaval. The initial mobilisation was partly organised by the youth and by the Montonero groups, but it also had a very important element of spontaneity. It was an explosion of pent-up demands in which outbursts of festivity, wild dreams, diffuse aspirations and sheer recklessness were mixed. The streets became one of the main centres of political developments. Violence, either actual or potential, was an important element; even the way in which violence was described tinted it with a kind of redeeming quality. As was perceptively said, 'peace is for them disturbing, they see it as a kind of corruption . . . they [prefer to] live dangerously' (*Mayoría*, 30 June 1973).

Peronism tried to give the impression that it was the only channel for these rampant forces, and that it would be able to keep some kind of control over them. This was the great risk taken by the military and by the Lanusse government. They were over-optimistic, however, about the extent to which the new mood of violence could be contained. A collision was bound to take place. When it did so it was extremely intense, culminating in the public rupture between Perón and the Peronist Youth at the rally of 1 May 1974. Probably that was the day when the Lanusse strategy was in the main vindicated, as from then on the guerrilla movements were fully isolated from the main body, not only of the country, but of the popular forces as well. One should imagine an alternative scenario in which Perón would have died in exile maintaining an ambiguous but a good relationship with the guerrilla forces, with an undemocratic government in power in Argentina.

The mobilisation process described here had very little, if any, workers' participation. The impression was that the youth group was the only one to retain the traditional mobilising capacity of Peronism. The union leaders were accused of having become 'bureaucrats and bourgeois' and of having lost their former fervour. What is true is that they did not have the same illusions as the youth had. They were at this stage clearly part of the system and behaved much more as accepted members of it. They made an effort, however, to compete with the youth, but what to the youth came easily to them came only with effort. After the May confrontation theirs became the sole responsibility for mobilisation and they had to double their efforts to produce the crowds, such as those at the rally of 12 June 1974, the last before the death of Perón.

However, this cannot be described as a part of the period of mobilisation; these rallies were highly artificial and had to be arranged by the union leaders more than is usual in 'spontaneous' mobilisations. In 1975, on the other hand, when the President tried to crush the union leadership and make a sharp turn to the right, the unions were quite easily able to mobilise large crowds to fight for their rights. The downfalls of López Rega and Rodrigo were partly the consequence of these mobilisations, in which numbers of workers abandoned their workplaces and gathered in a very menacing public rally in the Plaza de Mayo. Thus the capacity to mobilise the rank and file was still there, but restricted to a few practical issues of direct concern to workers.

The high tension of the period was also owing to the extraordinarily violent reactions against some of the distributionist and mildly nationalistic measures taken by the Government and against the access that new groups were given to positions of power. Some would be tempted to attribute these reactions to the failings of the Govern-

ment and to the particular ways in which some of the measures were
carried out. It is not easy, and may not be very useful, to try to
imagine the reaction to the attempted changes had they been made in a
more orderly and moderate way, even allowing for the less than
'good' behaviour of most new groups. At the risk of putting forward
one more unsubstantiated opinion, it may be, however, that the established groups were also very 'ill behaved'. This can be seen in their
intolerant attitude to anything that would have meant sharing power
with the new groups or allowing any moderate measures that would
have diminished their share of the national income. If one thinks that
during the 1930s the country was torn apart for not allowing the
Radicals under Alvear to contest elections, and that both the right-of-
centre government of Frondizi and the extremely moderate middle-
class government of Illia were deposed, one may become sceptical of
the willingness of the established groups to yield and negotiate. One
may reach the unfortunate conclusion that Argentina is basically an
intolerant society, where power, once it is grabbed and by any group,
is exercised immoderately, no matter what the group's position in
society, its tradition or its ideological shade. Such a view might offer
more significant, but probably gloomier, avenues to explore.

Whether Peronism had an insufficiently reformist character is a
question that has been heatedly discussed. It has been criticised for
being too tame, for lacking reforming zeal, for not having dared 'to
jump out of the capitalist system' (O'Donnell, 1976), implying that
things would have been in some unexplained way better if such a
'jump' had taken place. More specifically, it has been criticised for
having 'never set itself the task of going beyond the limits of a mixed
economy ... leaving practically intact the pre-existing pattern of
ownership' (Ferrer, 1977). Here the impression is given that non-
reformist regimes are intrinsically non-viable, and that a more
reformist and more radical version of Peronism would have been
more viable. This pair of propositions is not clearly substantiated by
any set of known facts, no matter how unfortunate this might be. It
does not really seem that these were really the problems at stake. What
was at issue was simply the possibility of a labour-based government,
not dedicated to any structural changes – and by this is meant changes
in ownership, land reform, workers' management, and so on – but
bent on improving economic and political distribution, in itself a most
challenging proposition capable of stirring heated controversies. If a
distributionist objective is in itself sufficient to justify a reformist
label, then Peronism can easily qualify, but, if a structural objective is

required, it certainly does not. To suggest that Peronism could, or should, have attempted reform in the structural sense is not realistic given its social base and the social context of the country. It would have been a sure way towards a more abrupt end, arousing much more violent opposition on a wider front. With limited objectives, the going was rough enough; Peronism had enough problems as it was. These criticisms and suggestions miss the crucial point that the 'mere' distribution of money and power is what most of the discussion, in any country, is about. More transcendent issues are relevant in a few instances, in a few countries, but they are not the common staple.

It may be tempting, just before we end, to make an assessment of the commitment of Peronism to reform, even if defined in a modest and mild way. It is true that it channelled the forces that had the potential and the will to introduce changes in the social and economic system. Moreover, it was able to bring together towards this end a broad coalition which far exceeded the trade union base. It was bound to meet strong opposition; Argentina's establishment has shown a relatively high social mobility (Mora, 1980), but has at the same time shown very little inclination to accept economic change or to share either power or money with other, newer groups, particularly if they retain their social identity. All establishments are reluctant to share in this way, but some are more stubborn than others and more willing to break the rules of the political game if necessary. At the same time, it is quite clear that the way in which Peronism put forward its proposals, the flamboyant rhetoric in which some of these mild reforms were shrouded, its abusive treatment of the opposition during the first presidencies and the violations of the dearly felt liberal democratic values that were part of the social consensus created a tremendous antagonism, even in sectors which would have naturally supported the more reformist measures regarding a greater role for the unions, the redistribution of income and interference with market forces.

It is difficult to think of a scenario in which Peronism would not have arisen. In the 1940s the social pressure was there and a change was bound to take place. A more 'well behaved' left-of-centre movement based on the trade unions, even with a narrower base, might have advanced social progress, initially at a slower pace, but in the end it might have obtained less contested and more permanent and effective results. But popular movements do not have ideal characteristics; they have those that social forces, struggles, and at times chance factors give to them. Peronism is what Argentina was able to produce; this is a fact of life and one of its dilemmas. Peronism may be a good example of the high cost to social reform when it is indulged in a rhetorical and at times high-handed and arbitrary way. It may have served the psychological needs of vast sectors; certainly it did so at a high cost to its avowed objectives.

The attitude of some of the Argentine intelligentsia has been to treat Peronism as an abnormality, intrinsically evil like the Nazi or fascist regimes, an abnormality that could and should have been destroyed simply by showing the people its nature. However, Peronism, despite some fascist overtones, is by no means in the same class as Nazism or fascism. Another view, not so prevalent, has been that in due time Peronism, with all its faults, may still form the basis of a reasonably democratic union-based party. As was said at the time,

> The party may, after the death of Perón, splinter into a thousand pieces, but one of these – organised labour – [has] the potential to draw together 80 per cent of the movement. If it can attract professionals and intellectuals, it can hopefully become a British-type Labour party. (di Tella, *New York Times*, 25 May 1973)

This, however, is the realm of wishful thinking of the kind that prompted the author to collaborate with such an 'animal'. It has to be humbly admitted that the story told here unfortunately provides too little evidence for such a view and to support such a decision. *Eppur....*

BIBLIOGRAPHY

Clutterbuck, R. (1975) *Living with Terrorism* (London).
Crozier, M., Huntington, S. and Watanabi, J. (1975) *The Crisis of Democracy – A Report on the Governability of Democracies to the Trilateral Commission* (New York).
Ferrer, A. (1977) *Crisis y alternativas en la política económica argentina* (Buenos Aires).
Halperín, T. (1964) *La Argentina en el callejón* (Montevideo).
Mora, M. (1980) 'El estatismo y los problemas políticos del desarrollo argentino' (Buenos Aires, mimeo).
O'Donnell, G. (1973) *Modernization and Bureaucratic Authoritarianism: Studies in South American Politics* (Berkeley, Calif.: Institute of International Politics).
O'Donnell, G. (1976) *Estado y alianzas en la Argentina 1956–76*, Documento CEDES no. 5 (Buenos Aires).

Statistical Appendix

LIST OF ABBREVIATIONS (SOURCES)

BCRA	Banco Central de la República Argentina
CEMA	Centro de Estudios Macro-económicos de Argentina of the Fundación PAÍS
CEMYB	Centro de Estudios Monetarios y Bancarios, of the BCRA
FIEL	Fundación de Investigaciones Económicas Latinoamericanas
IBRD	International Bank of Reconstruction and Development
IEERAL	Research Centre of the Fundación Mediterránea
IFS	International Financial Statistics
INDEC	Instituto Nacional de Estadísticas y Censos

TABLE A.1.1 Rate of Change of GNP and Investment

Period	$\dfrac{\triangle GNP}{GNP}$	Agriculture	Industry	Construction	Investment
1966	0.6	−3.7	0.7	6.2	−7.2
1967	2.7	4.3	1.5	12.9	4.5
1968	4.3	−5.4	6.5	18.1	10.6
1969	8.5	5.5	10.8	19.1	21.5
1970	5.4	5.6	6.3	9.4	7.4
1971	4.6	−5.0	9.7	−3.4	10.2
1972	3.1	−7.9	6.0	4.9	5.2
I	4.7	−4.3	8.9	12.9	−0.4
II	1.3	−13.2	7.6	8.0	−3.0
III	1.5	−3.7	5.2	1.6	−2.3
IV	3.3	4.0	2.9	−2.4	37.3
1973	5.8	13.5	6.4	−5.1	−1.3
I	6.1	12.2	7.4	−3.5	0.7
II	6.3	21.8	6.6	−12.7	0.5
III	4.1	12.1	4.6	−10.2	−14.8
IV	6.6	7.3	7.0	6.8	9.8

1974	6.5	6.2	6.1	12.2	3.9
I	4.3	8.8	3.2	6.9	-4.6
II	7.5	8.6	7.3	11.0	2.8
III	7.3	6.9	6.5	15.3	7.5
IV	6.8	-0.6	7.0	15.8	9.5
1975	-1.3	-3.5	-2.8	-9.6	-7.2
I	3.3	-5.7	2.9	8.2	4.3
II	1.4	-5.9	1.4	-6.7	-2.2
III	-3.2	-3.6	-5.6	-11.3	-8.1
IV	-6.3	2.8	-8.9	-26.3	-20.2
1976	-2.9	3.5	-4.5	-14.1	-6.2
I	-4.4	7.9	-6.7	-26.7	-16.9
II	-5.2	-0.1	-6.3	-15.0	-12.6
III	-1.7	0.8	-2.9	-10.7	0.5
IV	-0.2	5.9	-2.0	-0.3	5.4
1977	4.4	7.1	3.8	13.3	19.5
I	1.4	5.7	-0.4	6.3	19.4
II	4.5	11.0	2.2	10.5	22.9
III	7.9	8.8	9.3	14.1	25.0
IV	2.5	-2.1	2.8	16.7	8.4

Source: Departamento de Cuentas Nacionales, BCRA.

TABLE A.1.2 Investment as a Percentage of GNP

| Period | Total | | Private | Public |
	(including stock variation)	*(not including stock variation)*	*(not including stock variation)*	
1966	17.9	17.8	11.7	6.1
1967	18.2	18.1	11.0	7.1
1968	19.3	19.5	11.6	7.9
1969	21.6	21.7	13.6	8.1
1970	22.0	21.5	13.3	8.2
1971	23.1	22.5	14.0	8.5
1972	21.6	23.0	14.2	8.8
I	21.8			
II	21.7			
III	22.6			
IV	20.8			
1973	22.0	21.8	14.1	7.7
I	22.6			
II	22.4			
III	20.2			
IV	22.8			

1974	21.4	21.2	11.3	9.9
I	20.6			
II	21.4			
III	20.2			
IV	23.4			
1975	20.2	20.0	8.5	11.5
I	20.8			
II	20.6			
III	19.2			
IV	19.9			
1976	19.5	19.6	7.7	11.9
I	18.1			
II	19.0			
III	19.7			
IV	21.0			
1977	22.3			
I	21.3			
II	22.4			
III	22.8			
IV	22.3			

Source: Departamento de Cuentas Nacionales, BCRA.

TABLE A.2   Rates of Change of Consumer and Wholesale Price Indexes

		Yearly change	Jan	Feb	Mar	Apr	May	June	July	Aug	Sep	Oct	Nov	Dec
1966	CPI	29.9												
	WPI	22.7												
1967	CPI	27.3												
	WPI	20.6												
1968	CPI	9.6												
	WPI	3.9												
1969	CPI	10.7												
	WPI	7.2												
1970	CPI	12.2												
	WPI	26.9												
1971	CPI	39.2												
	WPI	48.2												
1972	CPI	64.2	10.9	3.9	4.5	5.4	2.5	5.6	5.1	1.0	2.6	3.8	4.0	1.6
	WPI	75.9	6.3	6.3	3.8	5.2	3.4	6.6	4.0	2.3	4.7	3.2	1.8	3.3
1973	CPI	43.7	10.3	7.9	2.9	5.0	4.4	−2.8	0.1	1.9	0.6	0.5	—	0.9
	WPI	30.8	4.9	6.9	6.5	0.4	0.6	−1.4	−0.6	1.2	0.4	0.1	1.1	1.3
1974	CPI	40.0	−0.6	1.9	1.5	3.4	4.3	3.9	2.4	3.0	3.4	2.7	3.3	5.2
	WPI	36.1	0.4	0.4	0.4	2.5	4.2	3.7	2.8	2.8	3.5	3.6	4.3	2.9
1975	CPI	335.0	2.9	4.6	8.1	9.7	3.9	21.3	34.9	23.8	10.9	12.6	8.1	11.5
	WPI	348.0	5.7	12.5	5.6	3.5	5.2	42.5	32.2	15.3	13.1	9.2	9.7	9.5
1976	CPI	364.0	14.8	19.3	38.0	34.6	13.1	28.0	4.3	6.7	10.7	7.4	7.1	6.7
	WPI	386.0	19.5	28.6	54.1	26.3	4.8	4.7	6.1	8.0	8.8	4.4	6.9	6.4
1977	CPI	160.0	13.8	8.6	7.9	6.0	6.5	7.6	10.7	11.3	10.8	12.5	9.0	7.3
	WPI	147.0	13.8	6.9	3.8	5.7	6.3	6.6	5.6	11.3	7.1	13.6	7.8	4.2

Monthly changes span the Jan–Dec columns.

CPI: Consumer price index, December to December, seasonally adjusted.
WPI: Wholesale price index, December to December.

Year	Series													
1972	CPI/WPI	105	109	103	102	103	105	104	105	102	130	101	105	110
	AGR/IND	129	125	116	117	119	119	125	131	130	137	138	136	135
	IMP/NAT	96	90	89	94	99	97	94	92	101	100	101	102	100
	G+L/CAT	58	47	47	52	54	54	51	55	60	64	66	66	70
1973	CPI/WPI	112	110	110	113	113	117	108	109	111	110	111	113	121
	AGR/IND	120	134	135	132	126	122	112	112	115	116	117	112	114
	IMP/NAT	105	99	95	92	100	100	107	109	110	109	110	112	114
	G+L/CAT	61	65	59	50	51	56	62	65	67	65	64	63	71
1974	CPI/WPI	116	114	113	116	116	115	116	115	114	114	114	114	125
	AGR/IND	106	113	113	112	109	110	110	107	109	104	100	100	97
	IMP/NAT	121	116	117	118		120	121	122	123	126	125	120	118
	G+L/CAT	73	70	71	73	71	71	72	73	70	68	70	80	88
1975	CPI/WPI	112	121	112	121	121	119	101	103	109	107	112	111	121
	AGR/IND	85	103	95	89	90	95	77	69	78	83	90	91	85
	IMP/NAT	149	112	108	114	114	118	145	150	158	156	159	159	174
	G+L/CAT	91	81	77	83	84	82	67	69	81	75	64	135	150
1976	CPI/WPI	125	116	102	91	97	96	95	93	92	94	96	96	97
	AGR/IND	93	89	97	82	79	102	102	86	93	103	102	97	99
	IMP/NAT	200	167	202	247	236	234	207	203	195	184	182	172	178
	G+L/CAT	86	112	86	59	63	68	76	129	102	85	96	77	85
1977	CPI/WPI	112	106	107	111	111	111	112	112	113	114	113	114	117
	AGR/IND	101	102	100	101	100	104	105	104	103	99	98	95	90
	IMP/NAT	185	175	173	198	218	215	202	204	179	178	161	158	158
	G+L/CAT	92	80	90	100	105	107	97	97	86	88	80	90	92

CPI/WPI: Consumer price index/wholesale price index.
AGR/IND: Agricultural/industrial prices.
IMP/NAT: Imported/national prices.
G+L/CAT: Grain and linseed prices/cattle prices.

Source: INDEC.

TABLE A.4.1 Balance of Payments, 1966–77 (yearly figures, US $ million)

		1966	1967	1968	1969	1970	1971	1972	1973	1974	1975	1976	1977
(1)	Merchandise account	469	369	198	36	79	−128	37	1031	435	−985	852	1727
	Exports	1593	1464	1367	1612	1773	1740	1941	3266	4005	2960	3762	5677
	Imports	1124	1095	1169	1576	1694	1868	1904	2235	3570	3946	2909	3950
(2)	Services	−275	−234	−243	−258	−225	−258	−255	−327	−190	−304	−287	−182
(3)	Current transactions (1) + (2)	194	−135	−45	−222	−156	−386	−218	704	245	−1289	565	1545
(4)	Non-compensatory transfers	−171	234	214	117	414	−190	−75	25	−172	502	380	934
(5)	International payments (3) + (4)*	24	416	160	−111	260	−560	−285	729	73	−787	945	2479
(6)	International Reserves (variation)	−5	480	57	−260	185	−385	167	921	−51	−791	945	2227
(7)	Compensatory transfers	28	−64	103	149	75	−175	−452	−192	124	4	—	252

*Includes unilateral transfers and errors and omissions.

Source: BCRA and INDEC.

TABLE A.4.2 Balance of Payments, 1972–7 (half-yearly figures, US $ million)

		1972		1973		1974		1975		1976		1977	
		I	II	I	II	I	II	I	II	I	II	I	II
(1)	Merchandise account	−4.3	41.3	565.6	417.0	467.2	−171.4	−663.1	−322.1	413.7	469.4	1045.8	681.2
	Exports	913.2	1027.8	1436.0	1780.0	1956.2	1974.5	1440.5	1520.8	1719.7	2196.4	2951.8	2725.2
	Imports	917.5	986.5	920.5	1309.0	1489.0	2145.9	2103.6	1842.9	1306.0	1727.0	1906.0	2044.0
(2)	Services	−121.8	−133.2	−172.6	−153.9	−72.3	−96.6	−210.1	−93.9	−129.1	−122.9	−144.3	−80.7
(3)	Current transactions (1) + (2)	−126.1	−91.9	393.0	317.0	395.0	−268.0	−874.0	−426.0	289.0	361.0	901.0	601.0
(4)	Non-compensatory transfers	−124.1	49.1	−145.3	160.3	196.8	−250.5	184.3	6.8	−109.4	−406.5	−108.6	1042.6
(5)	International payments (3) + (4)*	−254.4	−30.6	249.0	482.2	596.2	−501.5	−711.7	−382.8	177.5	−52.8	813.1	1665.9
(6)	International reserves (variation)	−17.8	184.8	409.1	511.9	564.1	−615.4	−694.8	−96.3	543.8	648.6	731.7	1495.3
(7)	Compensatory transfers	−236.6	−215.4	−160.1	−29.7	32.1	113.9	−16.9	−286.5	−366.3	−701.4	81.4	170.6

*Includes unilateral transfers and errors and omissions.

217

TABLE A.5 External Debt (US $ million)

	1972	1973	1974	1975	1976
Total debt	5788	6233	7968	9149	9738
Public sector	3089	3426	4558	5295	6648
less than 180 days	162	243	379	717	675
more than 180 days	2922	3183	4179	4578	5973
Private sector	2699	2807	3410	3854	3090
less than 180 days	930	1230	1759	2124	1066
more than 180 days	1769	1577	1651	1730	2024

Source: J. Sommer, 'La deuda externa argentina entre 1972 y 1976', paper presented to the XIVth Meeting of Central Bank Economists, Bariloche, Argentina (1977).

TABLE A.6   International Reserves

Period	US $ million
1966	251.1
1967	763.4
1968	792.4
1969	560.2
1970	724.7
1971	316.7
1972 I	300.3
II	321.5
III	300.7
IV	529.0
1973 I	694.8
II	892.7
III	1285.1
IV	1412.4
1974 I	1582.9
II	1972.3
III	1629.6
IV	1446.4
1975 I	1057.6
II	732.7
III	529.5
IV	678.0
1976 I	725.7
II	1114.2
III	1266.2
IV	1943.9
1977 I	2051.9
II	2436.1
III	3146.2
IV	3862.0

Source: BCRA.

TABLE A.7   Terms of Trade

Period	Export prices	Import prices	Terms of trade
1966	95.8	94.9	118.1
1967	90.7	93.0	114.1
1968	88.0	93.8	109.8
1969	139.0	99.5	104.3
1970	100.0	100.0	100.0
1971	101.0	96.4	104.9
1972	121.5	103.5	117.4
I	106	104	105
II	117	102	114
III	126	105	120
IV	138	107	129
1973	180.3	165.5	108.9
I	151	121	112
II	168	140	120
III	205	181	114
IV	197	220	89
1974	195.7	272.3	71.9
I	214	258	83
II	113	283	65
III	196	239	69
IV	188	265	71
1975	170.2	239.0	71.2
I	166	265	66
II	171	240	71
III	175	230	76
IV	168	235	72
1976	179.0	256.0	69.3
I	179	248	72
II	187	260	73
III	177	264	69
IV	164	257	64

Sources: 1966–9, BCRA, based on the 1958 trade mix; 1970 onwards, FIEL and IFS based on the 1970 trade mix.

TABLE A.8.1   Real Rates of Exchange (Dec 1976 = 100)

Year	Type of exchange	Year's average	Mar	June	Sep	Dec
1967	R_x	111.3	115.0	116.1	110.7	103.5
	R_m	112.3	117.4	116.6	110.9	104.2
1968	R_x	93.6	98.6	96.2	91.5	88.0
	R_m	94.7	99.7	97.2	92.8	89.2
1969	R_x	86.8	87.1	87.0	86.6	86.5
	R_m	88.1	88.4	88.5	87.5	87.8
1970	R_x	91.7	86.2	92.8	95.2	92.5
	R_m	93.2	87.3	95.2	96.4	93.7
1971	R_x	87.1	80.2	82.8	89.6	95.8
	R_m	89.8	81.1	84.5	89.5	104.0
1972	R_x	101.0	101.6	107.7	100.3	94.5
	R_m	105.9	116.3	107.8	103.8	95.5
1973	R_x	81.4	85.7	75.0	84.8	80.2
	R_m	76.8	82.4	75.2	76.6	73.0
1974	R_x	73.0	81.0	76.5	72.0	62.3
	R_m	67.5	75.4	71.0	66.5	57.2
1975	R_x	95.1	77.9	109.4	98.2	94.7
	R_m	88.9	59.4	102.5	102.4	91.4
1976	R_x	115.4	134.4	117.1	110.0	100.0
	R_m	107.7	128.7	105.6	96.6	100.0
1977	R_x	98.3	101.9	101.0	94.4	95.8
	R_m	96.8	100.6	99.4	93.1	94.0

Sources: R_x (real rate for exports), IEERAL; R_m (real rate for imports), IEERAL, and Parino and Cartas (1979).

TABLE A.8.2   Nominal Rates of Exchange (pesos per US dollar)

Year	Type of exchange	Yearly average	Jan	Feb	Mar	Apr	May	June	July	Aug	Sep	Oct	Nov	Dec
1966	free	2.08												
	b	2.44												
1967	free	3.31												
	b	2.42												
1968	free	3.50												
	b	3.50												
1969	free	3.50												
	b	3.51												
1970	free	3.82												
	b	3.86												
1971	free	4.19												
	c	5.00												
	f	7.51												
	b	6.14												
1972	c	5.00	5.00	5.00	5.00	5.00	5.00	5.00	5.00	5.00	5.00	5.00	5.00	5.00
	f	9.85	9.32	9.67	9.74	9.77	9.88	9.94	9.95	9.96	9.98	9.98	9.98	9.98
	b	11.50	10.15	10.00	10.00	10.15	11.95	11.75	11.20	13.00	13.70	12.90	11.88	11.25
1973	c	5.00	5.00	5.00	5.00	5.00	5.00	5.00	5.00	5.00	5.00	5.00	5.00	5.00
	f	9.98	9.98	9.98	9.98	9.98	9.98	9.98	9.98	9.98	9.98	9.98	9.98	9.98
	b	11.30	13.13	11.45	11.43	12.50	12.50	10.88	10.10	10.95	11.10	10.60	10.58	11.80
1974	c	5.00	5.00	5.00	5.00	5.00	5.00	5.00	5.00	5.00	5.00	5.00	5.00	5.00
	f	9.98	9.98	9.98	9.98	9.98	9.98	9.98	9.98	9.98	9.98	9.98	9.98	9.98
	b	16.25	11.90	12.30	12.40	13.30	14.40	14.90	16.60	17.55	18.70	20.05	20.90	22.00

Year	Rate													
1975	c	21.36	5.00	5.00	10.00	10.00	10.00	23.33	27.13	31.99	35.21	37.23	38.45	—
	f	30.67	9.98	9.98	15.10	15.10	15.10	27.59	33.04	40.74	45.32	47.87	51.08	57.00
	fs	69.94	22.65	—	—	—	—	—	—	63.18	64.56	68.15	72.82	81.01
	b	72.15	23.45	28.35	36.45	47.00	53.00	66.50	76.00	110.00	142.50	—	132.50	127.50
1976	c	140.33	140.33	140.33	140.33	140.33	140.33	140.33	140.33	140.33	140.33	140.33	140.33	140.33
	f	69.63	69.90	75.70	—	—	—	—	—	—	—	—	—	—
	fs	99.00	99.39	107.67	—	—	—	—	—	—	—	—	—	—
	b	257.80	270.00	325.00	255.00	245.00	247.56	250.00	263.00	247.00	245.50	—	273.00	276.50
	free	246.58	247.00	274.87	247.50	249.75	252.00	252.00	250.10	251.00	252.00	—	254.00	270.97
1977	free	409.90	304.75	327.78	347.32	365.14	383.71	405.00	427.73	451.27	499.38	—	538.00	580.00
	b	423.10	332.50	342.50	364.50	372.50	390.00	411.50	437.50	468.50	510.50	—	550.50	599.50

c	Commercial exchange rate.
f	Financial exchange rate.
fs	Financial special rate.
free	Free exchange rate.
b	Black-market rate.

Sources: c, f, fs, and free, BCRA; b, TECHINT.

TABLE A.9 Liquidity Coefficient

Period	$\dfrac{M_1}{Y}$	$\dfrac{M_2}{Y}$	$\dfrac{M_3}{Y}$	$\dfrac{M_4}{Y}$
1966	0.1269	0.1932		
1967	0.1306	0.2002		
1968	0.1486	0.2343		
1969	0.1564	0.2580		
1970	0.1467	0.2503		
1971	0.1245	0.2158		
1972	0.0948	0.1661	0.1751	
I			0.1752	
II			0.1636	
III			0.1599	
IV			0.1667	
1973	0.1025	0.1779	0.1982	0.2000
I	0.0933	0.1635	0.1822	0.1829
II	0.0910	0.1567	0.1749	0.1758
III	0.1078	0.1863	0.2076	0.2084
IV	0.1219	0.2128	0.2364	0.2371

	M_1	M_2	M_3	M_4
1974	0.1377	0.2451	0.2725	0.2738
I	0.1440	0.2550	0.2826	0.2834
II	0.1339	0.2432	0.2686	0.2694
III	0.1416	0.2526	0.2787	0.2801
IV	0.1377	0.2420	0.2680	0.2706
1975	0.0902	0.1371	0.1520	0.1614
I	0.1416	0.2400	0.2653	0.2724
II	0.1119	0.1828	0.2028	0.2119
III	0.0791	0.1170	0.1305	0.1419
IV	0.0875	0.1181	0.1310	0.1490
1976	0.0621	0.0842	0.0944	0.1244
I	0.0793	0.1025	0.1129	0.1339
II	0.0551	0.0709	0.0790	0.0117
III	0.0666	0.0941	0.1073	0.1380
IV	0.0674	0.1050	0.1207	0.1555
1977			0.1436	0.1679
I	0.0702	0.1161	0.1349	0.1695
II	0.0699	0.1272	0.1425	0.1670
III	0.0684	0.1455	0.1479	0.1668
IV	0.0600	0.1450	0.1482	0.1687

M_1 = currency and demand deposits.
M_2 = M_1 + interest-yielding deposits.
M_3 = M_2 + bank acceptances.
M_4 = M_3 + VNAs (indexed Government bonds) + Treasury bonds.

Source: CEMYB.

TABLE A.10   Shares of M_1, M_2, M_3 and M_4 (as a proportion of GNP)

Period	M_1	$M_2 - M_1$	$M_3 - M_2$	$M_4 - M_3$	Total
1966	0.6569	0.3431			1.0000
1967	0.6525	0.3475			1.0000
1968	0.6344	0.3656			1.0000
1969	0.6060	0.3940			1.0000
1970	0.5859	0.4141			1.0000
1971	0.5770	0.4230			1.0000
1972	0.5222	0.3925	0.0853		1.0000
1973	0.5151	0.3791	0.1018	0.0040	1.0000
I	0.5105	0.3836	0.1024	0.0036	1.0000
II	0.5177	0.3735	0.1032	0.0056	1.0000
III	0.5174	0.3767	0.1023	0.0036	1.0000
IV	0.5143	0.3834	0.0991	0.0031	1.0000
1974	0.5055	0.3946	0.0954	0.0045	1.0000
I	0.5082	0.3916	0.0973	0.0029	1.0000
II	0.4973	0.4054	0.0943	0.0030	1.0000
III	0.5058	0.3958	0.0934	0.0050	1.0000
IV	0.5090	0.3850	0.0961	0.0099	1.0000

1975	0.5576	0.2902	0.0939	0.0583	1.0000

1975	0.5576	0.2902	0.0939	0.0583	1.0000
I	0.5199	0.3611	0.0929	0.0261	1.0000
II	0.5285	0.3343	0.0944	0.0428	1.0000
III	0.5576	0.2670	0.0951	0.0803	1.0000
IV	0.5876	0.2053	0.0867	0.1204	1.0000
1976	0.4965	0.1765	0.0859	0.2411	1.0000
I	0.5921	0.1732	0.0779	0.1568	1.0000
II	0.4978	0.1426	0.0732	0.2864	1.0000
III	0.4829	0.1988	0.0956	0.2227	1.0000
IV	0.4337	0.2420	0.1007	0.2236	1.0000
1977					
I	0.4168	0.2725	0.1079	0.2028	1.0000
II	0.4167	0.3416	0.0954	0.1462	1.0000
III	0.3990	0.4506	0.0387	0.1117	1.0000
IV	0.3530	0.5070	0.0170	0.1210	1.0000

Source: CEMYB.

TABLE A.11 Sources of Money Creation
(changes, in million pesos and as a percentage of the total increase in M_2)

Period	Foreign sector US$ million	%	Government sector US$ million	%	Private sector US$ million	%	Banks net worth and other US$ million	%	Total increase in M_2 (US$ million)
1967	1,153	35	230	7	2,322	71	−423	−13	3,282
1968	323	8	249	6	4,234	102	−651	−16	4,155
1969	−609	−21	439	15	4,014	130	−945	−33	2,899
1970	771	17	697	16	3,770	84	−768	−17	4,470
1971	−1,080	−13	2,232	26	9,364	110	−1,976	−23	8,540
1972	1,004	6	4,999	31	15,399	95	−5,151	−32	16,251
I	−74	3	1,142	41	3,146	113	−1,428	−51	2,786
II	−20	−1	632	24	3,123	118	−1,092	−41	2,643
III	254	8	1,093	33	3,453	104	−1,482	−45	3,318
IV	844	11	2,132	28	5,677	76	−1,149	−15	7,504
1973	5,736	12	15,398	33	26,415	57	−1,448	−3	46,101
I	798	13	1,705	27	4,486	70	−621	−10	6,368
II	1,154	11	4,182	40	7,223	69	−2,102	−20	10,457
III	2,851	24	2,167	18	5,004	42	−1,755	15	11,777
IV	933	5	7,344	42	9,702	55	−480	−3	17,499

1974	4,317	8	20,383	39	40,793	77	-12,619	-24	52,874
I	1,581	19	4,512	53	5,121	60	-2,723	-32	8,491
II	4,499	28	3,490	22	7,946	50	-119	-1	15,816
III	-2,354	-21	2,403	22	13,896	127	-2,967	-27	10,978
IV	591	3	9,978	57	13,830	79	-6,810	-39	17,589
1975	-14,420	-8	118,525	63	174,154	92	-88,914	-47	189,345
I	-4,946	-55	10,404	115	9,716	107	-6,119	-68	9,055
II	-5,530	-30	8,455	46	23,074	127	-7,788	-43	18,211
III	-4,706	-9	30,472	59	60,942	118	-35,082	-68	51,626
IV	762	1	69,194	63	80,422	73	-39,925	-36	110,453
1976	387,144	35	113,782	10	922,612	82	-304,405	-27	1,119,133
I	17,315	15	77,022	65	87,861	74	-64,220	-54	117,978
II	146,078	54	23,809	9	165,153	61	-62,972	-23	272,068
III	136,250	49	-32,922	-12	247,686	90	-74,444	-27	276,570
IV	87,501	19	45,873	10	421,912	93	-102,769	-23	452,517
1977	886,145	25	554,444	16	24,003,521	91	-1,137,265	-32	3,543,359
I	145,086	42	55,924	16	320,218	92	-173,594	-50	347,634
II	161,856	16	240,200	24	751,562	75	-152,351	-15	1,001,267
III	275,230	32	-14,418	-2	1,025,772	119	-423,462	-49	863,122
IV	303,973	23	272,738	20	1,142,483	86	-387,858	-29	1,331,336

Source: BCRA.

TABLE A.12   Share of the National Income
Accruing to Wage-earners

Year	% of GNP
1950	49.7
1955	47.7
1960	38.0
1965	40.6
1966	43.8
1967	45.5
1968	44.9
1969	44.6
1970	45.8
1971	46.6
1972	42.7
1973	46.9
1974	46.7
1975	44.8
1976	n.a.

Source: Ministerio de Economía.

TABLE A.13 Transfer of Income from Debtors to Creditors

Year	Real rate of interest on deposits (1)	Implicit tax on interest-yielding deposits (% of GNP) (2)	Interest-yielding deposits (million new pesos) (3)	GDP (million new pesos) (4)	Implicit tax on interest-yielding deposits (% of GDP) (5) = (2) · (3)/(4)
1966	− 15.2	17.2	2,852	41,494	1.18
1967	− 13.5	15.5	3,857	53,006	1.13
1968	0.3	1.7	5,433	60,614	0.15
1969	3.0	− 1.0	7,421	71,831	− 0.10
1970	− 9.8	11.8	9,096	84,623	1.27
1971	− 18.8	20.8	11,710	120,163	2.03
1972	− 27.1	29.1	16,693	200,767	2.42
1973	− 17.1	19.1	28,123	334,147	1.61
1974	− 16.7	18.7	51,479	448,000	2.15
1975	− 72.4	74.4	64,427	1,294,000	3.70
1976	− 65.1	67.1	175,557	7,100,000	1.66

(2) derived from (1) assuming a positive equilibrium rate of 2 per cent.

Source: E. Gaba (1977), 'Indexación y sistema financiero', *Revista argentina de finanzas* (June).

TABLE A.14   Percentage Variation in the Number of Government Employees

Year	Total (1)+(2)	National sector (1)					Provinces (2)
		Central administration	Special accounts	Decentralised accounts	State enterprises	Total of national sector	
1967	−0.05	−0.23	1.51	3.31	−3.53	−0.72	1.25
1968	−1.19	0.37	12.28	1.66	−5.61	−1.51	−0.60
1969	−0.57	−0.10	20.72	−1.79	−2.83	−1.26	0.73
1970	−1.23	−2.57	27.93	−3.96	−1.27	−1.94	0.07
1971	1.57	−0.09	5.00	5.46	−0.37	1.25	2.14
1972	3.15	4.48	−17.33	5.16	2.32	3.47	2.48
1973	9.37	5.83	10.35	−3.11	10.89	5.45	16.49
1974	5.25	−13.35	12.34	1.22	20.33	3.25	8.54
1975	8.89	5.50	3.41	11.68	5.29	6.78	12.19
1976	0.67	−1.36	18.65	−0.72	0.99	0.20	1.37

Source: Ministerio de Economía, *Informe Estadístico*, no. 10.

TABLE A.15 Unemployment (as a percentage of total employed)

	1966 Apr	1966 Oct	1967 Apr	1967 Oct	1968 Apr	1968 Oct	1969 Apr	1969 Oct	1970 Apr	1970 Oct	1971 Apr	1971 Oct
Greater Buenos Aires	6.7	6.0	6.8	6.9	6.1	5.0	4.2	4.5	5.7	5.3	5.7	
Córdoba	7.3	6.6	8.9	7.3	7.3	4.3	6.1	3.2	4.2	4.7	5.0	4.4
Rosario	7.2	5.8	6.5	6.1	4.7	5.9	5.5	5.5	5.5	4.9	5.3	3.5
Tucumán	9.5	7.4	10.3	10.2	10.8	12.7	12.4	11.4	10.9	10.4	11.7	12.2
Greater Mendoza	3.8	2.7	2.4	2.6	2.5	2.4	2.5	2.7	3.8	3.3	4.3	3.6

	1972 Apr	1972 Oct	1973 Apr	1973 Oct	1974 Apr	1974 Oct	1975 Apr	1975 Oct	1976 Apr	1976 Oct	1977 Apr	1977 Oct
Greater Buenos Aires	7.4	5.8	6.1	4.5	4.2	2.5	2.3	2.7	4.8	4.2	3.4	2.2
Córdoba	7.2	5.2	5.3	6.1	7.0	5.4	7.2	7.5	6.5	5.6	5.9	
Rosario	6.2	5.8	5.3	5.5	4.7	3.8	5.5	5.6	5.3	4.1	3.5	
Tucumán	14.2	11.7	12.5	11.3	10.5	7.5	8.6	6.8	7.4	5.5	7.2	
Greater Mendoza	4.8	4.3	4.1	3.2	4.9	4.7	4.0	4.1	5.9	4.8	4.4	
Total	7.8	6.1	6.1	5.4	4.7	3.1	3.2	3.5	5.3	4.5		

Source: INDEC.

TABLE A.16 Real Wages (1973 = 100)

Year		Jan	Feb	Mar	Apr	May	June	July	Aug	Sep	Oct	Nov	Dec
1966	(a)	107.1											
1967	(a)	100.2											
1968	(a)	39.7											
1969	(a)	103.7											
1970	(a)	103.7											
1971	(a)	108.0											
1972	(a)	97.0											
1973	(a)	100.0	97.8	110.7	86.3	89.9	90.6	109.2	108.0	107.7	106.7	105.7	97.8
	(b)	100.0	97.5	98.2	96.9	98.8	96.6	96.3	99.4	100.0	102.8	105.8	107.1
1974	(a)	103.8	102.1	101.1	120.2	116.6	112.3	110.0	105.4	102.1	98.5	125.5	111.3
	(b)	111.4	105.8	106.8	108.3	109.8	112.0	113.5	119.7	122.2	121.5	122.8	124.0
1975	(a)	118.6	103.4	111.0	101.7	97.2	155.9	114.3	102.1	92.2	91.6	99.1	86.6
	(a^1)					98.7	169.2	124.1	110.4	99.7	98.2	105.1	91.8
	(b)	139.7	133.2	133.8	132.6	129.5	124.0	104.3	110.2	106.5	102.8	110.3	95.7
1976	(a)	101.8	85.3	74.1	60.9	54.0	60.3	57.6	54.0	54.7	51.1	54.7	51.4
	(a^1)	107.9	90.4	78.5									
	(b)	109.5	95.4	99.1	99.7	99.4	97.8	83.1	83.1	81.8	72.0	68.6	70.8

(a) Unskilled married workers; (a^1) Unskilled married workers with wage drift (when in existence).
(b) All workers, of a specific case, in the metallurgical industry.

Source: IBRD (1977) *Argentina, Reconstruction and Development.*

TABLE A.17 Public Sector Operations (Treasury, Provinces and State enterprises, as a percentage of GNP)

Year	Revenue (I)			Expenditures (II)			*	Deficit (I) (II)	Borrowing		Deficit financing
	Total	Taxes	Other	Total	Current	Investment			External	Internal	
1966	26.7	15.9	10.8	31.3	25.3	6.0	0.1	-4.6	0.3	—	-4.3
1967	30.3	19.0	11.3	32.3	25.2	7.1	—	-1.9	-0.3	0.1	-2.1
1968	30.2	18.4	11.8	32.3	24.6	7.7	0.2	-2.1	—	0.4	-1.7
1969	29.5	17.3	12.2	34.2	23.6	7.6	0.4	-1.6	0.3	0.5	-0.8
1970	29.4	18.0	11.4	31.1	23.3	7.8	0.4	-1.7	0.8	0.1	-0.8
1971	26.7	16.1	10.6	31.0	23.3	7.7	0.8	-4.3	1.1	0.7	-2.5
1972	25.0	14.3	10.7	30.2	22.1	8.1	0.7	-5.2	1.0	0.9	-3.5
1973	26.5	16.2	10.3	33.8	26.5	7.3	0.4	-7.3	0.1	0.9	-6.3
1974	30.2	19.3	10.9	38.0	29.4	8.6	1.3	-7.8	0.9	1.0	-5.9
1975	25.7	14.3	11.4	41.7	32.4	9.3	2.2	-16.2	0.1	1.7	-14.4
1976	30.0	17.5	12.5	41.1	28.2	12.9	-1.0	-11.1	0.6	2.6	-7.9
1977†	35.4	20.9	14.5	40.5	27.6	13.4	n.a.	-5.6	1.6	1.2	-2.8

*Excess of BCRA's public-investment figures over IBRD's.

† Estimate.

Source: IBRD (1977), *Argentina, Reconstruction and Development.*

TABLE A.18   Central Government's Treasury Operations
(as a percentage of GNP)

Period	Expenditures (I)	Income (II)	Deficit (I) − (II)
1972	8.64	6.21	2.43
I	7.79	5.69	2.10
II	8.65	7.00	1.65
III	8.84	6.28	2.56
IV	8.96	5.84	3.12
1973	10.95	5.54	5.43
I	8.75	4.89	3.86
II	9.41	4.39	5.01
III	11.93	6.35	5.58
IV	13.24	6.31	6.93
1974	13.12	6.58	6.54
I	11.37	5.94	5.43
II	13.22	7.87	5.34
III	13.32	6.77	6.35
IV	14.06	5.82	8.24
1975	15.98	4.27	11.71
I	12.15	5.03	7.12
II	12.22	4.40	6.92
III	13.81	4.06	9.75
IV	20.17	3.80	16.38
1976	13.66	5.65	8.01
I	16.97	4.03	12.94
II	11.34	4.32	7.02
III	13.91	6.13	7.79
IV	13.90	6.73	7.18
1977	10.41	6.74	3.67
I	12.62	6.80	5.18
II	10.50	7.25	3.73
III	10.59	7.33	3.26
IV	9.11	5.89	3.23

Source: BCRA.

Index